PORTRAITS OF PLACES

PORTRAITS OF PLACES

Henry James

Duckworth

This edition published in 2001 by
Gerald Duckworth & Co. Ltd.
61 Frith Street, London W1D 3JL
Tel: 020 7434 4242
Fax: 020 7434 4420
Email: enquiries@duckworth-publishers.co.uk
www.ducknet.co.uk

First published in 1883 by
Macmillan and Co.

A catalogue record for this book is available
from the British Library

ISBN 0 7156 3083 0

Typeset by Derek Doyle & Associates, Liverpool
Printed in Great Britain by
Bookcraft (Bath) Limited, Midsomer Norton, Somerset

NOTE TO THE ENGLISH EDITION.

The papers contained in this volume were first published in various American magazines and journals: and it is especially true of several articles embodying impressions – it is to be feared very superficial – received during the early months of a residence in England, that they were at that time addressed altogether to an American public. It is probable that they can have but a limited interest for English readers, familiar, naturally, to satiety with many of those minor characteristics to which the author has ventured to call the attention of his less initiated countrymen. It may be added that such pages represent a stage of observation on the writer's part which belongs to freshness of acquaintance. His impressions have been modified and enlarged, and he would not to-day have the temerity to write letters upon England. The four last sketches, dealing with American scenes, were the earliest written, and their only merit at present is that of testimony to the past. A period of thirteen years in the United States produces extraordinary changes, and the places in question would have now to be described in very different terms.

CONTENTS.

I.	VENICE	9
II.	ITALY REVISITED	41
III.	OCCASIONAL PARIS	71
IV.	RHEIMS AND LAON: A LITTLE TOUR	88
V.	CHARTRES	108
VI.	ROUEN	116
VII.	ETRETAT	124
VIII.	FROM NORMANDY TO THE PYRENEES	132
IX.	AN ENGLISH EASTER	161
X.	LONDON AT MIDSUMMER	183
XI.	TWO EXCURSIONS	198
XII.	IN WARWICKSHIRE	213
XIII.	ABBEYS AND CASTLES	232
XIV.	ENGLISH VIGNETTES	246
XV.	AN ENGLISH NEW YEAR	263
XVI.	AN ENGLISH WINTER WATERING-PLACE	270
XVII.	SARATOGA	277
XVIII.	NEWPORT	288
XIX.	QUEBEC	298
XX.	NIAGARA	310

I.

VENICE.

1882.

It is a great pleasure to write the word; but I am not sure there is not a certain impudence in pretending to add anything to it. Venice has been painted and described many thousands of times, and of all the cities of the world it is the easiest to visit without going there. Open the first book and you will find a rhapsody about it; step into the first picture-dealer's and you will find three or four high-coloured "views" of it. There is nothing more to be said about it. Every one has been there, and every one has brought back a collection of photographs. There is as little mystery about the Grand Canal as about our local thoroughfare; and the name of St. Mark is as familiar as the postman's ring. It is not forbidden, however, to speak of familiar things, and I believe that, for the true Venice-lover, Venice is always in order. There is nothing new to be said about it certainly, but the old is better than any novelty. It would be a sad day, indeed, when there should be something new to say. I write these lines with the full consciousness of having no information whatever to offer. I do not pretend to enlighten the reader; I pretend only to give a fillip to his memory; and I hold any writer sufficiently justified who is himself in love with his topic.

I.

Mr. Ruskin has given it up, that is very true; but it is only after extracting half a life-time of pleasure and an immeasurable quantity of fame from it. We all may do the same, after it has served our turn, which it probably will not cease to do for many a year to come. Meantime, it is Mr. Ruskin who, beyond any one, helps us to enjoy. He has, indeed, lately produced several aids to depression in the shape of certain little humorous – ill-humorous – pamphlets (the series of *St. Mark's Rest*), which embody his latest reflections on the subject of Venice and describe the latest atrocities that have been perpetrated there. These latter are numerous and deeply to be deplored; but to admit that they have spoiled Venice would be to admit that Venice may be spoiled – an admission pregnant, as it seems to us, with disloyalty. Fortunately, one reacts against the Ruskinian contagion, and one hour of the lagoon is worth a hundred pages of demoralised prose. This queer, late-coming prose of Mr. Ruskin (including the revised and condensed issue of the *Stones of Venice*, only one little volume of which has appeared or, perhaps, will ever appear) is all to be read, though much of it seems to be addressed to children of tender age. It is pitched in the nursery-key, and might be supposed to emanate from an angry governess. It is, however, all suggestive, and much of it is delightfully just. There is an inconceivable want of form in it, though the author has spent his life in laying down the principles of form, and scolding people for departing from them; but it throbs and flashes with the love of his subject – a love disconcerted and abjured, but which has still some of the force of inspiration. Among the many strange things that have befallen Venice, she has had the good fortune to become the object of a passion to a man of splendid genius, who has made her his own, and, in doing so, has made her the world's. There is no better reading at Venice, therefore, as I say, than Ruskin, for every true Venice-lover can separate the wheat from the chaff. The narrow theological spirit, the moralism *à tout propos*, the queer provincialities and pruderies, are mere wild weeds in a mountain of flowers. One may doubtless be very happy in Venice without reading at all – without criticism or analysing or thinking a strenuous thought. It is a city in which, I suspect, there is very little strenuous thinking, and yet it is a city in which there must be almost as much happiness as misery. The misery of Venice stands there for all the world to see; it is part of the spectacle – a thorough-going devotee of local colour might consistently say it is part of the pleasure. The Venetian people have little to call their own – little more than the bare privilege of leading their lives in the most beautiful of towns. Their habitations are decayed; their taxes heavy; their pockets light; their opportunities few. One receives an impression, however, that life presents itself to them with attractions not accounted for in this meagre train of advantages, and that they are on better terms with it than many people who have made a better bargain. They lie in the sunshine; they dabble in the sea; they wear bright rags; they fall into attitudes and harmonies; they assist at an eternal *conversazione*. It is not easy to say that one would have them other than they are, and it certainly would make an immense difference should they be better fed. The number of persons in Venice who evidently never have enough to eat is painfully large; but it would be more painful if we did not equally perceive that the rich Venetian temperament may bloom upon a dog's allowance. Nature has been kind to it, and sunshine and leisure and conversation and beautiful views form the greater part of its sustenance. It takes a great deal to make a successful American; but to make a happy Venetian takes only a handful of quick sensibility. The Italian people have, at once, the good and evil fortune to be conscious of few wants; so that if the civilisation of a society is measured by the number of its needs, as seems to be the common opinion to-day, it is to be feared that the children of the lagoon would make but a poor figure in a set of comparative tables. Not their misery, doubtless, but the way they elude their misery, is what pleases the sentimental tourist, who is gratified by the sight of a beautiful race that lives by the aid of its imagination. The way to enjoy Venice is to follow the example of these people and make the most of simple pleasures. Almost all the pleasures of the place are simple; this may be maintained even under the imputation of ingenious paradox. There is no simpler pleasure than looking at a fine Titian – unless it be looking at a fine Tintoret, or strolling into St. Mark's – it is abominable, the way one falls into the habit – and resting one's light-wearied eyes upon the windowless gloom; or than floating in a gondola, or hanging over a balcony, or taking one's coffee at Florian's. It is of these superficial pastimes that a Venetian day is composed, and the pleasure of the matter is in the emotions to which they minister. These, fortunately, are of the finest; otherwise, Venice would be insufferably dull. Reading Ruskin is good; reading the old records is, perhaps, better; but the best thing of all is simply staying on. The only way to care for Venice as she deserves it, is to give her a chance to touch you often – to linger and remain and return.

II.

The danger is that you will not linger enough – a danger of which the author of these lines had known something. It is possible to dislike Venice, and to entertain the sentiment in a responsible and intelligent manner. There are travellers who think the place odious, and those who are not of this opinion often find themselves wishing that the others were only more numerous. The sentimental tourist's only quarrel with his Venice is that he has too many competitors there. He likes to be alone; to be original; to have (to himself, at least) the air of making discoveries. The Venice of to-day is a vast museum where the little wicket that admits you is perpetually turning and creaking, and you march through the institution with a herd of fellow-gazers. There is nothing left to discover or describe, and originality of attitude is completely impossible. This is often very annoying; you can only turn your back on your impertinent playfellow and curse his want of delicacy. But this is not the fault of Venice; it is the fault of the rest of the world. The fault of Venice is that, though it is easy to admire it, it is not so easy to live in it. After you have been there a week, and the bloom of novelty has rubbed off, you wonder whether you can accommodate yourself to the peculiar conditions. Your old habits become impracticable, and you find yourself obliged to form new ones of an undesirable and unprofitable character. You are tired of your gondola (or you think you are), and you have seen all the principal pictures and heard the names of the palaces announced a dozen times by your gondolier, who brings them out almost as impressively as if he were an English butler bawling titles into a drawing-room. You have walked several hundred times round the Piazza, and bought several bushels of photographs. You have visited the antiquity-mongers whose horrible signboards dishonour some of the grandest vistas in the Grand Canal; you have tried the opera and found it very bad; you have bathed at the Lido and found the water flat. You have begun to have a shipboard-feeling – to regard the Piazza as an enormous saloon and the Riva degli Schiavoni as a promenade-deck. You are obstructed and encaged; your desire for space is unsatisfied; you miss your usual exercise. You try to take a walk, and you fail, and meantime, as I say, you have come to regard your gondola as a sort of magnified baby's cradle. You have no desire to be rocked to sleep, though you are sufficiently kept awake by the irritation produced, as you gaze across the shallow lagoon, by the attitude of the perpetual gondolier, with his turned-out toes, his protruded chin, his absurdly unscientific stroke. The canals have a horrible smell, and the everlasting Piazza, where you have looked repeatedly at every article in every shop-window and found them all rubbish, where the young Venetians who sell bead-bracelets and "panoramas" are perpetually thrusting their wares at you, where the same tightly-buttoned officers are for ever sucking the same black weeds, at the same empty tables, in front of the same *caffès* – the Piazza, as I say, has resolved itself into a sort of magnificent tread-mill. This is the state of mind of those shallow inquirers who find Venice all very well for a week; and if in such a state of mind you take your departure, you act with fatal rashness. The loss is your own, moreover; it is not – with all deference to your personal attractions – that of your companions who remain behind; for though there are some disagreeable things in Venice, there is nothing so disagreeable as the visitors. The conditions are peculiar, but your intolerance of them evaporates before it has had time to become a prejudice. When you have called for the bill to go, pay it and remain, and you will find on the morrow that you are deeply attached to Venice. It is by living there from day to day that you feel the fulness of its charm; that you invite its exquisite influence to sink into your spirit. The place is as changeable as a nervous woman, and you know it only when you know all the aspects of its beauty. It has high spirits or low, it is pale or red, gray or pink, cold or warm, fresh or wan, according to the weather or the hour. It is always interesting and almost always sad; but it has a thou-

sand occasional graces and is always liable to happy accidents.
You become extraordinarily fond of these things; you count
upon them; they make part of your life. Tenderly fond you
become; there is something indefinable in those depths of
personal acquaintance that gradually establish themselves.
The place seems to personify itself, to become human and
sentient, and conscious of your affection. You desire to
embrace it, to caress it, to possess it; and finally, a soft sense
of possession grows up, and your visit becomes a perpetual
love-affair. It is very true that if you go there, like the author
of these lines, about the middle of March, a certain amount
of disappointment is possible. He had not been there for several years, and in the interval the beautiful and helpless city
had suffered all increase of injury. The barbarians are in full
possession, and you tremble for what they may do. You are
reminded, from the moment of your arrival, that Venice
scarcely exists any more as a city at all; that it exists only as a
battered peep-show and bazaar. There was a horde of savage
Germans encamped in the Piazza, and they filled the Ducal
Palace and the Academy with their uproar. The English and
Americans came a little later. They came in good time, with a
great many French, who were discreet enough to make very
long repasts at the Caffè Quadri, during which they were out
of the way. The months of April and May of the year 1881
were not, as a general thing, a favourable season for visiting
the Ducal Palace and the Academy. The valet-de-place had
marked them for his own, and held triumphant possession of
them. He celebrates his triumphs in a terrible brassy voice,
which resounds all over the place, and has, whatever language he be speaking, the accent of some other idiom. During
all the spring months in Venice these gentry abound in the
great resorts, and they lead their helpless captives through
churches and galleries in dense irresponsible groups. They

infest the Piazza; they pursue you along the Riva; they hang about the bridges and the doors of the *caffès*. In saying just now that I was disappointed at first, I had chiefly in mind the impression that assails me to-day in the whole precinct of St. Mark's. The condition of this ancient sanctuary is surely a great scandal. The pedlars and commissioners ply their trade – often a very unclean one – at the very door of the temple; they follow you across the threshold, into the sacred dusk, and pull your sleeve, and hiss into your ear, scuffling with each other for customers. There is a great deal of dishonour about St. Mark's altogether, and if Venice, as I say, has become a great bazaar, this exquisite edifice is now the biggest booth.

III.

It is treated as a booth in all ways, and if it had not, somehow, a great spirit of solemnity within it, the traveller would soon have little warrant for regarding it as a religious affair. The restoration of the outer walls, which has lately been so much attacked and defended, is certainly a great shock. Of the necessity of the work only an expert is, I suppose, in a position to judge; but there is no doubt that, if a necessity it be, it is one that is deeply to be regretted. To no more distressing necessity have people of taste lately had to resign themselves. Wherever the hand of the restorer has been laid all semblance of beauty has vanished; which is a sad fact, considering that the external loveliness of St. Mark's has been for ages less impressive only than that of the still comparatively uninjured interior. I know not what is the measure of necessity in such a case, and it appears indeed to be a very delicate question. To-day, at any rate, that admirable harmony of faded mosaic and marble, which, to the eye of the traveller emerging from the narrow streets that lead to the Piazza, filled all the farther end of it with a sort of dazzling, silvery presence – to-day this lovely vision is in a way to be completely reformed and, indeed, well-nigh abolished. The old softness and mellowness of colour – the work of the quiet centuries and of the breath of the salt sea – is giving way to large crude patches of new material, which have the effect of a monstrous malady rather than of a restoration to health. They look like blotches of red and white paint and dishonourable smears of chalk on the cheeks of a noble matron. The face toward the Piazzetta is in especial the newest-looking thing conceivable – as new as a new pair of boots, or as the morning's paper. We do not profess, however, to undertake a scientific quarrel with these changes; we admit that our complaint is a purely sentimental one. The march of industry in united Italy must doubtless be looked at as a whole, and one must endeavour to believe that it is through innumerable lapses of taste that this deeply interesting country is groping her way to her place among the nations. For the present, it is not to be denied, certain odd phases of the process are more visible than the result, to arrive at which it seems necessary that, as she was of old a passionate votary of the beautiful, she should to-day burn everything that she has adored. It is, doubtless, too soon to judge her, and there are moments when one is willing to forgive her even the restoration of St. Mark's. Inside, as well, there has been a considerable attempt to make the place more tidy; but the general effect, as yet, has not seriously suffered. What I chiefly remember is the straightening out of that dark and rugged old pavement – those deep undulations of primitive mosaic, in which the wondering tourist was thought to perceive an intended resemblance to the waves of the ocean. Whether intended or not, the analogy was an image the more in a treasure-house of images; but from a considerable portion of the church it has now disappeared. Throughout the greater part, indeed, the pavement remains as recent generations have known it – dark, rich, cracked, uneven, spotted with porphyry and time-blackened malachite, and polished by the knees of innumerable worshippers; but in other large sections the idea imitated by the restorers is that of the ocean in a dead calm, and the model they have taken, the floor of a London clubhouse or of a New York hotel. I think no Venetian and scarcely any Italian cares much for such differences; and when, a year ago, people in England were writing to the *Times* about the whole business, and holding meetings to protest against it, the dear children of the lagoon (so far as they heard, or heeded, the rumour) thought them partly busy-bodies and partly asses. Busy-bodies they doubtless were, but they took a good deal of disinterested trouble. It never occurs to the Venetian mind of to-day that such trouble may be worth taking; the Venetian mind vainly endeavours to conceive a state of existence in which personal questions are so insipid that people have to look for grievances in the wrongs of brick and marble. I must not, however, speak of St. Mark's as if I had the pretension of giving a description of it, or as if the reader desired one. The reader has been too well served already. It is surely the best-described building in the world. Open the *Stones of Venice*, open Théophile Gautier's *Italia*, and you will see. These writers take it very seriously, and it is only because there is another way of taking it that I venture to speak of it; the way that offers itself after you have been in Venice a couple of months, and the light is hot in the great Square, and you pass in under the pictured porticoes with a feeling of habit and friendliness, and a desire for something cool and dark. There are moments, after all, when the church is comparatively quiet and empty, when you may sit there with an easy consciousness of its beauty. From the moment, of course, that you go into any Italian church for any purpose but to say your prayers or look at the ladies, you rank yourself among the trooping barbarians I just spoke of; you treat the place like an orifice in the peep-show. Still, it is almost a spiritual function – or, at the worst, an amorous one – to feed one's eyes on the molten colour that drops from the hollow vaults and thickens the air with its richness. It is all so quiet and sad and faded; and yet it is all so brilliant and living. The strange figures in the mosaic pictures, bending with the curve of niche and vault, stare down through the glowing dimness; and the burnished gold that stands behind them catches the light on its little uneven cubes. St. Mark's owes nothing of its character to the beauty of proportion or perspective; there is nothing grandly balanced or far-arching; there are no long lines nor triumphs of the perpendicular. The church arches indeed; but it arches like a dusky cavern. Beauty of surface, of tone, of detail, of things near enough to touch and kneel upon and lean against – it is from this the effect proceeds. In this sort of beauty the place is incredibly rich, and you may go there every day and find afresh some lurking pictorial nook. It is a treasury of bits, as the painters say; and there are usually three or four painters, with their easels set up in uncertain equilibrium on the undulating floor. It is not easy to catch the real complexion of St. Mark's, and these laudable attempts at portraiture are apt to look either lurid or livid. But, if you cannot paint the old loose-looking marble slabs, the great panels of basalt and jasper, the crucifixes, of which the lonely anguish looks deeper in the vertical light, the tabernacles whose open doors disclose a dark Byzantine image, spotted with dull, crooked gems – if you cannot paint these things you can, at least, grow fond of them. You grow fond even of the old benches of red marble, partly worn away by the breeches of many generations, and

attached to the base of those wide pilasters, of which the precious plating, delightful in its faded brownness, with a faint
gray bloom upon it, bulges and yawns a little with honourable
age.

IV.

Even at first, when the vexatious sense of the city of the Doges
having been reduced to earning its living as a curiosity-shop
was in its keenness, there was a great deal of entertainment to
be got from lodging on the Riva degli Schiavoni and looking
out at the far-shimmering lagoon. There was entertainment
indeed in simply getting into the place and observing the
queer incidents of a Venetian installation. A great many persons contribute indirectly to this undertaking, and it is
surprising how they spring out at you during your novitiate to
remind you that they are bound up in some mysterious
manner with the constitution of your little establishment. It
was an interesting problem, for instance, to trace the subtle
connection existing between the niece of the landlady and the
occupancy of the fourth floor. Superficially, it was not easily
visible, as the young lady in question was a dancer at the
Fenice theatre – or, when that was closed, at the Rossini – and
might have been supposed to be absorbed by her professional
duties. It proved to be necessary, however, that she should
hover about the premises in a velvet jacket and a pair of black
kid gloves, with one little white button; as also, that she
should apply a thick coating of powder to her face, which had
a charming oval and a sweet, weak expression, like that of
most of the Venetian maidens, who, as a general thing (it was
not a peculiarity of the landlady's niece), are fond of
besmearing themselves with flour. It soon became plain that it
is not only the many-twinkling lagoon that you behold from a

habitation on the Riva; you see a little of everything Venetian. Straight across, before my windows, rose the great pink mass of San Giorgio Maggiore, which, for an ugly Palladian church, has a success beyond all reason. It is a success of position, of colour, of the immense detached Campanile, tipped with a tall gold angel. I know not whether it is because San Giorgio is so grandly conspicuous, and because it has a great deal of worn, faded-looking brickwork; but for many persons the whole place has a kind of suffusion of rosiness. If we were asked what is the leading colour at Venice we should say pink, and yet, after all, we cannot remember that this elegant tint occurs very often. It is a faint, shimmering, airy, watery pink; the bright sea-light seems to flush with it, and the pale whitish-green of lagoon and canal to drink it in. There is, indeed, in Venice a great deal of very evident brickwork, which is never fresh or loud in colour, but always burnt out, as it were, always exquisitely mild. There are certain little mental pictures that rise before the sentimental tourist at the simple mention, written or spoken, of the places he has loved. When I hear, when I see, the magical name I have written above these pages, it is not of the great Square that I think, with its strange basilica and its high arcades, nor of the wide mouth of the Grand Canal, with the stately steps and the well-poised dome of the Salute; it is not of the low lagoon, nor the sweet Piazzetta, nor the dark chambers of St. Mark's. I simply see a narrow canal in the heart of the city – a patch of green water and a surface of pink wall. The gondola moves slowly; it gives a great, smooth swerve, passes under a bridge, and the gondolier's cry, carried over the quiet water, makes a kind of splash in the stillness. A girl is passing over the little bridge, which has an arch like a camel's back, with an old shawl on her head, which makes her look charming; you see her against the sky as you float beneath. The pink of the old wall seems to fill the whole place; it sinks even into the opaque water. Behind the wall is a garden, out of which the long arm of a white June rose – the roses of Venice are splendid – has flung itself by way of spontaneous ornament. On the other side of this small water-way is a great shabby façade of Gothic windows and balconies – balconies on which dirty clothes are hung and under which a cavernous-looking doorway opens from a low flight of slimy water-steps. It is very hot and still, the canal has a queer smell, and the whole place is enchanting. It is poor work, however, talking about the colour of things in Venice. The sentimental tourist is perpetually looking at it from his window, when he is not floating about with that delightful sense of being for the moment a part of it, which any gentleman in a gondola is free to entertain. Venetian windows and balconies are a dreadful lure, and while you rest your elbows on these cushioned ledges the precious hours fly away. But, in truth, Venice is not, in fair weather, a place for concentration of mind. The effort required for sitting down to a writing-table is heroic, and the brightest page of MS. looks dull beside the brilliancy of your *milieu*. All nature beckons you forth, and murmurs to you sophistically that such hours should be devoted to collecting impressions. Afterward, in ugly places, at unprivileged times, you can convert your impressions into prose. Fortunately for the present proser, the weather was not always fine; the first month was wet and windy, and it was better to look at the lagoon from an open casement than to respond to the advances of persuasive gondoliers. Even then, however, there was a constant entertainment in the view. It was all cold colour, and the steel-gray floor of the lagoon was stroked the wrong way by the wind. Then there were charming cool intervals, when the churches, the houses, the anchored fishing-boats, the whole gently-curving line of the Riva, seemed to be washed with a pearly white. Later it all turned warm – warm to the eye as well as to other senses. After the middle of May the whole place was in a glow. The sea took on a thousand shades, but they were only infinite variations of blue, and those rosy walls I just spoke of began to flush in the thick sunshine. Every patch of colour, every yard of weather-stained stucco, every glimpse of nestling garden or daub of sky above a *calle*, began to shine and sparkle – began, as the painters say, to "compose". The lagoon was streaked with odd currents, which played across it like huge, smooth finger-marks. The gondolas multiplied and spotted it all over; every gondola and every gondolier looking, at a distance, precisely like every other. There is something strange and fascinating in this mysterious impersonality of the gondola. It has an identity when you are in it, but, thanks to their all being of the same size, shape, and colour, and of the same deportment and gait, it has none, or as little as possible, as you see it pass before you. From my windows on the Riva there was always the same silhouette – the long, black, slender skiff, lifting its head and throwing it back a little, moving yet seeming not to move, with the grotesquely-graceful figure on the poop. This figure inclines, as may be, more to the graceful or to the grotesque – standing in the "second position" of the dancing-master, but indulging, from the waist upward, in a freedom of movement which that functionary would deprecate. One may say, as a general thing, that there is something rather awkward in the movement of even the most graceful gondolier, and something graceful in the movement of the most awkward. In the graceful men of course the grace predominates, and nothing can be finer than the large firm way in which, from their point of vantage, they throw themselves over their tremendous oar. It has the boldness of a plunging bird, and the regularity of a pendulum. Sometimes, as you see this movement in profile, in a gondola

that passes you – see, as you recline on your own low cush-
ions, the arching body of the gondolier lifted up against the
sky – it has a kind of nobleness which suggests an image on a
Greek frieze. The gondolier at Venice is your very good friend
– if you choose him happily – and on the quality of the personage depends a good deal that of your impressions. He is a
part of your daily life, your double, your shadow, your com-
plement. Most people, I think, either like their gondolier or
hate him – and if they like him, like him very much. In this
case they take an interest in him after his departure; wish him
to be sure of employment, speak of him as the gem of gondoliers, and tell their friends to be certain to "secure" him. There
is usually no difficulty in securing him; there is nothing elusive
or reluctant about a gondolier. They are, for the most part,
excellent fellows, and the sentimental tourist must always have
a kindness for them. More than the rest of the population, of
course, they are the children of Venice; they are associated
with its idiosyncrasy, with its essence, with its silence, with its
melancholy. When I say they are associated with its silence, I
should immediately add that they are associated also with its
sound. Among themselves they are an extraordinarily talkative
company. They chatter at the *traghetti*, where they always
have some sharp point under discussion; they bawl across the
canals; they bespeak your commands as you approach; they
defy each other from afar. If you happen to have a *traghetto*
under your window, you are well aware that they are a vocal
race. I should go even farther than I went just now, and say
that the voice of the gondolier is, in fact, the sound of Venice.
There is scarcely any other, and that, indeed, is part of the
interest of the place. There is no noise there save distinctly
human noise; no rumbling, no vague uproar, nor rattle of
wheels and hoofs. It is all articulate, personal sound. One may
say, indeed, that Venice is, emphatically, the city of conversa-

tion; people talk all over the place, because there is nothing to interfere with their being heard. Among the populace it is a kind of family party. The still water carries the voice, and good Venetians exchange confidences at a distance of half a mile. It saves a world of trouble, and they don't like trouble. Their delightful garrulous language helps them to make Venetian life a long *conversazione*. This language, with its soft elisions, its odd transpositions, its kindly contempt for consonants and other disagreeables, has in it something peculiarly human and accommodating. If your gondolier had no other merit, he would have the merit that he speaks Venetian. This may rank as a merit, even – some people perhaps would say especially – when you don't understand what he says. But he adds to it other graces which make him an agreeable feature in your life. The price he sets on his services is touchingly small, and he has a happy art of being obsequious, without being, or, at least, without seeming, abject. For occasional liberalities he evinces an almost lyrical gratitude. In short, he has delightfully good manners, a merit which he shares, for the most part, with Venetians at large. One grows very fond of these people, and the reason of one's fondness is the frankness and sweetness of their address. That of the Italian people, in general, has much to recommend it; but in the Venetian manner there is some-thing peculiarly ingratiating. One feels that the race is old, that it has a long and rich civilisation in its blood, and that if it has not been blessed by fortune, it has at least been polished by time. It has not a genius for morality, and indeed makes few pretensions in that direction. It scruples not to represent the false as the true, and is liable to confusion in the attribution of property. It is peculiarly susceptible to the tender sentiment, which it cultivates with a graceful disregard of the more rigid formalities. I am not sure that it is very brave, and was not struck with its being very industrious. But it has an unfailing sense of the amenities of life; the poorest Venetian is a natural man of the world. He is better company than persons of his class are apt to be among the nations of industry and virtue – where people are also, sometimes, perceived to lie and steal. He has a great desire to please and to be pleased.

V.

In this latter point the cold-blooded stranger begins at last to imitate him; he begins to lead a life that is, before all things, good-humoured: unless, indeed, he allow himself, like Mr. Ruskin, to be put out of his good-humour by Titian and Tiepolo. The hours he spends among the pictures are his best hours in Venice, and I am ashamed of myself to have written so much of common things when I might have been making festoons of the names of the masters. But, when we have covered our page with such festoons, what more is left to say? When one has said Carpaccio and Bellini, the Tintoret and the Veronese, one has struck a note that must be left to resound at will. Everything has been said about the mighty painters, and it is of little importance to record that one traveller the more has found them to his taste. "Went this morning, to the Academy; was very much pleased with Titian's 'Assumption'." That honest phrase has doubtless been written in many a traveller's diary, and was not indiscreet on the part of its author. But it appeals little to the general reader, and we must, moreover, not expose our deepest feelings. Since I have mentioned Titian's "Assumption", I must say that there are some people who have been less pleased with it than the gentleman we have just imagined. It is one of the possible disappointments of Venice, and you may, if you like, take advantage of your privilege of not caring for it. It imparts a look of great richness to the side of the beautiful room of the Academy on which it hangs; but the same room contains two or three works less known to fame which are equally capable of inspiring a passion. "The 'Annunciation' struck me as coarse and superficial": that was once written in a simple-minded traveller's note-book. At Venice, strange to say, Titian is altogether a disappointment; the city of his adoption is far from containing the best of him. Madrid, Paris, London, Florence, Dresden, Munich – these are the homes of his greatness. There are other painters who have but a single home, and the greatest of these is the Tintoret. Close beside him sit Carpaccio and Bellini, who make with him the dazzling Venetian trio. The Veronese may be seen and measured in other places; he is most splendid in Venice, but he shines in Paris and in Dresden. You may walk out of the noon-day dusk of Trafalgar Square in November, and in one of the chambers of the National Gallery see the family of Darius rustling and pleading and weeping at the feet of Alexander. Alexander is a beautiful young Venetian in crimson pantaloons, and the picture sends a glow into the cold London twilight. You may sit before it for an hour, and dream you are floating to the water-gate of the Ducal Palace, where a certain old beggar, with one of the handsomest heads in the world – he has sat to a hundred painters for Doges, and for personages more sacred – has a prescriptive right to pretend to pull your gondola to the steps and to hold out a greasy, immemorial cap. But you must go to Venice, in fact, to see the other masters, who form part of your life while you are there, and illuminate your view of the universe. It is difficult to express one's relation to them; for the whole Venetian art-world is so near, so familiar, so much an extension and adjunct of the actual world, that it seems almost invidious to say one owes more to one of them than to another. Nowhere (not even in Holland, where the correspondence between the real aspects and the little polished canvases is so constant and so exquisite) do art and life seem so interfused and, as it were, so consanguineous. All the splendour of light and colour, all the Venetian air and the Venetian history, are on the walls and ceilings of the palaces, and all the genius of the masters, all the images and visions they have left upon canvas, seem to tremble in the sunbeams and dance upon the waves. That is the perpetual interest of the place – that you live in a certain sort of knowledge as in a rosy cloud. You don't go into the churches and galleries by way of a change from the streets; you go into them because they offer you an exquisite reproduction of the things that surround you. All Venice was both model and painter, and life was so pictorial that art could not help becoming so. With all diminutions life is pictorial still, and this fact gives an extraordinary freshness to one's perception of the great Venetian works. You judge of them not as a connoisseur, but as a man of the world, and you enjoy them because they are so social and so actual. Perhaps, of all works of art that are equally great, they demand least reflection on the part of the spectator – they make least of a mystery of being enjoyed. Reflection only confirms your admiration, but it is almost ashamed to show its head. These things speak so frankly and benignantly to the sense that we feel there is reason as well in such an address. But it is hard, as I say, to express all this, and it is painful as well to attempt it – painful, because in the memory of vanished hours so filled with beauty the sense of present loss is overwhelming. Exquisite hours, enveloped in light and silence, to have known them once is to have always a terrible standard of enjoyment. Certain lovely mornings of May and June come back with an ineffaceable fairness. Venice is not smothered in flowers at this season, in the manner of Florence and Rome; but the sea and sky themselves seem to blossom and rustle. The gondola waits at the wave-washed steps, and if you are wise you will take your place beside a discriminating companion. Such a companion, in Venice, should, of course, be of the sex that discriminates most finely. An intelligent woman who knows her Venice seems doubly intelligent, and it makes no woman's perceptions less keen to be aware that she cannot help looking graceful as she glides over the waves. The handsome Pasquale, with uplifted oar, awaits your command, knowing, in a general way, from observation of your habits, that your intention is to go to see a picture or two. It perhaps does not immensely matter what picture you choose: the whole affair is so charming. It is charming to wander through the light and shade of intricate canals, with perpetual architecture above you and perpetual fluidity beneath. It is charming to disembark at the polished steps of a little empty *campo* – a sunny, shabby square, with an old well in the middle, an old church on one side, and tall Venetian windows looking down. Sometimes the windows are tenantless; sometimes a lady in a faded dressing-gown is leaning vaguely on the sill. There is always an old man holding out his hat for coppers; there are always three or four small boys dodging possible umbrella-pokes while they precede you, in the manner of custodians, to the door of the church.

VI.

The churches of Venice are rich in pictures, and many a masterpiece lurks in the unaccommodating gloom of side-chapels and sacristies. Many a noble work is perched behind the dusty candles and muslin roses of a scantily-visited altar; some of them, indeed, are hidden behind the altar, in a darkness that can never be explored. The facilities offered you for approaching the picture, in such cases, are a kind of mockery of your irritated desire. You stand on tip-toe on a three-legged stool, you climb a rickety ladder, you almost mount upon the shoulders of the *custode*. You do everything but see the picture. You see just enough to perceive that it is beautiful. You catch a glimpse of a divine head, of a fig-tree against a mellow sky; but the rest is impenetrable mystery. You renounce all hope, for instance, of approaching the magnificent Cima da Coneliano in San Giovanni in Bragora; and bethinking yourself of the immaculate purity that dwells in the works of this master, you renounce it with chagrin and pain. Behind the high altar, in that church, there hangs a Baptism of Christ, by Cima, which, I believe, has been more or less repainted. You can make the thing out in spots; you can see that it has a fulness of perfection. But you turn away from it with a stiff neck, and promise yourself consolation in the Academy and at the Madonna dell' Orto, where two noble pictures, by the same hand – pictures as clear as a summer twilight – present themselves in better circumstances. It may be said, as a general thing, that you never see the Tintoret. You admire him, you adore him, you think him the greatest of painters, but, in the great majority of cases, you don't see him. This is partly his own fault; so many of his works have turned to blackness and are positively rotting in their frames. At the Scuola di San Rocco, where there are acres of the Tintoret, there is scarcely anything at all adequately visible save the immense "Crucifixion" in the upper story. It is true that in looking at this huge composition you look at many pictures; it has not only a multitude of figures, but a wealth of episodes; and you pass from one of these to the other as if you were "doing" a gallery. Surely, no single picture in the world contains more of human life; there is everything in it, including the most exquisite beauty. It is one of the greatest things of art; it is always interesting. There are pictures by the Tintoret which contain touches more exquisite, revelations of beauty more radiant, but there is no other vision of so intense a reality and execution so splendid. The interest, the impressiveness, of that whole corner of Venice, however melancholy the effect of its gorgeous and ill-lighted chambers, gives a strange importance to a visit to the Scuola. Nothing that all travellers go to see appears to suffer less from the incursions of travellers. It is one of the loneliest booths of the bazaar, and the author of these lines has always had the good fortune, which he wishes to every other traveller, of having it to himself. I think most visitors find the place rather alarming and wicked-looking. They walk about a while among the fitful figures that gleam here and there out of the great tapestry (as it were) with which the painter has hung all the walls, and then, depressed and bewildered by the portentous solemnity of these objects, by strange glimpses of unnatural scenes, by the echo of their lonely footsteps on the vast stone floors, they take a hasty departure, and find themselves again, with a sense of release from danger, and of the *genius loci* having been a sort of mad white-washer, who worked with a bad mixture, in the bright light of the *campo*, among the beggars, the orange-vendors, and the passing gondolas. Solemn, indeed, is the place, solemn and strangely suggestive, for the simple reason that we shall scarcely find four walls elsewhere that inclose within a like area an equal quantity of genius. The air is thick with it, and dense and difficult to breathe; for it was genius that was not happy, inasmuch as it lacked the art to fix itself for ever. It is not immortality that we breathe at the Scuola di San Rocco, but conscious, reluctant mortality. Fortunately, however, we have the Ducal Palace, where everything is so brilliant and splendid that the poor dusky Tintoret is lifted in spite of himself into the concert. This deeply original building is, of course, the loveliest thing in Venice, and a morning's stroll there is a

wonderful illumination. Cunningly select your hour – half the
enjoyment of Venice is a question of dodging – and go at
about one o'clock, when the tourists have gone to lunch and
the echoes of the charming chambers have gone to sleep
among the sunbeams. There is no brighter place in Venice; by
which I mean that, on the whole, there is none half so bright.
The reflected sunshine plays up through the great windows
from the glittering lagoon, and shimmers and twinkles over
gilded walls and ceilings. All the history of Venice, all its
splendid, stately past, glows around you in a strong sea-light.
Every one here is magnificent, but the great Veronese is the
most magnificent of all. He swims before you in a silver
cloud; he thrones in an eternal morning. The deep blue sky
burns behind him, streaked across with milky bars; the white
colonnades sustain the richest canopies, under which the first
gentlemen and ladies in the world both render homage and
receive it. Their glorious garments rustle in the air of the sea,
and their sun-lighted faces are the very complexion of Venice.
The mixture of pride and piety, of politics and religion, of art
and patriotism, gives a magnificent dignity to every scene.
Never was a painter more nobly joyous, never did an artist
take a greater delight in life, seeing it all as a kind of breezy
festival and feeling it through the medium of perpetual success. He revels in the gold-framed ovals of the ceilings, with
the fluttering movement of an embroidered banner that
tosses itself into the blue. He was the happiest of painters,
and he produced the happiest picture in the world. The
"Rape of Europa" surely deserves this title; it is impossible to
look at it without aching with envy. Nowhere else in art is
such a temperament revealed; never did inclination and
opportunity combine to express such enjoyment. The mixture of flowers and gems and brocade, of blooming flesh and
shining sea and waving groves, of youth, health, movement,

desire – all this is the brightest vision that ever descended
upon the soul of a painter. Happy the artist who could entertain such a vision; happy the artist who could paint it as the
"Rape of Europa" is painted. The Tintoret's visions were not
so bright as that; but he had several that were radiant enough.
In the room that contains the "Rape of Europa" are several
smaller canvases by the greatly more complex genius of the
Scuola di San Rocco, which are almost simple in their loveliness, almost happy in their simplicity. They have kept their
brightness through the centuries, and they shine with their
neighbours in those golden rooms. There is a piece of
painting in one of them which is one of the sweetest things in
Venice, and which reminds one afresh of those wild flowers
of execution that bloom so profusely and so unheeded in the
dark corners of all of the Tintoret's work. "Pallas chasing
away Mars" is, I believe, the name that is given to the picture;
and it represents in fact a young woman of noble appearance
administering a gentle push to a fine young man in armour,
as if to tell him to keep his distance. It is of the gentleness of
this push that I speak, the charming way in which she puts
out her arm, with a single bracelet on it, and rests her young
hand, with its rosy fingers parted, upon his dark breastplate.
She bends her enchanting head with the effort – a head which
has all the strange fairness that the Tintoret always sees in
women – and the soft, living, flesh-like glow of all these
members, over which the brush has scarcely paused in its
course, is as pretty an example of genius as all Venice can
show. But why speak of the Tintoret when I can say nothing
of the great "Paradise", which unfolds its somewhat smoky
splendour, and the wonder of its multitudinous circles, in one
of the other chambers? If it were not one of the first pictures
in the world, it would be about the biggest, and it must be
confessed that at first the spectator gets from it chiefly an

impression of quantity. Then he sees that this quantity is
really wealth; that the dim confusion of faces is a magnificent
composition, and that some of the details of this composition
are supremely beautiful. It is impossible, however, in a retrospect of Venice, to specify one's happiest hours, though, as
one looks backward, certain ineffaceable moments start here
and there into vividness. How is it possible to forget one's
visits to the sacristy of the Frari, however frequent they may
have been, and the great work of John Bellini which forms
the treasure of that apartment?

VII.

Nothing in Venice is more perfect than this, and we know of
no work of art more complete. The picture is in three com-
partments: the Virgin sits in the central division with her
child; two venerable saints, standing close together, occupy
each of the others. It is impossible to imagine anything more
finished or more ripe. It is one of those things that sum up the
genius of a painter, the experience of a life, the teaching of a
school. It seems painted with molten gems, which have only
been clarified by time, and it is as solemn as it is gorgeous,
and as simple as it is deep. John Bellini is, more or less, everywhere in Venice, and wherever he is, he is almost certain to
be first – first, I mean, in his own line; he paints little else
than the Madonna and the saints; he has not Carpaccio's care
for human life at large, nor the Tintoret's, nor that of the
Veronese. Some of his greater pictures, however, where several figures are clustered together, have a richness of sanctity
that is almost profane. There is one of them on the dark side
of the room at the Academy, containing Titian's
"Assumption", which, if we could only see it – its position is
an inconceivable scandal – would evidently be one of the

mightiest of so-called sacred pictures. So, too, is the
Madonna of San Zaccaria, hung in a cold, dim, dreary place,
ever so much too high, but so mild and serene, and so grandly
disposed and accompanied, that the proper attitude for even
the most critical amateur, as he looks at it, seems to be the
bended knee. There is another noble John Bellini, one of the
very few in which there is no Virgin, at San Giovanni
Crisostomo – a St. Jerome, in a red dress, sitting aloft upon
the rocks, with a landscape of extraordinary purity behind
him. The absence of the peculiarly erect Madonna makes it
an interesting surprise among the works of the painter, and
gives it a somewhat less strenuous air. But it has brilliant
beauty, and the St. Jerome is a delightful old personage. The
same church contains another great picture, for which he
must find a shrine apart in his memory; one of the most interesting things he will have seen, if not the most brilliant.
Nothing appeals more to him than three figures of Venetian
ladies which occupy the foreground of a smallish canvas of
Sebastian del Piombo, placed above the high altar of San
Giovanni Crisostomo. Sebastian was a Venetian by birth, but
few of his productions are to be seen in his native place; few,
indeed, are to be seen anywhere. The picture represents the
patron-saint of the church, accompanied by other saints, and
by the worldly votaries I have mentioned. These ladies stand
together on the left, holding in their hands little white cas-
kets; two of them are in profile, but the foremost turns her
face to the spectator. This face and figure are almost unique
among the beautiful things of Venice, and they leave the susceptible observer with the impression of having made, or
rather having missed, a strange, a dangerous, but a most valuable, acquaintance. The lady, who is superbly handsome, is
the typical Venetian of the sixteenth century, and she remains
in the mind as the perfect flower of that society. Never was

there greater air of breeding, a deeper expression of tranquil superiority. She walks like a goddess – as if she trod, without sinking, the waves of the Adriatic. It is impossible to conceive a more perfect expression of the aristocratic spirit, either in its pride or in its benignity. This magnificent creature is so strong and secure that she is gentle, and so quiet that, in comparison, all minor assumptions of calmness suggest only a vulgar alarm. But for all this, there are depths of possible disorder in her light-coloured eye. I had meant, however, to say nothing about her, for it is not right to speak of Sebastian when one has not found room for Carpaccio. These visions come to one, and one can neither hold them nor brush them aside. Memories of Carpaccio, the magnificent, the delightful – it is not for want of such visitations, but only for want of space, that I have not said of him what I would. There is little enough need of it for Carpaccio's sake, his fame being brighter to-day – thanks to the generous lamp Mr. Ruskin has held up to it – than it has ever been. Yet there is something ridiculous in talking of Venice without making him, almost, the refrain. He and the Tintoret are the two great realists, and it is hard to say which is the more human, the more various. The Tintoret had the mightier temperament, but Carpaccio, who had the advantage of more newness and more responsibility, sailed nearer to perfection. Here and there he quite touches it, as in the enchanting picture, at the Academy, of St. Ursula asleep in her little white bed, in her high, clean room, where the angel visits her at dawn; or in the noble St. Jerome in his study, at S. Giorgio degli Schiavoni. This latter work is a pearl of sentiment, and I may add, without being fantastic, a ruby of colour. It unites the most masterly finish with a kind of universal largeness of feeling, and he who has it well in his memory will never hear the name of Carpaccio without a throb of almost personal affection. This, indeed, is the feeling that descends upon you in that wonderful little chapel of St. George of the Slaves, where this most personal and sociable of artists has expressed all the sweetness of his imagination. The place is small and incommodious, the pictures are out of sight and ill-lighted, the custodian is rapacious, the visitors are mutually intolerable, but the shabby little chapel is a palace of art. Mr. Ruskin has written a pamphlet about it which is a real aid to enjoyment, though I cannot but think the generous artist, with his keen senses and his just feeling, would have suffered at hearing his eulogist declare that one of his other productions – in the Museo Civico in Palazzo Correr, a delightful portrait of two Venetian ladies, with pet animals – is the "finest picture in the world". It has no need of that to be thought admirable; and what more can a painter desire?

VIII.

May in Venice is better than April, but June is best of all. Then the days are hot, but not too hot, and the nights are more beautiful than the days. Then Venice is rosier than ever in the morning and more golden than ever as the day descends. It seems to expand and evaporate, to multiply all its reflections and iridescences. Then the life of its people and the strangeness of its constitution become a perpetual comedy, or, at least, a perpetual drama. Then the gondola is your sole habitation, and you spend days between sea and sky. You go to the Lido, though the Lido has been spoiled. When I was first in Venice, in 1869, it was a very natural place, and there was only a rough lane across the little island from the landing-place to the beach. There was a bathing-place in those days, and a restaurant, which was very bad, but where, in the warm evenings, your dinner did not much matter as you sat letting

it cool upon the wooden terrace that stretched out into the
sea. To-day the Lido is a part of united Italy, and has been
made the victim of villainous improvements. A little cockney
village has sprung up on its rural bosom, and a third-rate
boulevard leads from Santa Elisabetta to the Adriatic. There
are bitumen walls and gas-lamps, lodging-houses, shops, and a
teatro diurno. The bathing establishment is bigger than before,
and the restaurant as well; but it is a compensation, perhaps,
that the cuisine is no better. Such as it is, however, you will not
scorn occasionally to partake of it on the breezy platform
under which bathers dart and splash, and which looks out to
where the fishing-boats, with sails of orange and crimson
wander along the darkening horizon. The beach at the Lido is
still lonely and beautiful, and you can easily walk away from
the cockney village. The return to Venice in the sunset is classical and indispensable, and those who, at that glowing hour,
have floated toward the towers that rise out of the lagoon, will
not easily part with the impression. But you indulge in larger
excursions – you go to Burano and Torcello, to Malamocco
and Chioggia. Torcello, like the Lido, has been improved; the
deeply interesting little cathedral of the eighth century, which
stood there on the edge of the sea, as touching in its ruin, with
its grassy threshold and its primitive mosaics, as the bleached
bones of a human skeleton washed ashore by the tide, has now
been restored and made cheerful, and the charm of the place,
its strange and suggestive desolation, has well-nigh departed.
It will still serve you as a pretext, however, for a day on the
lagoon, especially as you will disembark at Burano and admire
the wonderful fisher-folk, whose good looks – and bad manners, I am sorry to say – can scarcely be exaggerated. Burano
is celebrated for the beauty of its women and the rapacity of
its children, and it is a fact that though some of the ladies are
rather bold about it, every one of them shows you a handsome

face. The children assail you for coppers, and, in their desire
to be satisfied, pursue your gondola into the sea. Chioggia is a
larger Burano, and you carry away from either place a half-
sad, half-cynical, but altogether pictorial impression; the
impression of bright-coloured hovels, of bathing in stagnant
canals, of young girls with faces of a delicate shape and a susceptible expression, with splendid heads of hair and
complexions smeared with powder, faded yellow shawls that
hang like old Greek draperies, and little wooden shoes that
click as they go up and down the steps of the convex bridges;
of brown-cheeked matrons with lustrous tresses and high tem-
pers, massive throats encased with gold beads, and eyes that
meet your own with a certain traditional defiance. The men
throughout the islands of Venice are almost as handsome as
the women; I have never seen so many good-looking fellows.
At Burano and Chioggia they sit mending their nets, or lounge
at the street corners, where conversation is always high-
pitched, or clamour to you to take a boat; and everywhere
they decorate the scene with their splendid colour – cheeks
and throats as richly brown as the sails of their fishing-smacks
– their sea-faded tatters which are always a "costume" – their
soft Venetian jargon, and the gallantry with which they wear
their hats – an article that nowhere sits so well as on a mass of
dense Venetian curls. If you are happy, you will find yourself,
after a June day in Venice (about ten o'clock), on a balcony
that overhangs the Grand Canal, with your elbows on the
broad ledge, a cigarette in your teeth, and a little good company beside you. The gondolas pass beneath, the watery
surface gleams here and there from their lamps, some of which
are coloured lanterns that move mysteriously in the darkness.
There are some evenings in June when there are too many
gondolas, too many lanterns, too many serenades in front of
the hotels. The serenading (in particular) is overdone; but on

such a balcony as I speak of you needn't suffer from it, for in the apartment behind you – an accessible refuge – there is more good company, there are more cigarettes. If you are wise you will step back there presently.

II.

ITALY REVISITED.

1877.

I.

I waited in Paris until after the elections for the new Chamber (they took place on the 14th of October); for only after one had learned that the celebrated attempt of Marshal MacMahon and his ministers to drive the French nation to the polls like a flock of huddling sheep, each with the white ticket of an official candidate round his neck, had not achieved the success which the energy of the process might have promised – only then was it possible to draw a long-breath and deprive the republican party of such support as might have been conveyed in one's sympathetic presence. Seriously speaking, too, the weather had been enchanting, and there were Italian sensations to be encountered without leaving the banks of the Seine. Day after day the air was filled with golden light, and even those chalkish vistas of the Parisian *beaux quartiers* assumed the iridescent tints of autumn. Autumn-weather in Europe is often such a very sorry affair that a fair-minded American will have it on his conscience to call attention to a rainless and radiant October.

The echoes of the electoral strife kept me company for a while after starting upon that abbreviated journey to Turin, which, as you leave Paris at night, in a train unprovided with encouragements to slumber, is a singular mixture of the odious and the charming. The charming, however, I think, prevails; for the dark half of the journey is, in fact, the least interesting. The morning light ushers you into the romantic gorges of the Jura, and after a big bowl of *café au lait* at Culoz you may compose yourself comfortably for the climax of your spectacle. The day before leaving Paris I met a French friend who had just returned from a visit to a Tuscan country-seat, where he had been watching the vintage. "Italy," he said, "is more lovely than words can tell, and France, steeped in this electoral turmoil, seems no better than a bear-garden." That part of the bear-garden through which you travel as you approach the Mont-Cenis seemed to me that day very beautiful. The autumn colouring, thanks to the absence of rain, had been vivid and crisp, and the vines that swung their low garlands between the mulberries, in the neighbourhood of Chambéry, looked like long festoons of coral and amber. The frontier station of Modane, on the farther side of the Mont-Cenis tunnel, is a very ill-regulated place; but even the most irritable of tourists, meeting it on his way southward, will be disposed to consider it good-naturedly. There is far too much bustling and scrambling, and the facilities afforded you for the obligatory process of ripping open your luggage before the officers of the Italian custom-house are much scantier than should be; but, for myself, there is something that deprecates irritation in the shabby green and gray uniforms of all the Italian officials who stand loafing about and watching the northern invaders scramble back into marching order. Wearing an administrative uniform does not necessarily spoil a man's temper, as in France one is sometimes led to believe; for these excellent under-paid Italians carry theirs as lightly as possible, and their answers to your inquiries do not in the least bristle with rapiers, buttons, and cockades. After leaving Modane you slide straight down-hill into the Italy of your desire; and there is something very impressive in the way the road edges along these great precipices which stand shoulder to shoulder, in a long perpendicular file, until they finally admit you to a distant glimpse of the ancient capital of Piedmont.

Turin is not a city to make, in vulgar parlance, a fuss about, and I pay an extravagant tribute to subjective emotion in speaking of it as ancient. But if the place is not so peninsular as Florence and Rome, at least it is more so than New York and Paris; and while the traveller walks about the great arcades and looks at the fourth-rate shop windows, he does not scruple to cultivate a shameless optimism. Relatively speaking Turin is diverting; but there is, after all, no reason in a large collection of shabbily-stuccoed houses, disposed in a rigidly rectangular manner, for passing a day of deep, still gaiety. The only reason, I am afraid, is the old superstition of Italy – that property in the very look of the written word, the evocation of a myriad images, that makes any lover of the arts take Italian satisfactions upon easier terms than any other. Italy is an idea to conjure with, and we play tricks upon our credulity even with such inferior apparatus as is offered to our hand at Turin. I walked about all the morning under the tall porticoes, thinking it sufficient entertainment to take note of the soft, warm air, of that colouring of things in Italy that is at once broken and harmonious, and of the comings and goings, the physiognomy and manners, of the excellent Turinese. I had opened the old book again; the old charm was in the style; I was in a more delightful world. I saw nothing surpassingly beautiful or curious; but the appreciative traveller finds a vividness in nameless details. And I must add that on the threshold of Italy he tastes of one solid and perfectly definable pleasure, in finding himself among the traditions of the grand style in architecture. It must be said that we have still to come to Italy to see great houses. (I am speaking more particularly of town-architecture.) In northern cities there are beautiful houses, picturesque and curious houses; sculptured gables that hang over the street, charming bay-windows, hooded doorways, elegant proportions, and a profusion of delicate ornament; but a good specimen of an old Italian palazzo has a nobleness that is all its own. We laugh at Italian "palaces", at their peeling paint, their nudity, their dreariness; but they have the great palatial quality – elevation and extent. They make smaller houses seem beggarly; they round their great arches and interspace their huge windows with a noble indifference to the cost of materials. These grand proportions – the colossal basements, the doorways that seem meant for cathedrals, the far-away cornices – impart by contrast a humble and *bourgeois* expression to those less exalted dwellings in which the air of grandeur depends largely upon the help of the upholsterer. At Turin my first feeling was really one of shame for the architectural manners of our northern lands. I have heard people who know the Italians well say that at bottom they despise all the rest of mankind and regard them as barbarians. I doubt of it, for the Italians strike me as having less national vanity than any other people in Europe; but if the charge had its truth there would be some ground for the feeling in the fact that they live in palaces.

An impression which, on coming back to Italy, I find even stronger than when it was first received is that of the contrast between the fecundity of the great artistic period and the vulgarity of the Italian genius of to-day. The first few hours spent on Italian soil are sufficient to renew it, and the phenomenon that I allude to is surely one of the most singular in human history. That the people who but three hundred years ago had the best taste in the world should now have the worst; that having produced the noblest, loveliest, costliest works, they should now be given up to the manufacture of objects at once ugly and paltry; that the race of which Michelangelo and Raphael, Leonardo and Titian were characteristic should have no other title to distinction than third-rate *genre* pictures and catch-penny statues – all this is a frequent perplexity to the observer of actual Italian life. The flower of art in these latter years has ceased to bloom very powerfully anywhere; but nowhere does it seem so drooping and withered as in the shadow of the immortal embodiments of the old Italian genius. You go into a church or a gallery and feast your fancy upon a splendid picture or an exquisite piece of sculpture, and on issuing from the door that has admitted you to the beautiful past you are confronted with something that has all the effect of a very bad joke. The aspect of your lodging (the carpets, the curtains, the upholstery in general, with their crude and violent colouring and their vulgar material), the third-rate look of the shops, the extreme bad taste of the dress of the women, the cheapness and baseness of every attempt at decoration in the cafés and railway stations, the hopeless frivolity of everything that pretends to be a work of art – all this modern crudity runs riot over the relics of the great period.

We can do a thing for the first time but once; it is but once for all that we can have a pleasure in its freshness. This is a law which is not on the whole, I think, to be regretted, for we sometimes learn to know things better by not enjoying them too much. It is certain, however, at the same time, that a traveller who has worked off the primal fermentation of his relish for this inexhaustibly interesting country has by no means entirely drained the cup. After thinking of Italy as historical and artistic, it will do him no great harm to think of her, for a while, as modern, an idea supposed (as a general thing correctly) to be fatally at variance with the Byronic, the Ruskinian, the artistic, poetic, æsthetic manner of considering this fascinating peninsula. He may grant – I don't say it is

absolutely necessary – that modern Italy is ugly, prosaic, pro-
vokingly out of relation to the diary and the album; it is
nevertheless true that, at the point things have come to,
modern Italy in a manner imposes herself. I had not been
many hours in the country before I became conscious of this
circumstance; and I may add that, the first irritation past, I
found myself able to accept it. And if we think of it, nothing
is more easy to understand than a certain displeasure on the
part of the young Italy of to-day at being looked at by all the
world as a kind of soluble pigment. Young Italy, preoccupied
with its economical and political future, must be heartily tired
of being admired for its eyelashes and its pose. In one of
Thackeray's novels there is mention of a young artist who sent
to the Royal Academy a picture representing "A Contadino
dancing with a Trasteverina at the door of a Locanda, to the
music of a Pifferaro." It is in this attitude and with these conventional accessories that the world has hitherto seen fit to
represent young Italy, and I do not wonder that, if the youth
has any spirit, he should at last begin to resent our insufferable
æsthetic patronage. He has established a line of tram-cars in
Rome, from the Porta del Popolo to the Ponte Molle, and it is
on one of these democratic vehicles that I seem to see him
taking his triumphant course down the vista of the future. I
will not pretend to rejoice with him any more than I really do;
I will not pretend, as the sentimental tourists say about it all,
as if it were the setting of an intaglio or the border of a Roman
scarf, to "like" it. Like it or not, as we may, it is evidently destined to be; I see a new Italy in the future which in many
important respects will equal, if not surpass, the most enter-
prising sections of our native land. Perhaps by that time
Chicago and San Francisco will have acquired a pose, and
their sons and daughters will dance at the doors of *locande*.
However this may be, a vivid impression of an accomplished

schism between the old Italy and the new is, as the French say, *le plus clair* of a new visit to this ever-suggestive part of the world. The old Italy has become more and more of a museum, preserved and perpetuated in the midst of the new, but without any further relation to it – it must be admitted, indeed, that such a relation is considerable – than that of the stock on his shelves to the shopkeeper, or of the Siren of the South to the showman who stands before his booth. More than once, as we move about nowadays in the Italian cities, there seems to pass before our eyes a vision of the coming years. It represents to our satisfaction an Italy united and prosperous, but altogether commercial. The Italy, indeed, that we sentimentalise and romance about was an ardently mercantile country; though I suppose it loved not its ledgers less, but its frescoes and altar-pieces more. Scattered through this brilliantly economical community – this country of a thousand ports – we see a large number of beautiful buildings, in which an endless series of dusky pictures are darkening, dampening, fading, failing through the years. At the doors of the beautiful buildings are little turnstiles, at which there sit a great many men in uniform, to whom the visitor pays a ten-penny fee. Inside, in the vaulted and frescoed chambers, the art of Italy lies buried, as in a thousand mausoleums. It is well taken care of; it is constantly copied; sometimes it is "restored" – as in the case of that beautiful boy-figure of Andrea del Sarto, at Florence, which may be seen at the gallery of the Uffizi, with its honourable duskiness quite peeled off and heaven knows what raw, bleeding cuticle laid bare. One evening lately, in Florence, in the soft twilight, I took a stroll among those encircling hills on which the massive villas are mingled with the vaporous olives. Presently I arrived where three roads met at a wayside shrine, in which, before some pious daub of an old-time Madonna, a little votive lamp glimmered through the evening air. The hour, the lovely evening, the place, the twin-kling taper, the sentiment of the observer, the thought that some one had been rescued here from an assassin, or from some other peril, and had set up a little grateful altar in con-sequence, in the yellow-plastered wall of a tangled *podere*; all this led me to approach the shrine with a reverent, an emo-tional step. I drew near it, but after a few steps I paused. I became conscious of an incongruous odour; it seemed to me that the evening air was charged with a perfume which, although to a certain extent familiar, had not hitherto associ-ated itself with rustic frescoes and wayside altars. I gently interrogated the atmosphere, and the operation left me no doubts. The odour was that of petroleum; the votive taper was nourished with the national fluid of Pennsylvania. I confess that I burst out laughing, and a picturesque contadino, wending his homeward way in the dusk, stared at me as if I were an iconoclast. If he noticed the petroleum, it was only, I imagine, to sniff it gratefully; but to me the thing served as a symbol of the Italy of the future. There is a horse-car from the Porta del Popolo to the Ponte Molle, and the Tuscan shrines are fed with kerosene.

II.

If it is very well to come to Turin first, it is still better to go to Genoa afterwards. Genoa is the queerest place in the world, and even a second visit helps you little to straighten it out. In the wonderful crooked, twisting, climbing, soaring, burrowing Genoese alleys the traveller is really up to his neck in the old Italian sketchability. Genoa is, I believe, a port of great capacity, and the bequest of the late Duke of Galliera, who left four millions of dollars for the purpose of improving and enlarging it, will doubtless do much toward converting it into one of the great commercial stations of Europe. But as, after leaving my hotel the afternoon I arrived, I wandered for a long time at hazard through the tortuous byways of the city, I said to myself, not without an accent of private triumph, that here was something it would be almost impossible to modernise. I had found my hotel, in the first place, extremely entertaining – the Croce di Malta, as it was called, established in a gigantic palace on the edge of the swarming and not over-clean harbour. It was the biggest house I had ever entered, and the basement alone would have contained a dozen American caravansaries. I met an American gentleman in the vestibule who (as he had indeed a perfect right to be) was annoyed by its troublesome dimensions – one was a quarter of an hour ascending out of the basement – and desired to know whether it was a "fair sample" of the Genoese inns. It appeared to be an excellent specimen of Genoese architecture generally; so far as I observed, there were few houses perceptibly smaller than this Titanic tavern. I lunched in a dusky ballroom, whose ceiling was vaulted, frescoed and gilded with the fatal facility of a couple of centuries ago, and which looked out upon another ancient house-front, equally huge and equally battered, from which it was separated only by a little wedge of dusky space (one of the principal streets, I believe, of Genoa), out of the bottom of which the Genoese populace sent up to the windows – I had to crane out very far to see it – a perpetual clattering, shuffling, chaffering sound. Issuing forth, presently, into this crevice of a street, I found an abundance of that soft local colour for the love of which one revisits Italy. It offered itself, indeed, in a variety of tints, some of which were not remarkable for their freshness or purity. But their combined effect was highly pictorial, and the picture was a very rich and various representation of southern low-life. Genoa is the crookedest and most incoherent of cities; tossed about on the sides and crests of a dozen hills, it is seamed with gullies and ravines that bristle with those innumerable palaces for which we have heard from our earliest years that the place is celebrated. These great edifices, with their mottled and faded complexions, lift their big ornamental cornices to a tremendous height in the air, where, in a certain indescribably forlorn and desolate fashion, overtopping each other, they seem to reflect the twinkle and glitter of the warm Mediterranean. Down about the basements, in the little dim, close alleys, the people are for ever moving to and fro, or standing in their cavernous doorways and their dusky, crowded shops, calling, chattering, laughing, scrambling, living their lives in the conversational Italian fashion. For a long time I had not received such an impression of the human agglomeration. I had not for a long time seen people elbowing each other so closely, or swarming so thickly out of populous hives. A traveller is very often disposed to ask himself whether it has been worth while to leave his home – whatever his home may have been – only to see new forms of human suffering, only to be reminded that toil and privation, hunger and sorrow and sordid effort, are the portion of the great majority of his fellow-men. To travel is, as it were, to go to the play, to attend a spectacle; and there is something heartless in stepping forth into the streets of a foreign town to feast upon novelty when the novelty consists simply of the slightly different costume in which hunger and labour present themselves. These reflections were forced upon me as I strolled about in those crepuscular, stale-smelling alleys of Genoa; but after a time they ceased to bear me company. The reason of this, I think, is because (at least to foreign eyes) the sum of Italian misery is, on the whole, less than the sum of the Italian knowledge of life. That people should thank you, with a smile of striking sweetness, for the gift of twopence is a proof, certainly, of an extreme and constant destitution; but (keeping in mind the sweetness) it is also a proof of an enviable ability not to be depressed by circumstances. I know that this may possibly be great nonsense; that half the time that we are admiring the brightness of the Italian smile the romantic natives may be, in reality, in a sullen frenzy of impatience and pain. Our observation in any foreign land is extremely superficial, and our remarks are happily not addressed to the inhabitants themselves, who would be sure to exclaim upon the impudence of the fancy-picture. The other day I visited a very picturesque old city upon a mountain-top, where, in the course of my wanderings, I arrived at an old disused gate in the ancient town-wall. The gate had not been absolutely forfeited; but the recent completion of a modern road down the mountain led most vehicles away to another egress. The grass-grown pavement, which wound into the plain by a hundred graceful twists and plunges, was now given up to ragged contadini and their donkeys, and to such wayfarers as were not alarmed at the disrepair into which it had fallen. I stood in the shadow of the tall old gateway admiring the scene, looking to right and left at the wonderful walls of the little town, perched on the edge of a shaggy precipice; at the circling mountains over against them; at the road dipping downward among the chestnuts and olives. There was no one within sight but a young man, who was slowly trudging upward, with his coat slung over his shoulder and his hat upon his ear, like a cavalier in an opera. Like an operatic performer, too, he was singing as he came; the spectacle, generally, was operatic, and as his vocal flourishes reached my ear I said to myself that in Italy accident was always picturesque, and that such a figure had been exactly what was wanted to set off the landscape. It suggested in a high degree that knowledge of life for which I just now commended the Italians. I was turning back, under the old gateway, into the town, when the young

man overtook me, and, suspending his song, asked me if I
could favour him with a match to light the hoarded remnant
of a cigar. This request led, as I walked back to the inn, to my
having some conversation with him. He was a native of the
ancient city, and answered freely all my inquiries as to its manners and customs and the state of public opinion there. But the
point of my anecdote is that he presently proved to be a
brooding young radical and communist, filled with hatred of
the present Italian government, raging with discontent and
crude political passion, professing a ridiculous hope that Italy
would soon have, as France had had, her " '89," and declaring
that he, for his part, would willingly lend a hand to chop off
the heads of the king and the royal family. He was an unhappy,
underfed, unemployed young man, who took a hard, grim
view of everything, and was operatic only quite in spite of
himself. This made it very absurd of me to have looked at him
simply as a graceful ornament to the prospect, an harmonious
little figure in the middle distance. Damn the prospect, damn
the middle distance! would have been all his philosophy. Yet,
but for the accident of my having a little talk with him, I
should have made him do service, in memory, as an example
of sensuous optimism!

I am bound to say, however, that I believe that a great deal
of the sensuous optimism that I noticed in the Genoese alleys
and beneath the low, crowded arcades along the port was very
real. Here every one was magnificently sunburnt, and there
were plenty of those queer types, mahogany-coloured, bare-
chested mariners, with earrings and crimson girdles, that make
a southern seaport entertaining. But it is not fair to speak as
if at Genoa there were nothing but low-life to be seen, for
the place is the residence of some of the grandest people in the
world. Nor are all the palaces ranged upon dusky alleys;
the handsomest and most impressive form a splendid series on

each side of a couple of very proper streets, in which there is plenty of room for a coach-and-four to approach the big doorways. Many of these doorways are open, revealing great marble staircases, with couchant lions for balustrades, and ceremonious courts surrounded by walls of sun-softened yellow. One of the palaces is coloured a goodly red, and contains, in particular, the grand people I just now spoke of. They live, indeed, in the third story; but here they have suites of wonderful painted and gilded chambers, in which there are many foreshortened frescoes in the vaulted ceilings, and the walls are embossed with the most florid mouldings. These distinguished tenants bear the name of Vandyke, though they are members of the noble family of Brignole-Sale, one of whose children (the Duchess of Galliera) has lately given proof of nobleness in presenting the gallery of the Red Palace to the city of Genoa.

III.

On leaving Genoa I repaired to Spezia, chiefly with a view of accomplishing a sentimental pilgrimage, which I, in fact, achieved, in the most agreeable conditions. The Gulf of Spezia is now the headquarters of the Italian fleet, and there were several big iron-plated frigates riding at anchor in front of the town. The streets were filled with lads in blue flannel, who were receiving instruction at a school-ship in the harbour, and in the evening – there was a brilliant moon – the little breakwater which stretched out into the Mediterranean offered a promenade to the naval functionaries. But this fact is, from the tourist's point of view, of little account, for since it has become prosperous Spezia has grown ugly. The place is filled with long, dull stretches of dead wall and great raw expanses of artificial land. It wears that look of monstrous, of more than Occidental, newness which distinguishes all the creations of

the young Italian state. Nor did I find any great compensation
in an immense new inn, which has lately been deposited by the
edge of the sea, in anticipation of a *passeggiata* which is to
come that way some five years hence, the region being in the
meantime of the most primitive formation. The inn was filled
with grave English people, who looked respectable and bored,
and there was of course a Church of England service in the
gaudily-frescoed parlour. Neither was it the drive to Porto
Venere that chiefly pleased me – a drive among vines and
olives – over the hills and beside the sea, to a queer little crumbling village on a headland, as sweetly desolate and
superannuated as the name it bears. There is a ruined church
near the village, which occupies the site (according to tradition) of an ancient temple of Venus; and if Venus ever revisits
her desecrated shrines she must sometimes pause a moment in
that sunny stillness, and listen to the murmur of the tideless
sea at the base of the narrow promontory. If Venus sometimes
comes there, Apollo surely does as much; for close to the
temple is a gateway, surmounted by an inscription in Italian
and English which admits you to a curious (and it must be confessed rather cockneyfied) cave among the rocks. It was here,
says the inscription, that the great Byron, swimmer and poet,
"defied the waves of the Ligurian sea." The fact is interesting,
though not supremely so; for Byron was always defying something, and if a slab had been put up where ever this
performance came off, these commemorative tablets would
be, in many parts of Europe, as thick as milestones. No; the
great merit of Spezia, to my eye, is that I engaged a boat there
of a lovely October afternoon, and had myself rowed across
the gulf – it took about an hour and a half – to the little bay
of Lerici, which opens out of it. This bay of Lerici is charming;
the bosky gray-green hills close it in, and on either side of the
entrance, perched upon a bold headland, a wonderful old

crumbling castle keeps ineffectual guard. The place is classic for all English travellers, for in the middle of the curving shore is the now desolate little villa in which Shelley spent the last months of his short life. He was living at Lerici when he started on that short southern cruise from which he never returned. The house he occupied is strangely shabby, and as sad as you may choose to find it. It stands directly upon the beach, with scarred and battered walls, and a loggia of several arches opening upon a little terrace with a rugged parapet, which, when the wind blows, must be drenched with the salt spray. The place is very lonely – all overwearied with sun and breeze and brine – very close to nature, as it was Shelley's passion to be. I can fancy a great lyric poet sitting on the terrace, of a warm evening, far from England, in the early years of the century. In that place, and with his genius, he would, as a matter of course, have heard in the voice of nature a sweetness which only the lyric movement could translate. It is a place where an English-speaking traveller may very honestly be sentimental and feel moved, himself, to lyric utterance. But I must content myself with saying in halting prose that I remember few episodes of Italian travel more sympathetic, as they have it here, than that perfect autumn afternoon; the half-hour's station on the little battered terrace of the villa; the climb to the singularly picturesque old castle that hangs above Lerici; the meditative lounge, in the fading light, on the vine-decked platform that looked out toward the sunset and the darkening mountains, and, far below, upon the quiet sea, beyond which the pale-faced villa stared up at the brightening moon.

IV.

I had never known Florence more charming than I found her for a week in that brilliant October. She sat in the sunshine beside her yellow river like the little treasure-city that she has always seemed, without commerce, without other industry than the manufacture of mosaic paper-weights and alabaster Cupids, without actuality, or energy, or earnestness, or any of those rugged virtues which in most cases are deemed indispensable for civic robustness; with nothing but the little unaugmented stock of her mediaeval memories, her tender-coloured mountains, her churches and palaces, pictures and statues. There were very few strangers; one's detested fellow sight-seer was infrequent; the native population itself seemed scanty; the sound of wheels in the streets was but occasional; by eight o'clock at night, apparently, every one had gone to bed, and the wandering tourist, still wandering, had the place to himself – had the thick shadow-masses of the great palaces, and the shafts of moonlight striking the polygonal paving-stones, and the empty bridges, and the silvered yellow of the Arno, and the stillness broken only by a homeward step, accompanied by a snatch of song from a warm Italian voice. My room at the inn looked out on the river, and was flooded all day with sunshine. There was an absurd orange-coloured paper on the walls; the Arno, of a hue not altogether different, flowed beneath; and on the other side of it rose a line of sallow houses, of extreme antiquity, crumbling and mouldering, bulging and protruding over the stream. (I seem to speak of their fronts; but what I saw was their shabby backs, which were exposed to the cheerful flicker of the river, while the fronts stood for ever in the deep, damp shadow of a narrow mediæval street.) All this brightness and yellowness was a perpetual delight; it was a part of that indefinably charming colour which Florence always seems to wear as you look up and down at it from the river, from the bridges and quays. This is a kind of grave brilliancy – a harmony of high tints – which I know not how to describe. There are yellow walls and green blinds and red roofs, and intervals of brilliant brown and natural-looking blue; but the picture is not spotty nor gaudy, thanks to the colours being distributed in large and comfortable masses, and to its being washed over, as it were, by some happy softness of sunshine. The river-front of Florence is, in short, a delightful composition. Part of its charm comes, of course, from the generous aspect of those high-based Tuscan palaces which a renewal of acquaintance with them has again commended to me as the most dignified dwellings in the world. Nothing can be finer than that look of giving up the whole immense ground-floor to simple purposes of vestibule and staircase, of court and high-arched entrance; as if this were all but a massive pedestal for the real habitation, and people were not properly housed unless, to begin with, they should be lifted fifty feet above the pavement. The great blocks of the basement; the great intervals, horizontally and vertically, from window to window (telling of the height and breadth of the rooms within); the armorial shield hung forward at one of the angles; the wide-brimmed roof, overshadowing the narrow street; the rich old browns and yellows of the walls – these definite elements are put together with admirable art.

Take one of these noble structures out of its oblique situation in the town; call it no longer a palace, but a villa; set it down upon a terrace, on one of the hills that encircle Florence, with a row of high-waisted cypresses beside it, a grassy courtyard, and a view of the Florentine towers and the valley of the Arno, and you will think it perhaps even more worthy of your esteem. It was a Sunday noon, and brilliantly warm, when I arrived in Florence; and after I had looked from my windows a while at that quietly-basking river-front I have spoken of, I took my way across one of the bridges and then out of one of the gates – that immensely tall Roman Gate, in

which the space from the top of the arch to the cornice
(except that there is scarcely a cornice, it is all a plain, massive
piece of wall) is as great (or seems to be) as that from the
ground to the former point. Then I climbed a steep and
winding way – much of it a little dull, if one likes, being
bounded by mottled, mossy garden-walls – to a villa on a hill-
top, where I found various things that touched me with almost
too fine a point. Seeing them again, often, for a week, both by
sunlight and moonshine, I never quite learned not to covet
them; not to feel that not being a part of them was somehow
to miss an exquisite chance. What a tranquil, contented life it
seemed, with romantic beauty as a part of its daily texture! –
the sunny terrace, with its tangled *podere* beneath it; the bright
gray olives against the bright blue sky; the long, serene, horizontal lines of other villas, flanked by their upward cypresses,
disposed upon the neighbouring hills; the richest little city in
the world in a softly-scooped hollow at one's feet, and beyond
it the most appealing of views, the most majestic, yet the most
familiar. Within the villa was a great love of art and a painting-
room full of successful work, so that if human life there
seemed very tranquil, the tranquillity meant simply contentment and devoted occupation. A beautiful occupation in that
beautiful position, what could possibly be better? That is what
I spoke just now of envying – a way of life that is not afraid of
a little isolation and tolerably quiet days. When such a life presents itself in a dull or an ugly place, we esteem it, we admire
it, but we do not feel it to be the ideal of good fortune. When,
however, the people who lead it move as figures in an ancient,
noble landscape, and their walks and contemplations are like
a turning of the leaves of history, we seem to have before us
an admirable case of virtue made easy; meaning here by virtue,
contentment and concentration, the love of privacy and study.
One need not be exacting if one lives among local conditions

that are of themselves constantly suggestive. It is true, indeed, that I might, after a certain time, grow weary of a regular afternoon stroll among the Florentine lanes; of sitting on low parapets, in intervals of flower-topped wall, and looking across at Fiesole, or down the rich-hued valley of the Arno; of pausing at the open gates of villas and wondering at the height of cypresses and the depth of loggias; of walking home in the fading light and noting on a dozen westward-looking surfaces the glow of the opposite sunset. But for a week or so all this was delightful. The villas are innumerable, and if one is a stranger half the talk is about villas. This one has a story; that one has another; they all look as if they had stories. Most of them are offered to rent (many of them for sale) at prices unnaturally low; you may have a tower and a garden, a chapel and an expanse of thirty windows, for five hundred dollars a year. In imagination, you hire three or four; you take possession, and settle, and live there. About the finest there is something very grave and stately; about two or three of the best there is something even solemn and tragic. From what does this latter impression come? You gather it in as you stand there in the early dusk, looking at the long, pale-brown façade, the enormous windows, the iron cages fastened upon the lower ones. Part of the brooding expression of these great houses comes, even when they have not fallen into decay, from their look of having outlived their original use. Their extraordinary largeness and massiveness are a satire upon their present fate. They were not built with such a thickness of wall and depth of embrasure, such a solidity of staircase and superfluity of stone, simply to afford an economical winter residence to English and American families. I know not whether it was the appearance of these stony old villas, which seemed so dumbly conscious of a change of manners, that threw a tinge of melancholy over the general prospect; certain it is that, having always found this plaintive note in the view of Florence, it seemed to me now particularly distinct. "Lovely, lovely, but it makes me blue," the fanciful stranger could not but murmur to himself as, in the late afternoon, he looked at the landscape from over one of the low parapets, and then, with his hands in his pockets, turned away indoors to candles and dinner.

V.

Below, in the city, in wandering about in the streets and churches and museums, it was impossible not to have a good deal of the same feeling; but here the impression was more easy to analyse. It came from a sense of the perfect separateness of all the great productions of the Renaissance from the present and the future of the place, from the actual life and manners, the native ideal. I have already spoken of the way in which the great aggregation of beautiful works of art in the Italian cities strikes the visitor nowadays (so far as present Italy is concerned) as the mere stock-in-trade of an impecunious but thrifty people. It is this metaphysical desertedness and loneliness of the great works of architecture and sculpture that deposits a certain weight upon the heart; when we see a great tradition broken we feel something of the pain with which we hear a stifled cry. But regret is one thing and resentment is another. Seeing one morning in a shop-window, the series of *Mornings in Florence*, published a few years since by Mr. Ruskin, I made haste to enter and purchase these amusing little books, some passages of which I remembered formerly to have read. I could not turn over many pages without observing that the "separateness" of the new and old which I just mentioned had produced in their author the liveliest irritation. With the more acute phases of this sentiment it was difficult to sympathise, for the simple reason, it seems to me, that it savours of arrogance to demand of any people, as a right of one's own, that they shall be artistic. "Be artistic your-selves!" is the very natural reply that young Italy has at hand for English critics and censors. When a people produces beau-tiful statues and pictures it gives us something more than is set down in the bond, and we must thank it for its generosity; and when it stops producing them or caring for them we may cease thanking, but we hardly have a right to begin and abuse it. The wreck of Florence, says Mr. Ruskin, "is now too ghastly and heart-breaking to any human soul that remembers the days of old"; and these desperate words are an allusion to the fact that the little square in front of the cathedral, at the foot of Giotto's Tower, with the grand Baptistery on the other side, is now the resort of a number of hackney-coaches and omnibuses. This fact is doubtless lamentable, and it would be a hundred times more agreeable to see among people who have been made the heirs of so priceless a work of art as the sublime campanile some such feeling about it as would keep it free even from the danger of defilement. A cab-stand is a very ugly and dirty thing, and Giotto's Tower should have nothing in common with such conveniences. But there is more than one way of taking such things, and a quiet traveller, who has been walking about for a week with his mind full of the sweet-ness and suggestiveness of a hundred Florentine places, may feel at last, in looking into Mr. Ruskin's little tracts that, dis-cord for discord, there is not much to choose between the importunity of the author's personal ill-humour and the incongruity of horse-pails and bundles of hay. And one may say this without being at all a partisan of the doctrine of the inevitableness of new desecrations. For my own part, I believe there are few things in this line that the new Italian spirit is not capable of, and not many, indeed, that we are not destined to see. Pictures and buildings will not be completely destroyed, because in that case foreigners with full pockets would cease to visit the country, and the turn-stiles at the doors of the old palaces and convents, with the little patented slit for absorbing your half-franc, would grow quite rusty, and creak with disuse. But it is safe to say that the new Italy, growing into an old Italy again, will continue to take her elbow-room wherever she finds it.

I am almost ashamed to say what I did with Mr. Ruskin's little books. I put them into my pocket and betook myself to Santa Maria Novella. There I sat down, and after I had looked about for a while at the beautiful church, I drew them forth one by one, and read the greater part of them. Occupying one's self with light literature in a great religious edifice is perhaps as bad a piece of profanation as any of those rude dealings which Mr. Ruskin justly deplores; but a traveller has to make the most of odd moments, and I was waiting for a friend in whose company I was to go and look at Giotto's beautiful frescoes in the cloister of the church. My friend was a long time coming, so that I had an hour with Mr. Ruskin, whom I called just now a light *littèrateur*, because in these little Mornings in Florence he is for ever making his readers laugh. I remembered, of course, where I was; and, in spite of my latent hilarity, I felt that I had rarely got such a snubbing. I had really been enjoying the good old city of Florence; but I now learned from Mr. Ruskin that this was a scandalous waste of charity. I should have gone about with an imprecation on my lips, I should have worn a face three yards long. I had taken great pleasure in certain frescoes by Ghirlandaio, in the choir of that very church; but it appeared from one of the little books that these frescoes were as naught. I had much admired Santa Croce, and I had thought the Duomo a very noble affair; but I had now the most positive assurance I knew nothing about it. After a while, if it was only ill-humour that was needed for doing honour to the city of the Medici, I felt that I had risen to a proper level; only now it was Mr. Ruskin himself I had lost patience with, and not the stupid Brunelleschi and the vulgar Ghirlandaio. Indeed, I lost patience altogether, and asked myself by what right this informal votary of form pretended to run riot through a quiet traveller's relish for the noblest of pleasures – his wholesome enjoyment of the loveliest of cities. The little books seemed invidious and insane, and it was only when I remembered that I had been under no obligation to buy them that I checked myself in repenting of having done so. Then, at last, my friend arrived, and we passed together out of the church, and through the first cloister beside it, into a smaller enclosure, where we stood a while to look at the tomb of the Marchesa Strozzi-Ridolfi, upon which the great Giotto has painted four superb little pictures. It was easy to see the pictures were superb; but I drew forth one of my little books again, for I had observed that Mr. Ruskin spoke of them. Hereupon I recovered my tolerance; for what could be better in this case, I asked myself, than Mr. Ruskin's remarks? They are, in fact, excellent and charming, and full of appreciation of the deep and simple beauty of the great painter's work. I read them aloud to my companion; but my companion was rather, as the phrase is, "put off" by them. One of the frescoes (it is a picture of the birth of the Virgin) contains a figure coming through a door. "Of ornament," I quote, "there is only the entirely simple outline of the vase which the servant carries; of colour two or three masses of sober red and pure white, with brown and gray. That is all," Mr. Ruskin continues. "And if you are pleased with this you can see Florence. But if not, by all means amuse yourself there, if you find it amusing, as long as you like; you can never see it." You can never see it. This

seemed to my friend insufferable, and I had to shuffle away
the book again, so that we might look at the fresco with the
unruffled geniality it deserves. We agreed afterwards, when in
a more convenient place I read aloud a good many more passages from Mr. Ruskin's tracts, that there are a great many
ways of seeing Florence, as there are of seeing most beautiful
and interesting things, and that it is very dry and pedantic to
say that the happy vision depends upon our squaring our toes
with a certain particular chalk-mark. We see Florence wherever and whenever we enjoy it, and for enjoying it we find a
great many more pretexts than Mr. Ruskin seems inclined to
allow. My friend and I agreed also, however, that the little
books were an excellent purchase, on account of the great
charm and felicity of much of their incidental criticism; to say
nothing, as I hinted just now, of their being extremely
amusing. Nothing, in fact, is more comical than the familiar
asperity of the author's style and the pedagogic fashion in
which he pushes and pulls his unhappy pupils about, jerking
their heads toward this, rapping their knuckles for that,
sending them to stand in corners, and giving them Scripture
texts to copy. But it is neither the felicities nor the aberrations
of detail, in Mr. Ruskin's writings, that are the main affair for
most readers; it is the general tone that, as I have said, puts
them off or draws them on. For many persons he will never
bear the test of being read in this rich old Italy, where art, so
long as it really lived at all, was spontaneous, joyous, irresponsible. If the reader is in daily contact with those beautiful
Florentine works which do still, in a way, force themselves
into notice through the vulgarity and cruelty of modern profanation, it will seem to him that Mr. Ruskin's little books are
pitched in the strangest falsetto key. "One read a hundred
pages of this sort of thing," said my friend, "without ever
dreaming that he is talking about *art*. You can say nothing

worse about it than that." And that is very true. Art is the one corner of human life in which we may take our ease. To justify our presence there the only thing that is demanded of us is that we shall have a passion for representation. In other places our passions are conditioned and embarrassed; we are allowed to have only so many as are consistent with those of our neighbours; with their convenience and well-being, with their convictions and prejudices, their rules and regulations. Art means an escape from all this. Wherever her brilliant standard floats the need for apologies and exonerations is over; there it is enough simply that we please or that we are pleased. There the tree is judged only by its fruits. If these are sweet, one is welcome to pluck them.

One may read a great many pages of Mr. Ruskin without getting a hint of this delightful truth; a hint of the not unimportant fact that art, after all, is made for us, and not we for art. This idea of the value of a work of art being the amount of illusion it yields is conspicuous by its absence. And as for Mr. Ruskin's world of art being a place where we may take life easily, woe to the luckless mortal who enters it with any such disposition. Instead of a garden of delight, he finds a sort of assize-court, in perpetual session. Instead of a place in which human responsibilities are lightened and suspended, he finds a region governed by a kind of Draconic legislation. His responsibilities, indeed, are tenfold increased; the gulf between truth and error is for ever yawning at his feet; the pains and penalties of this same error are advertised, in apocalyptic terminology, upon a thousand sign-posts; and the poor wanderer soon begins to look back with infinite longing to the lost paradise of the artless. There can be no greater want of tact in dealing with those things with which men attempt to ornament life than to be perpetually talking about "error". A truce to all rigidities is the law of the place; the only thing that is absolute there is sensible charm. The grim old bearer of the scales excuses herself; she feels that this is not her province. Differences here are not iniquity and righteousness; they are simply variations of temperament and of point of view. We are not under theological government.

VI.

It was very charming, in the bright, warm days, to wander from one corner of Florence to another, paying one's respects again to remembered masterpieces. It was pleasant also to find that memory had played no tricks, and that the beautiful things of an earlier year were as beautiful as ever. To enumerate these beautiful things would take a great deal of space; for I never had been more struck with the mere quantity of brilliant Florentine work. Even giving up the Duomo and Santa Croce to Mr. Ruskill as very ill-arranged edifices, the list of the Florentine treasures is almost inexhaustible. Those long outer galleries of the Uffizi had never seemed to me more delectable; sometimes there were not more than two or three figures standing there, Baedeker in hand, to break the charming perspective. One side of this upstairs-portico, it will be remembered, is entirely composed of glass; a continuity of old-fashioned windows, draped with white curtains of rather primitive fashion, which hang there till they acquire a perceptible "tone". The light, passing through them, is softly filtered and diffused; it rests mildly upon the old marbles – chiefly antique Roman busts – which stand in the narrow intervals of the casements. It is projected upon the numerous pictures that cover the opposite wall, and that are not by any means, as a general thing, the gems of the great collection; it imparts a faded brightness to the old ornamental arabesques upon the painted wooden ceiling, and it makes a great soft shining upon the marble floor, in which, as you look up and down, you see the strolling tourists and the motionless copyists almost reflected. I don't know why I should find all this very pleasant, but, in fact, I have seldom gone into the Uffizi without walking the length of this third-story cloister, between the (for the most part) third-rate pictures and the faded cotton curtains. Why is it that in Italy we see a charm in things in regard to which in other countries we always take vulgarity for granted? If in the city of New York a great museum of the arts were to be provided, by way of decoration, with a species of verandah inclosed on one side by a series of smallpaned windows, draped in dirty linen, and furnished on the other with an array of pictorial feebleness, the place being surmounted by a thinly-painted wooden roof, strongly suggestive of summer heat, of winter cold, of frequent leakage, those amateurs who had had the advantage of foreign travel would be at small pains to conceal their contempt. Contemptible or respectable, to the judicial mind, this quaint old loggia of the Uffizi admitted me into twenty chambers where I found as great a number of ancient favourites. I do not know that I had a warmer greeting for any old friend than for Andrea del Sarto, that most touching of painters who is not one of the first. But it was on the other side of the Arno that I found him in force, in those dusky drawing-rooms of the Pitti Palace, to which you take your way along the tortuous tunnel that wanders through the houses of Florence, and is supported by the little goldsmiths' booths on the Ponte Vecchio. In the rich, insufficient light of these beautiful rooms, where, to look at the pictures, you sit in damask chairs and rest your elbows on tables of malachite, Andrea del Sarto becomes peculiarly effective. Before long, you feel a real affection for him. But the great pleasure, after all, was to revisit the earlier masters, in those specimens of them chiefly that bloom so unfadingly on the big, plain walls

of the Academy. Fra Angelico and Filippo Lippi, Botticelli, and
Lorenzo di Credi are the sweetest and best of all painters; as I
sat for an hour in their company, in the cold great hall of the
institution I have mentioned – there are shabby rafters above
and an immense expanse of brick tiles below, and many bad
pictures as well as good ones – it seemed to me more than ever
that if one really had to choose one could not do better than
choose here. You may sit very quietly and comfortably at the
Academy, in this big first room – at the upper end, especially,
on the left – because more than many other places it savours
of old Florence. More for instance, in reality, than the
Bargello, though the Bargello makes great pretensions.
Beautiful and picturesque as the Bargello is, it smells too
strongly of restoration, and, much of old Italy as still lurks in
its furbished and renovated chambers, it speaks even more distinctly of the ill-mannered young kingdom that has (as
unavoidably as you please) lifted down a hundred delicate
works of sculpture from the convent-walls where their pious
authors placed them. If the early Tuscan painters are exquisite,
I can think of no praise generous enough for the sculptors of
the same period, Donatello and Luca della Robbia, Matteo
Civitale and Mino da Fiesole, who, as I refreshed my memory
of them, seemed to me to leave absolutely nothing to be
desired in the way of purity of inspiration and grace of invention. The Bargello is full of early Tuscan sculpture, most of the
pieces of which have come from suppressed convents; and
even if the visitor be an ardent liberal, he is uncomfortably
conscious of the rather brutal process by which it has been col-
lected. One can hardly envy young Italy the number of
disagreeable things she has had to do.

The railway journey from Florence to Rome has been
altered both for the better and for the worse; for the better, in
that it has been shortened by a couple of hours; for the worse,

inasmuch as, when about half the distance has been traversed, the train deflects to the west, and leaves the beautiful old cities of Assisi, Perugia, Terni, Narni, unvisited. Of old, it was possible to visit these places, in a manner, from the window of the train; even if you did not stop, as you probably could not, every time you passed, the picturesque fashion in which, like a loosened belt on an aged and shrunken person, their old red walls held them easily together was something well worth noting. Now, however, by way of compensation, the express-train to Rome stops at Orvieto, and in consequence . . . In consequence what? What is the consequence of an express train stopping at Orvieto? As I glibly wrote that sentence I suddenly paused, with a sense of the queer stuff I was uttering. That an express train would graze the base of the horrid purple mountain from the apex of which this dark old Catholic city uplifts the glittering front of its cathedral – that might have been foretold by a keen observer of contemporary manners. But that it would really have the grossness to stop there, this is a fact over which, as he records it, a sentimental chronicler may well make what is vulgarly called an ado. The train does stop at Orvieto, not very long, it is true, but long, enough to let you out. The same phenomenon takes place on the following day, when, having visited the city, you get in again. I availed myself of both of these occasions, having formerly neglected to drive to Orvieto in a post-chaise. And really, the railway-station being in the plain, and the town on the summit of an extraordinary hill, you have time to forget all about the triumphs of steam, while you wind upwards to the city-gate. The position of Orvieto is superb; it is worthy of the "middle distance" of a last-century landscape. But, as every one knows, the beautiful cathedral is the proper attraction of the place, which, indeed, save for this fine monument, and for its craggy and crumbling ramparts, is a meanly arranged and, as Italian cities go, not particularly impressive little town. I spent a beautiful Sunday there, and I looked at the charming church. I looked at it a great deal – a great deal considering that on the whole I found it inferior to its fame. Intensely brilliant, however, is the densely carved front; densely covered with the freshest-looking mosaics. The old white marble of the sculptured portions is as softly yellow as ancient ivory; the large, exceedingly bright pictures above them flashed and twinkled in the splendid weather. Very beautiful and interesting are the theological frescoes of Luca Signorelli, though I have seen pictures that struck me as more attaching. Very enchanting, finally, are the clear-faced saints and seraphs, in robes of pink and azure, whom Fra Angelico has painted upon the ceiling of the great chapel, along with a noble sitting figure – more expressive of movement than most of the creations of this pictorial peace-maker – of Christ in judgment. But the interest of the cathedral of Orvieto is mainly not the visible result, but the historical process that lies behind it; those three hundred years of devoted popular labour of which an American scholar has written an admirable account.[1]

[1] Charles Eliot Norton: *Study and Travel in Italy.*

III.

OCCASIONAL PARIS.

1877.

It is hard to say exactly what is the profit of comparing one race with another, and weighing in opposed groups the manners and customs of neighbouring countries; but it is certain that as we move about the world we constantly indulge in this exercise. This is especially the case if we happen to be infected with the baleful spirit of the cosmopolite – that uncomfortable consequence of seeing many lands and feeling at home in none. To be a cosmopolite is not, I think, an ideal; the ideal should be to be a concentrated patriot. Being a cosmopolite is an accident, but one must make the best of it. If you have lived about, as the phrase is, you have lost that sense of the absoluteness and the sanctity of the habits of your fellow-patriots which once made you so happy in the midst of them. You have seen that there are a great many *patriae* in the world, and that each of these is filled with excellent people for whom the local idiosyncrasies are the only thing that is not rather barbarous. There comes a time when one set of customs, wherever it may be found, grows to seem to you about as provincial as another; and then I suppose it may be said of you that you have become a cosmopolite. You have formed the habit of comparing, of looking for points of difference and of resemblance, for present and absent advantages, for the virtues that go with certain defects, and the defects that go with certain virtues. If this is poor work compared with the active practice, in the sphere to which a discriminating Providence has assigned you, of the duties of a tax-payer, an elector, a juryman or a diner-out, there is nevertheless something to be said for it. It is good to think well of mankind, and this, on the whole, a cosmopolite does. If you limit your generalisations to the sphere I mentioned just now, there is a danger that your occasional fits of pessimism may be too sweeping. When you are out of humour the whole country suffers, because at such moments one is never discriminating, and it costs you very little bad logic to lump your fellow-citizens together. But if you are living about, as I say, certain differences impose themselves. The worst you can say of the human race is, for instance, that the Germans are a detestable people. They do not represent the human race for you, as in your native town your fellow-citizens do, and your unflattering judgment has a flattering reverse. If the Germans are detestable, you are mentally saying, there are those admirable French, or those charming Americans, or those interesting English. (Of course it is simply by accident that I couple the German name here with the unfavourable adjective. The epithets may be transposed at will.) Nothing can well be more different from anything else than the English from the French, so that, if you are acquainted with both nations, it may be said that on any special point your agreeable impression of the one implies a censorious attitude toward the other, and *vice versa*. This has rather a shocking sound; it makes the cosmopolite appear invidious and narrow-minded. But I hasten to add that there seems no real reason why even the most delicate conscience should take alarm. The consequence of the cosmopolite spirit is to initiate you into the merits of all peoples; to convince you that national virtues are numerous, though they may be very different, and to make downright

preference really very hard. I have, for instance, every disposition to think better of the English race than of any other
except my own. There are things which make it natural I
should; there are inducements, provocations, temptations,
almost bribes. There have been moments when I have almost
burned my ships behind me, and declared that, as it simplified
matters greatly to pin one's faith to a chosen people, I would
henceforth cease to trouble my head about the lights and
shades of the foreign character. I am convinced that if I had
taken this reckless engagement, I should greatly have regretted
it. You may find a room very comfortable to sit in with the
window open, and not like it at all when the window has been
shut. If one were to give up the privilege of comparing the
English with other people, one would very soon, in a moment
of reaction, make once for all (and most unjustly) such a comparison as would leave the English nowhere. Compare then, I
say, as often as the occasion presents itself. The result as
regards any particular people, and as regards the human race
at large, may be pronounced agreeable, and the process is both
instructive and entertaining.

So the author of these observations finds it on returning to
Paris after living for upwards of a year in London. He finds
himself comparing, and the results of comparison are several
disjointed reflections, of which it may be profitable to make a
note. Certainly Paris is a very old story, and London is a still
older one; and there is no great reason why a journey across
the channel and back should quicken one's perspicacity to an
unprecedented degree. I therefore will not pretend to have
been looking at Paris with new eyes, or to have gathered on
the banks of the Seine a harvest of extraordinary impressions.
I will only pretend that a good many old impressions have
recovered their freshness, and that there is a sort of renovated
entertainment in looking at the most brilliant city in the world

with eyes attuned to a different pitch. Never, in fact, have those qualities of brightness and gaiety that are half the stock-in-trade of the city by the Seine seemed to me more uncontestable. The autumn is but half over, and Paris is, in common parlance, empty. The private houses are closed, the lions have returned to the jungle, the Champs Elysées are not at all "mondains." But I have never seen Paris more Parisian, in the pleasantest sense of the word; better humoured, more open-windowed, more naturally entertaining. A radiant September helps the case; but doubtless the matter is, as I hinted above, in a large degree "subjective". For when one comes to the point there is nothing very particular just now for Paris to rub her hands about. The Exhibition of 1878 is looming up as large as a mighty mass of buildings on the Trocadéro can make it. These buildings are very magnificent and fantastical; they hang over the Seine, in their sudden immensity and glittering newness, like a palace in a fairy-tale. But the trouble is that most people appear to regard the Exhibition as in fact a fairy-tale. They speak of the wonderful structures on the Champ de Mars and the Trocadéro as a pre-destined monument to the folly of a group of gentlemen destitute of a sense of the opportune. The moment certainly does not seem very well chosen for inviting the world to come to Paris to amuse itself. The world is too much occupied with graver cares – with reciprocal cannonading and chopping, with cutting of throats and burning of homes, with murder of infants and mutilation of mothers, with warding off famine and civil war, with lamenting the failure of its resources, the dulness of trade, the emptiness of its pockets. Rome is burning altogether too fast for even its most irresponsible spirits to find any great satisfaction in fiddling. But even if there is (as there very well may be) a certain scepticism at headquarters as to the accomplishment of this graceful design, there is no

apparent hesitation, and everything is going forward as
rapidly as if mankind were breathless with expectation. That
familiar figure, the Parisian *ouvrier*, with his white, chalky
blouse, his attenuated person, his clever face, is more familiar
than ever, and I suppose, finding plenty of work to his hand,
is for the time in a comparatively rational state of mind. He
swarms in thousands, not only in the region of the Exhibition,
but along the great thoroughfare – the Avenue de l'Opéra –
which has just been opened in the interior of Paris. This is an
extremely Parisian creation, and as it is really a great convenience – it will save a great many steps and twists and turns –
I suppose it should be spoken of with gratitude and admiration. But I confess that to my sense it belongs primarily to that
order of benefits which during the twenty years of the Empire
gradually deprived the streets of Paris of nine-tenths of their
ancient individuality. The deadly monotony of the Paris that
M. Haussmann called into being – its huge, blank, pompous,
featureless sameness – sometimes comes over the wandering
stranger with a force that leads him to devote the author of
these miles of architectural commonplace to execration. The
new street is quite on the imperial system; it must make the
late Napoleon III smile with beatific satisfaction as he looks
down upon it from the Bonapartist corner of Paradise. It
stretches straight away from the pompous façade of the Opera
to the doors of the Théâtre Français, and it must be admitted
that there is something fine in the vista that is closed at one
end by the great sculptured and gilded mass of the former
building. But it smells of the modern asphalt; it is lined with
great white houses that are adorned with machine-made
arabesques, and each of which is so exact a copy of all the rest
that even the little white porcelain number on a blue ground,
which looks exactly like all the other numbers, hardly constitutes an identity. Presently there will be a long succession of

milliners' and chocolate-makers' shops in the basement of this homogeneous row, and the pretty bonnets and bonbonnières in the shining windows will have their ribbons knotted with a *chic* that you must come to Paris to see. Then there will be little glazed sentry-boxes at regular intervals along the curb-stone, in which churlish old women will sit selling half a dozen copies of each of the newspapers; and over the hardened bitumen the young Parisian of our day will constantly circu-late, looking rather pallid and wearing very large shirt-cuffs. And the new avenue will be a great success, for it will place in symmetrical communication two of the most important estab-lishments in France – the temple of French music and the temple of French comedy.

I said just now that no two things could well be more unlike than England and France; and though the remark is not orig-inal, I uttered it with the spontaneity that it must have on the lips of a traveller who, having left either country, has just dis-embarked in the other. It is of course by this time a very trite observation, but it will continue to be made so long as Boulogne remains the same lively antithesis of Folkestone. An American, conscious of the family-likeness diffused over his own huge continent, never quite unlearns his surprise at finding that so little of either of these two almost contiguous towns has rubbed off upon the other. He is surprised at cer-tain English people feeling so far away from France, and at all French people feeling so far away from England. I travelled from Boulogne the other day in the same railway-carriage with a couple of amiable and ingenuous young Britons, who had come over to spend ten days in Paris. It was their first landing in France; they had never yet quitted their native island; and in the course of a little conversation that I had with them I was struck with the scantiness of their information in regard to French manners and customs. They were very intelligent lads;

they were apparently fresh from a university; but in respect to the interesting country they were about to enter, their minds were almost a blank. If the conductor, appearing at the carriage door to ask for our tickets, had had the leg of a frog sticking out of his pocket, I think their only very definite preconception would have been confirmed. I parted with them at the Paris station, and I have no doubt that they very soon began to make precious discoveries; and I have alluded to them not in the least to throw ridicule upon their "insularity" – which indeed, being accompanied with great modesty, I thought a very pretty spectacle – but because having become, since my last visit to France, a little insular myself, I was more conscious of the emotions that attend on an arrival.

The brightness always seems to begin while you are still out in the channel, when you fairly begin to see the French coast. You pass into a region of intenser light – a zone of clearness and colour. These properties brighten and deepen as you approach the land, and when you fairly stand upon that good Boulognese quay, among the blue and red douaniers and soldiers, the small ugly men in cerulean blouses, the charming fishwives, with their folded kerchiefs and their crisp cap-frills, their short striped petticoats, their tightly-drawn stockings, and their little clicking sabots – when you look about you at the smokeless air, at the pink and yellow houses, at the white-fronted café, close at hand, with its bright blue letters, its mirrors and marble-topped tables, its white-aproned, alert, undignified waiter, grasping a huge coffee-pot by a long handle – when you perceive all these things you feel the additional savour that foreignness gives to the picturesque; or feel rather, I should say, that simple foreignness may itself make the picturesque; for certainly the elements in the picture I have just sketched are not especially exquisite. No matter; you are amused, and your amusement continues – being sensibly stimulated by a visit to the buffet at the railway station, which is better than the refreshment-room at Folkestone. It is a pleasure to have people offering you soup again, of their own movement; it is a pleasure to find a little pint of Bordeaux standing naturally before your plate; it is a pleasure to have a napkin; it is a pleasure, above all, to take up one of the good long sticks of French bread – as bread is called the staff of life, the French bake it literally in the shape of staves – and break off a loose, crisp, crusty morsel.

There are impressions, certainly, that imperil your good-humour. No honest Anglo-Saxon can like a French railway-station; and I was on the point of adding that no honest Anglo-Saxon can like a French railway-official. But I will not go so far as that; for after all I cannot remember any great harm that such a functionary has ever done me – except in locking me up as a malefactor. It is necessary to say, however, that the honest Anglo-Saxon, in a French railway-station, is in a state of chronic irritation – an irritation arising from his sense of the injurious effect upon the genial French nature of the possession of an administrative uniform. I believe that the consciousness of brass buttons on his coat and stripes on his trousers has spoiled many a modest and amiable Frenchman, and the sight of these aggressive insignia always stirs within me a moral protest. I repeat that my aversion to them is partly theoretic, for I have found, as a general thing, that an inquiry civilly made extracts a civil answer from even the most official-looking personage. But I have also found that such a personage's measure of the civility due to him is inordinately large; if he places himself in any degree at your service, it is apparently from the sense that true greatness can afford to unbend. You are constantly reminded that you must not presume. In England these intimations never proceed from one's "inferiors". In France the "administration" is the first thing

that touches you; in a little while you get used to it, but you
feel somehow that, in the process, you have lost the flower of
your self-respect. Of course you are under some obligation to
it. It has taken you off the steamer at Folkestone; made you
tell your name to a gentleman with a sword, stationed at the
farther end of the plank – not a drawn sword, it is true, but
still, at the bust, a very nasty weapon; marshalled you into the
railway-station; assigned you to a carriage – I was going to say
to a seat; transported you to Paris, marshalled you again out
of the train, and under a sort of military surveillance, into an
enclosure containing a number of human sheep-pens, in one
of which it has imprisoned you for some half-hour. I am
always on the point, in these places, of asking one of my
gaolers if I may not be allowed to walk about on parole. The
administration at any rate has finally taken you out of your
pen, and, through the medium of a functionary who
"inscribes" you in a little book, transferred you to a cab
selected by a logic of its own. In doing all this it has certainly
done a great deal for you; but somehow its good offices have
made you feel sombre and resentful. The other day, on
arriving from London, while I was waiting for my luggage, I
saw several of the porters who convey travellers' impedimenta
to the cab come up and deliver over the coin they had just
received for this service to a functionary posted *ad hoc* in a
corner, and armed with a little book in which he noted down
these remittances. The *pour-boires* are apparently thrown into
a common fund and divided among the guild of porters. The
system is doubtless an excellent one, excellently carried out;
but the sight of the poor round-shouldered man of burdens
dropping his coin into the hand of the official arithmetician
was to my fancy but another reminder that the individual, as
an individual, loses by all that the administration assumes.

    After living a while in England you observe the individual

in Paris with quickened attention; and I think it must be said that at first he makes an indifferent figure. You are struck with the race being physically and personally a poorer one than that great family of largely-modelled, fresh-coloured people you have left upon the other side of the channel. I remember that in going to England a year ago and disembarking of a dismal, sleety Sunday evening at Folkestone, the first thing that struck me was the good looks of the railway porters – their broad shoulders, their big brown beards, their well-cut features. In like manner, landing lately at Boulogne of a brilliant Sunday morning, it was impossible not to think the little men in numbered caps who were gesticulating and chattering in one's path, rather ugly fellows. In arriving from other countries one is struck with a certain want of dignity in the French face. I do not know, however, whether this is anything worse than the fact that the French face is expressive; for it may be said that, in a certain sense, to express anything is to compromise with one's dignity, which likes to be understood without taking trouble. As regards the lower classes, at any rate, the impression I speak of always passes away; you perceive that the good looks of the French working-people are to be found in their look of intelligence. These people, in Paris, strike me afresh as the cleverest, the most perceptive, and, intellectually speaking the most human of their kind. The Paris ouvrier, with his democratic blouse, his expressive, demonstrative, agreeable eye, his meagre limbs, his irregular, pointed features, his sallow complexion, his face at once fatigued and animated, his light, nervous organisation, is a figure that I always encounter again with pleasure. In some cases he looks depraved and perverted, but at his worst, he looks refined; he is full of vivacity of perception, of something that one can appeal to.

It takes some courage to say this, perhaps, after reading *L'Assommoir*; but in M. Emile Zola's extraordinary novel one

must make the part, as the French say, of the horrible uncleanness of the author's imagination. *L'Assommoir*, I have been
told, has had great success in the lower walks of Parisian life;
and if this fact is not creditable to the delicacy of M. Zola's
humble readers, it proves a good deal in favour of their intelligence. With all its grossness the book in question is
essentially a literary performance; you must be tolerably clever
to appreciate it. It is highly appreciated, I believe, by the
young ladies who live in the region of the Latin Quarter –
those young ladies who thirty years ago were called grisettes,
and now are called I don't know what. They know long passages by heart; they repeat them with infinite gusto. "Ce
louchon d'Augustine" – the horrible little girl with a squint,
who is always playing nasty tricks and dodging slaps and pro-
jectiles in Gervaise's shop, is their particular favourite; and it
must be admitted that "ce louchon d'Augustine" is, as regards
reality, a wonderful creation.

If Parisians, both small and great, have more of the intellectual stamp than the people one sees in London, it is striking,
on the other hand, that the people of the better sort in Paris
look very much less "respectable". I did not know till I came
back to Paris how used I had grown to the English cachet; but
I immediately found myself missing it. You miss it in the men
much more than in the women; for the well-to-do
Frenchwoman of the lower orders, as one sees her in public,
in the streets and in shops, is always a delightfully comfortable
and creditable person. I must confess to the highest admiration for her, an admiration that increases with acquaintance.
She, at least, is essentially respectable; the neatness, compact-
ness, and sobriety of her dress, the decision of her movement
and accent suggest the civic and domestic virtues – order,
thrift, frugality, the moral necessity of making a good appearance. It is, I think, an old story that to the stranger in France

the women seem greatly superior to the men. Their superiority, in fact, appears to be conceded; for wherever you turn you meet them in the forefront of action. You meet them, indeed, too often; you pronounce them at times obtrusive. It is annoying when you go to order your boots or your shirts, to have to make known your desires to even the most neat-waisted female attendant; for the limitations to the feminine intellect are, though few in number, distinct, and women are not able to understand certain masculine needs. Mr. Worth makes ladies' dresses; but I am sure there will never be a fashionable tailoress. There are, however, points at which, from the commercial point of view, feminine assistance is invaluable. For insisting upon the merits of an article that has failed to satisfy you, talking you over, and making you take it; for defending a disputed bill, for paying the necessary compliments or supplying the necessary impertinence – for all these things the neat-waisted sex has peculiar and precious faculties. In the commercial class in Paris the man always appeals to the woman; the woman always steps forward. The woman always proposes the conditions of a bargain. Go about and look for furnished rooms, you always encounter a concierge and his wife. When you ask the price of the rooms, the woman takes the words out of her husband's mouth, if indeed he have not first turned to her with a questioning look. She takes you in hand; she proposes conditions; she thinks of things he would not have thought of.

What I meant just now by my allusion to the absence of the "respectable" in the appearance of the Parisian population was that the men do not look like gentlemen, as so many Englishmen do. The average Frenchman that one encounters in public is of so different a type from the average Englishman that you can easily believe that to the end of time the two will not understand each other. The Frenchman has always, comparatively speaking, a Bohemian, empirical look; the expression of his face, its colouring, its movement, have not been toned down to the neutral complexion of that breeding for which in English speech we reserve the epithet of "good". He is at once more artificial and more natural; the former where the Englishman is positive, the latter where the Englishman is negative. He takes off his hat with a flourish to a friend, but the Englishman never bows. He ties a knot in the end of a napkin and thrusts it into his shirt-collar, so that, as he sits at breakfast, the napkin may serve the office of a pinafore. Such an operation as that seems to the Englishman as *naïf* as the flourishing of one's hat is pretentious.

I sometimes go to breakfast at a café on the Boulevard, which I formerly used to frequent with considerable regularity. Coming back there the other day, I found exactly the same group of habitués at their little tables, and I mentally exclaimed as I looked at them over my newspaper, upon their unlikeness to the gentlemen who confront you in the same attitude at a London club. Who are they? what are they? On these points I have no information; but the stranger's imagination does not seem to see a majestic social order massing itself behind them as it usually does in London. He goes so far as to suspect that what is behind them is not adapted for exhibition; whereas your Englishmen, whatever may be the defects of their personal character, or the irregularities of their conduct, are pressed upon from the rear by an immense body of private proprieties and comforts, of domestic conventions and theological observances. But it is agreeable all the same to come back to a café of which you have formerly been an habitué. Adolphe or Edouard, in his long white apron and his large patent-leather slippers, has a perfect recollection of "les habitudes de Monsieur." He remembers the table you preferred, the wine you drank, the newspaper you read. He greets you with the friendliest of smiles, and remarks that it is a long time since he has had the pleasure of seeing Monsieur. There is something in this simple remark very touching to a heart that has suffered from that incorruptible dumbness of the British domestic. But in Paris such a heart finds consolation at every step; it is reminded of that most classic quality of the French nature – its sociability; a sociability which operates here as it never does in England, from below upward. Your waiter utters a greeting because, after all, something human within him prompts him; his instinct bids him say something, and his taste recommends that it be agreeable. The obvious reflection is that a waiter must not say too much, even for the sake of being human. But in France the people always like to make the little extra remark, to throw in something above the simply necessary. I stop before a little man who is selling newspapers at a street-corner, and ask him for the *Journal des Débats*. His answer deserves to be literally given: "Je ne l'ai plus, Monsieur; mais je pourrai vous donner quelquechose à peu près dans le même genre – la *République Française*." Even a person of his humble condition must have had a lurking sense of the comicality of offering anything as an equivalent for the "genre" of the venerable, classic, academic *Débats*. But my friend could not bear to give me a naked, monosyllabic refusal.

There are two things that the returning observer is likely to do with as little delay as possible. One is to dine at some *cabaret* of which he retains a friendly memory; another is to betake himself to the Théâtre Français. It is early in the season; there are no new pieces; but I have taken great pleasure in seeing some of the old ones. I lost no time in going to see Mademoiselle Sarah Bernhardt in *Andromaque*. *Andromaque* is not a novelty, but Mademoiselle Sarah Bernhardt has a perennial freshness. The play has been revived, to enable her to represent not the great part, the injured and passionate Hermione, but that of the doleful, funereal widow of Hector. This part is a poor one; it is narrow and monotonous, and offers few brilliant opportunities. But the actress knows how to make opportunities, and she has here a very sufficient one for crossing her thin white arms over her nebulous black robes, and sighing forth in silver accents her dolorous rhymes. Her rendering of the part is one more proof of her singular intelligence – of the fineness of her artistic nature. As there is not a great deal to be done with it in the way of declamation, she has made the most of its plastic side. She understands the art of motion and attitude as no one else does, and her extra-ordinary personal grace never fails her. Her Andromaque has postures of the most poetic picturesqueness – something that suggests the broken stem and drooping head of a flower that had been rudely plucked. She bends over her classic confidant like the figure of Bereavement on a bas-relief, and she has a marvellous manner of lifting and throwing back her delicate arms, locking them together, and passing them behind her hanging head.

The *Demi-Monde* of M. Dumas *fils* is not a novelty either; but I quite agree with M. Francisque Sarcey that it is on the whole, in form, the first comedy of our day. I have seen it several times, but I never see it without being forcibly struck with its merits. For the drama of our time it must always remain the model. The interest of the story, the quiet art with which it is unfolded, the naturalness and soberness of the means that are used, and by which great effects are produced, the brilliancy and richness of the dialogue – all these things make it a singularly perfect and interesting work. Of course it is admirably well played at the Théâtre Français. Madame d'Ange was originally a part of too great amplitude for Mademoiselle Croizette; but she is gradually filling it out and taking possession of it; she begins to give a sense of the "calme infernal", which George Sand somewhere mentions as the leading attribute of the character. As for Delaunay, he does nothing better, more vividly and gallantly, than Olivier de Jalin. When I say gallantry I say it with qualification; for what a very queer fellow is this same M. de Jalin! In seeing the *Demi-Monde* again I was more than ever struck with the oddity of its morality and with the way that the ideal of fine conduct differs in different nations. The *Demi-Monde* is the history of the eager, the almost heroic, effort of a clever and superior woman, who has been guilty of what the French call "faults", to pass from the irregular and equivocal circle to which these faults have consigned her into what is distinctively termed "good society". The only way in which the passage can be effected is by her marrying an honourable man; and to induce an honourable man to marry her, she must suppress the more discreditable facts of her career. Taking her for an honest woman, Raymond de Nanjac falls in love with her, and honestly proposes to make her his wife. But Raymond de Nanjac has contracted an intimate friendship with Olivier de Jalin, and the action of the play is more especially De Jalin's attempt – a successful one – to rescue his friend from the ignominy of a union with Suzanne d'Ange. Jalin knows a great deal about her, for the simple reason that he has been her lover. Their relations have been most harmonious, but from the moment that Suzanne sets her cap at Nanjac, Olivier declares war. Suzanne struggles hard to keep possession of her suitor, who is very much in love with her, and Olivier spares no pains to detach him. It is the means that Olivier uses that excite the wonderment of the Anglo-Saxon spectator. He takes the ground that in such a cause all means are fair, and when, at the climax of the play, he tells a thumping lie in order to make Madame d'Ange compromise herself, expose herself, he is pronounced by the author "le plus honnête homme que je connaisse." Madame d'Ange, as I have said, is a superior woman; the interest of the play is in her being a superior woman. Olivier has been her lover; he himself is one of the reasons why she may not marry Nanjac; he has given her a push along the downward path. But it is curious how little this is held by the author to disqualify him from fighting the battle in which she is so much the weaker combatant. An English-speaking audience is more "moral" than a French, more easily scandalised; and yet it is a singular fact that if the *Demi-Monde* were represented before an English-speaking audience, its sympathies would certainly not go with M. de Jalin. It would pronounce him rather a coward. Is it because such an audience, although it has not nearly such a pretty collection of pedestals to place under the feet of the charming sex, has, after all, in default of this degree of gallantry, a tenderness more fundamental? Madame d'Ange has stained herself, and it is doubtless not at all proper that such ladies should be led to the altar by honourable young men. The point is not that the English-speaking audience would be disposed to condone Madame d'Ange's irregularities, but that it would remain perfectly cold before the spectacle of her ex-lover's masterly campaign against her, and quite fail to think it positively admirable, or to regard the fib by which he finally clenches his victory as a proof of exceptional honesty. The ideal of our own audience would be expressed in some such words as, "I say, that's not fair game. Can't you let the poor woman alone?"

IV.

RHEIMS AND LAON:
A LITTLE TOUR.

1877.

It was a very little tour, but the charm of the three or four old towns and monuments that it embraced, the beauty of the brilliant October, the pleasure of reminding one's self how much of the interest, strength and dignity of France is to be found outside of that huge pretentious caravansary called Paris (a reminder often needed), these things deserve to be noted. I went down to Rheims to see the famous cathedral, and to reach Rheims I travelled through the early morning hours along the charming valley of the Marne. The Marne is a pretty little green river, the vegetation upon whose banks, otherwise unadorned, had begun to blush with the early frosts in a manner that suggested the autumnal tints of American scenery. The trees and bushes were scarlet and orange; the light was splendid and a trifle harsh; I could have fancied myself immersed in an American "fall", if at intervals some gray old large-towered church had not lifted a sculptured front above a railway-station, to dispel the fond illusion. One of these church-fronts (I saw it only from the train) is particularly impressive; the little cathedral of Meaux, of which the great Bossuet was bishop, and along whose frigid nave he set his eloquence rolling with an impetus which it has not wholly lost to this day. It was entertaining, moreover, to enter the country of champagne; for Rheims is in the ancient province whose later fame is syllabled the world over in popping corks. A land of vineyards is not usually accounted sketchable; but the country about Epernay seemed to me to have a charm of its own. It stretched away in soft undulations that were pricked all over with little stakes muffled in leaves. The effect at a distance was that of vast surfaces, long, subdued billows, of pincushion; and yet it was very pretty. The deep blue sky was over the scene; the undulations were half in sun and half in shade; and here and there, among their myriad bristles, were groups of vintagers, who, though they are in reality, doubtless, a prosaic and mercenary body of labourers, yet assumed, to a fancy that glanced at them in the cursory manner permitted by the passage of the train, the appearance of joyous and disinterested votaries of Bacchus. The blouses of the men, the white caps of the women, were gleaming in the sunshine; they moved about crookedly among the tiny vine-poles. I thought them full of a charming suggestiveness. Of all the delightful gifts of France to the world, this was one of the most agreeable – the keen, living liquid in which the finest flower of sociability is usually dipped. It came from these sunny places; this little maze of curling-sticks supplied the world with half the world's gaiety. I call it little only in relation to the immense number of bottles with gilded necks in which this gaiety is annually stored up. The acreage of the champagne seemed to me, in fact, large; the bristling slopes went rolling away to new horizons in a manner that was positively reassuring. Making the handsomest allowance for the wine manufactured from baser elements, it was apparent that this big corner of a province represents a very large number of bottles.

As you draw near to Rheims the vineyards become sparser, and finally disappear, a fact not to be regretted, for there is something incongruous in the juxtaposition of champagne and gothic architecture. It may be said, too, that for the proper appreciation of a structure like the cathedral of Rheims you have need of all your head. As, after my arrival, I sat in my window at the inn, gazing up at the great façade, I found something dizzying in the mere climbing and soaring of one's astonished vision; and later, when I came to wander about in the upper regions of the church, and to peep down through the rugged lacework of the towers at the little streets and the small spots of public places, I found myself musing upon the beauty of soberness. My window at the Lion d'Or was like a proscenium-box at the play; to admire the cathedral at my leisure I had only to perch myself in the casement with a good opera-glass. I sat there for a long time watching the great architectural drama. A drama I may call it, for no church-front that I have seen is more animated, more richly figured. The density of the sculptures, the immense scale of the images, detract, perhaps, at first, in a certain sense, from the impressiveness of the cathedral of Rheims; the absence of large surfaces, of ascending lines, deceives you as to the elevation of the front, and the dimensions of some of the upper statues bring them unduly near the eye. But little by little you perceive that this great figured and storied screen has a mass proportionate to its detail, and that it is the grandest part of a structure which, as a whole, is one of the noblest works of man's hands. Most people remember to have seen some print or some photograph of this heavily-charged façade of Rheims, which is usually put forward as the great example of the union of the purity and the possible richness of gothic. I must first have seen some such print in my earliest years, for I have always thought of Rheims as the typical gothic cathedral. I had vague associations with it; it seemed to me that I had already stood there in the little overwhelmed *place*. One's literary associations with Rheims are indeed very vivid and impressive; they begin with the picture of the steel-clad Maid passing under the deeply-sculptured portal, with a banner in her hand which she has no need to lower, and while she stands amid the incense and the chants, the glitter of arms and the glow of coloured lights asking leave of the young king whom she has crowned to turn away and tend her flocks. And after that there is the sense of all the kings of France having travelled down to Rheims in their splendour to be consecrated; the great groups on the front of the church must have looked down on groups almost as stately – groups full of colour and movement – assembled in the square. (The square of Rheims, it must be confessed, is rather shabby. It is singular that the august ceremony of the *sacre* should not have left its mark upon the disposition of the houses, should not have kept them at a respectful distance. Louis XIV, smoothing his plumage before he entered the church, can hardly have had space to swing the train of his coronation-robe.) But when in driving into the town I reached the small precinct, such as it is, and saw the cathedral lift its spireless towers above the long rows of its carven saints, the huge wheel of its window, the three great caverns of its portals, with the high acute pediments above each arch, and the sides abutting outward like the beginning of a pyramid; when I looked at all this I felt that I had carried it in my mind from my earliest years, and that the stately vision had been implanted there by some forgotten glimpse of an old-fashioned water-colour sketch, in which the sky was washed in with expressive splashes, the remoter parts of the church tinted with a fascinating blueness, and the foundations represented as encumbered with little gabled and cross-timbered houses, inhabited by women in red petticoats and curious caps.

I shall not attempt any regular enumeration of the great details of the façade of Rheims; I cannot profess even to have fully apprehended them. They are a glorious company, and here and there, on its high-hung pedestal, one of the figures detaches itself with peculiar effectiveness. Over the central portal sits the Virgin Mary, meekly submitting her head to the ponderous crown which her Son prepares to place upon it; the attitude and movement of Christ are full of a kind of splendid politeness. The three great doorways are in themselves a museum of imagery, disposed in each case in five close tiers, the statues in each of the tiers packed perpendicularly against their comrades. The effect of these great hollowed and chiselled recesses is extremely striking; they are a proper vestibule to the dusky richness of the interior. The cathedral of Rheims, more fortunate than many of its companions, appears not to have suffered from the iconoclasts of the Revolution; I noticed no absent heads nor broken noses. It is very true that these members may have had adventures to which they do not, as it were, allude. But, like many of its companions, it is so pressed upon by neighbouring houses that it is not easy to get a general view of the sides and the rear. You may walk round it, and note your walk as a long one; you may observe that the choir of the church travels back almost into another quarter of the city; you may see the farspreading mass lose itself for a while in parasitic obstructions, and then emerge again with all its buttresses flying; but you miss that wide margin of space and light which should enable it to present itself as a consistent picture. Pictures have their frames, and poems have their margins; a great work of art, such as a gothic cathedral, should at least have elbow-room. You may, however, stroll beneath the walls of Rheims, along a narrow, dark street, and look up at the mighty structure and see its higher parts foreshortened into all kinds of delusive proportions. There is a grand entertainment in the view of the church which you obtain from the farthermost point to which you may recede from it in the rear, keeping it still within sight. I have never seen a cathedral so magnificently buttressed. The buttresses of Rheims are all double; they have a tremendous spring and are supported upon pedestals surmounted by immense crocketed canopies containing statues of wide-winged angels. A great balustrade of gothic arches connects these canopies one with another, and along this balustrade are perched strange figures of sitting beasts, unicorns and mermaids, griffins and monstrous owls. Huge, terrible gargoyles hang far over into the street, and doubtless some of them have a detail which I afterwards noticed at Laon. The gargoyle represents a grotesque beast – a creature partaking at once of the shape of a bird, a fish, and a quadruped. At Laon, on either side of the main entrance, a long-bellied monster cranes forth into the air with the head of a hippopotamus; and under its belly crouches a little man, hardly less grotesque, making up a rueful grimace and playing some ineffectual trick upon his terrible companion. One of these little figures has plunged a sword, up to the hilt, into the belly of the monster above him, so that when he draws it forth there will be a leak in the great stone gutter; another has suspended himself to a rope that is knotted round the neck of the gargoyle, and is trying in the same manner to interrupt its functions by pulling the cord as tight as possible. There was sure to be a spirit of life in an architectural conception that could range from the combination of clustering towers and opposing fronts to this infinitely minute play of humour.

There is no great play of humour in the interior of Rheims, but there is a great deal of beauty and solemnity. This interior is a spectacle that excites the sensibility, as our forefathers used to say; but it is not an easy matter to describe. It is no description of it to say that it is four hundred and sixty-six feet in length, and that the roof is one hundred and twenty-four feet above the pavement; nor is there any very vivid portraiture in the statement that if there is no coloured glass in the lower windows, there is, *per contra*, a great deal of the most gorgeous and most ancient in the upper ones. The long sweep of the nave, from the threshold to the point where the coloured light-shafts of the choir lose themselves in the gray distance, is a triumph of perpendicular perspective. The white light in the lower part of Rheims really contributes to the picturesqueness of the interior. It makes the gloom above look richer still, and throws that part of the roof which rests upon the gigantic piers of the transepts into mysterious remoteness. I wandered about for a long time; I sat first in one place and then in another; I attached myself to that most fascinating part of every great church, the angle at which the nave and transept divide. It was the better to observe this interesting point, I think, that I passed into the side gate of the choir – the gate that stood ajar in the tall gilded railing. I sat down on a stool near the threshold; I leaned back against the side of one of the stalls; the church was empty, and I lost myself in the large perfection of the place. I lost myself, but the beadle found me; he stood before me, and with a silent, imperious gesture, motioned me to depart. I risked an argumentative glance, whereupon he signified his displeasure, repeated his gesture, and pointed to an old gentleman with a red cape, who had come into the choir softly, without my seeing him, and had seated himself in one of the stalls. This old gentleman seemed plunged in pious thoughts; I was not, after all, very near him, and he did not look as if I disturbed him. A canon is at any time, I imagine, a more merciful man than a beadle. But of course I obeyed the beadle, and eliminated myself from this peculiarly sacred precinct. I found another chair, and I fell to admiring the cathedral again. But this time I think it was with a difference – a difference which may serve as an excuse for the triviality of my anecdote. Sundry other old gentlemen in red capes emerged from the sacristy and went into the choir; presently, when there were half a dozen, they began to chant, and I perceived that the impending vespers had been the reason of my expulsion. This was highly proper, and I forgave the beadle; but I was not so happy as before, for my thoughts had passed out of the architectural channel into – what shall I say? – into the political. Here they found nothing so sweet to feed upon. It was the 5th of October; ten days later the elections for the new Chamber were to take place – the Chamber which was to replace the Assembly dissolved on the 16th of May by Marshal MacMahon, on a charge of "latent" radicalism. Stranger though one was, it was impossible not to be much interested in the triumph of the republican cause; it was impossible not to sympathise with this supreme effort of a brilliant and generous people to learn the lesson of national self-control and self-government. It was impossible by the same token, not to have noted and detested the alacrity with which the Catholic party had rallied to the reactionary cause, and the unction with which the clergy had converted itself into the go-betweens of Bonapartism. The clergy was giving daily evidence of its devotion to arbitrary rule and to every iniquity that shelters itself behind the mask of "authority". These had been frequent and irritating reflections; they lurked in the folds of one's morning paper. They came back to me in the midst of that tranquil grandeur of Rheims, as I listened to the droning of the old gentlemen in the red capes. Some of the canons, it was painful to observe, had not been punctual; they came hurrying out of the sacristy after the service had begun. They looked like amiable and venerable men; their chanting and droning, as it spread itself under the great arches, was not disagreeable to listen to; I could certainly bear them no grudge. But their presence there was distracting and vexatious; it had spoiled my enjoyment of their church, in which I doubtless had no business. It had set me thinking of the activity and vivacity of the great organisation to which they belonged, and of all the odious things it would have done before the 15th of October. To what base uses do we come at last! It was this same organisation that had erected the magnificent structure around and above me, and which had then seemed an image of generosity and benignant power. Such an edifice might at times make one feel tenderly sentimental toward the Catholic church – make one remember how many of the great achievements of the past we owe to her. To lapse gently into this state of mind seems indeed always, while one strolls about a great cathedral, a proper recognition of its hospitality; but now I had lapsed gently out of it, and it was one of the exasperating elements of the situation that I felt, in a manner, called upon to decide how far such a lapse was unbecoming. I found myself even extending the question a little, and picturing to myself that conflict which must often occur at such a moment as the present – which is actually going on, doubtless, in many thousands of minds – between the actively, practically liberal instinct and what one may call the historic, æsthetic sense, the sense upon which old cathedrals lay a certain palpable obligation. How far should a lover of old cathedrals let his hands be tied by the sanctity of their traditions? How far should he let his imagination bribe him, as it were, from action? This of course is a question for each man to answer for himself; but as I sat listening to the drowsy old canons of Rheims, I was visited, I scarcely know why, by a kind of revelation of the anti-catholic passion, as it must burn to-day in the breasts of certain radicals. I felt that such persons must be intent upon war to the death; how that must seem the most sacred of all duties. Can anything, in the line of action, for a votary of the radical creed, be more sacred? I asked myself; and can any instruments be too trenchant? I raised my

eyes again to the dusky splendour of the upper aisles and measured their enchanting perspective, and it was with a sense of
doing them full justice that I gave my fictive liberal my good
wishes.

This little operation restored my equanimity, so that I
climbed several hundred steps and wandered lightly over the
roof of the cathedral. Climbing into cathedral-towers and
gaping at the size of the statues that look small from tile street
has always seemed to me a rather brutal pastime; it is not the
proper way to treat a beautiful building; it is like holding one's
nose so close to a picture that one sees only the grain of the
canvas. But when once I had emerged into the upper wilderness of Rheims the discourse of a very urbane and appreciative
old bellringer, whom I found lurking behind some gigantic
excrescence, gave an æsthetic complexion to what would otherwise have been a rather vulgar feat of gymnastics. It was very
well to see what a great cathedral is made of, and in these high
places of the immensity of Rheims I found the matter very
impressively illustrated. I wandered for half an hour over endless expanses of roof, along the edge of sculptured abysses,
through hugely-timbered attics and chambers that were in
themselves as high as churches. I stood knee-high to strange
images, of unsuspected proportions, and I followed the topmost staircase of one of the towers, which curls upward like
the groove of a cork-screw, and gives you at the summit a hint
of how a sailor feels at the masthead. The ascent was worth
making to learn the fulness of beauty of the church, the
solidity and perfection, the mightiness of arch and buttress,
the latent ingenuity of detail. At the angles of the balustrade
which ornaments the roof of the choir are perched a series of
huge sitting eagles, which from below, as you look up at them,
produce a great effect. They are immense, grim-looking birds,
and the sculptor has given to each of them a pair of very neatly

carved human legs, terminating in talons. Why did he give them human legs? Why did he indulge in this ridiculous conceit? I am unable to say, but the conceit afforded me pleasure. It seemed to tell of an imagination always at play, fond of the unexpected and delighting in its labour.

Apart from its cathedral Rheims is not an interesting city. It has a prosperous, modern, mercantile air. The streets look as if at one time M. Haussmann, in person, may have taken a good deal of exercise in them; they prove, however, that a French provincial town may be a wonderfully fresh, clean, comfortable-looking place. Very different is the aspect of the ancient city of Laon, to which you may, by the assistance of the railway, transfer yourself from Rheims in a little more than an hour. Laon is full of history, and the place, as you approach it, reminds you of a quaint woodcut in the text of an ancient folio. Out of the midst of a smiling plain rises a goodly mountain, and on the top of the mountain is perched the old feudal *commune*, from the centre of which springs, with infinite majesty, the many-towered cathedral. At Laon you are in the midst of old France; it is one of the most interesting chapters of the past. Ever since reading in the pages of M. Thierry the story of the fierce struggle for municipal independence waged by this ardent little city against its feudal and ecclesiastical lords, I had had the conviction that Laon was worthy of a visit. All the more so that her two hundred years of civic fermentation had been vainly spent, and that in the early part of the fourteenth century she had been disfranchised without appeal. M. Thierry's readers will remember the really thrilling interest of the story which he has selected as the most complete and typical among those of which the records of the mediaeval communities are full; the complications and fluctuations of the action, its brilliant episodes, its sombre, tragic *dénoûment*. I did not visit Laon with the *Lettres sur l'Histoire de France* in my pocket, nor had I any other historic texts for reference; but a vague notion of the vigorous manner in which for a couple of centuries the stubborn little town had attested its individuality supplied my observations with an harmonious background. Nothing can well be more picturesque than the position of this interesting city. The tourist who has learned his trade can tell a "good" place at a glance. The moment Laon became visible from the window of the train I perceived that Laon was good. And then I had the word for it of an extremely intelligent young officer of artillery, who shared my railway-carriage in coming from Rheims, and who spoke with an authority borrowed from three years of garrison-life on that windy hill-top. He affirmed that the only recreation it afforded was a walk round the ramparts which encircle the town; people went down the hill as little as possible – it was such a dreadful bore to come up again. But he declared, nevertheless, that, as an intelligent traveller, I should be enchanted with the place; that the cathedral was magnificent, the view of the surrounding country a perpetual entertainment, and the little town full of originality. After I had spent a day there I thought of this pleasant young officer and his familiar walk upon the city-wall; he gave a point to my inevitable reflections upon the degree to which at the present hour, in France, the front of the stage is occupied by the army. Inevitable reflections, I say, because the net result of any little tour that one may make just now is a vivid sense of red trousers and cropped heads. Wherever you go you come upon a military quarter, you stumble upon a group of young citizens in uniform. It is always a pretty spectacle; they enliven the scene; they touch it here and there with an effusion of colour. But this is not the whole of the matter, and when you have admitted that it is pictorial to be always *sous les armes*, you fall to wondering whether it is not very expensive. A million of defenders take up a good deal of room, even for defenders. It must be very uncomfortable to be always defending. How do the young men bear it; how does France bear it; how long will she be able to keep it up? Every young Frenchman, on reaching maturity, has to give up five years of his life to this bristling Minotaur of military service. It is hard for a nation of shameless civilians to understand how life is arranged among people who come into the world with this heavy mortgage upon the freshest years of their strength; it seems like drinking the wine of life from a vessel with a great leak in the bottom. Is such a *régime* inspiring, or is it demoralising? Is the effect of it to quicken the sentiment of patriotism, the sense of the dangers to which one's country is exposed and of what one owes to the common cause, or to take the edge from all ambition that is not purely military, to force young men to say that there is no use trying, that nothing is worth beginning, and that a young fellow condemned to pay such a tax as that has a right to refund himself in any way that is open to him? Reminded as one is at every step of the immensity of the military burden of France, the most interesting point seems to me not its economical but its moral bearing. Its effect upon the finances of the country may be accurately computed; its effect upon the character of the young generation is more of a mystery. As the analytic tourist wanders of an autumn afternoon upon the planted rampart of an ancient town and meets young soldiers strolling in couples or leaning against the parapet and looking off at the quiet country, he is apt to take the more genial view of the dreadful trade of arms. He is disposed to say that it teaches its votaries something that is worth knowing and yet is not learned in several other trades – the hardware, say, or the drygoods business. Five years is a good deal to ask of a young life as a sacrifice; but the sacrifice is in some ways a gain. Certainly, apart from the question of material defence, it may be said that no European nation, at present, can afford, morally, not to pass her young men, the hope of the country, through the military mill. It does for them something indispensable; it toughens, hardens, solidifies them; gives them an ideal of honour, of some other possibility in life than making a fortune. A country in which the other trades I spoke of have it all their own way appears, in comparison, less educated.

So I mused, as I strolled in the afternoon along the charming old city-wall at Laon; and if my meditations seem pretentious or fallacious, I must say in justice that I had been a good while coming to them. I had done a great many things first. I had climbed up the long straight staircase which has been dropped like a scaling-ladder from one of the town-gates to the bottom of the hill. Laon still has her gates as she still has her wall, and one of these, the old Porte d'Ardon, is a really precious relic of mediæval architecture. I had repaired to the sign of the *Hure* – a portrait of this inhospitable beast is swung from the front of the inn – and bespoken a lodging; I had spent a long time in the cathedral, in it and before it, beside it, behind it; I had walked all over the town, from the citadel, at one end of the lofty plateau on which it stands, to the artillery-barracks and the charming old church of St. Martin at the other. The cathedral of Laon has not the elaborate grandeur of that of Rheims; but it is a very noble and beautiful church. Nothing can be finer than its position; it would set off any church to stand on such a hill-crest. Laon has also a façade of many sculptures, which, however, has suffered greater violence than that of Rheims, and is now being carefully and delicately restored. Whole figures and bas-reliefs have lately been replaced by exact imitations in that fresh white French stone which looks at first like a superior sort of plaster. They were far gone, and I suppose the restorer's hand was imperiously called for. I do not know that it has been too freely used.

But half the charm of Laon is the magnificent colouring of brownish, weather-battered gray which it owes to the great exposure of its position, and it will be many a year before the chalky scars and patches will be wrought into dusky harmony with the rest of the edifice. Fortunately, however, they promise not to be very numerous; the principal restorations have taken place inside. I know not what all this labour costs; but I was interested in learning from the old bellringer at Rheims that the sum voted by the Chamber for furbishing up his own church was two millions of francs, to be expended during ten years. That is what it is to have "national monuments" to keep up. One is apt to think of the fourteenth century as a rather ill-appointed and comfortless period; but the fact that at the present time the mere repair of one of its buildings costs forty thousand dollars a year would indicate that the original builders had a great deal of money to spend. The cathedral of Laon was intended to be a wonderful cluster of towers, but only two of these ornaments – the couple above the west front – have been carried to a great altitude; the pedestals of the rest, however, detach themselves with much vigour, and contribute to the complicated and somewhat fantastic look which the church wears at a distance, and which makes its great effectiveness. The finished towers are admirably light and graceful; with the sky shining through their large interstices they suggest an imitation of timber in masonry. They have one very quaint feature. From their topmost portions, at each angle, certain carven heads of oxen peep forward with a startling naturalness – a tribute to the patient, powerful beasts who dragged the material of the building up the long zig-zags of the mountain. We perhaps treat our dumb creatures better to-day than was done five hundred years ago; but I doubt whether a modern architect, in settling his accounts, would have "remembered", as they say, the oxen.

The whole precinct of the cathedral of Laon is picturesque. There is a charming Palais de Justice beside it, separated from it by a pleasant, homely garden, in which, as you walk about, you have an excellent view of the towering back and sides of the great church. The Palais de Justice, which is an ancient building, has a fine old gothic arcade, and on the other side, directly upon the citywall, a picturesque, irregular rear, with a row of painted windows, through which, from the *salle d'audience*, the judge on the bench and the prisoner in the dock may enjoy a prospect, admonitory, inspiring, or depressing, as the case may be, of the expanded country. This great sea-like plain that lies beneath the town on all sides constitutes, for Laon, a striking resemblance to those Italian cities – Siena, Volterra, Perugia – which the traveller remembers so fondly as a dark silhouette lifted high against a glowing sunset. There is something Italian, too, in the mingling of rock and rampart in the old foundations of the town, and in the generous verdure in which these are muffled. At one end of the hill-top the plateau becomes a narrow ridge; the slope makes a deep indentation, which contributes to the effect of a thoroughly Italian picture. A line of crooked little red-roofed houses stands on the edge of this indentation, with their feet in the tangled verdure that blooms in it; and above them rises a large, florid, deserted-looking church, which you may be sure has a little empty, grass-grown, out-of-the-way *place* before it. Almost opposite, on another spur of the hill, the gray walls of a suppressed convent peep from among the trees. I might have been at Perugia.

There came in the evening to the inn of the Hure a very worthy man who had vehicles to hire. The Hure was decidedly a provincial hostelry, and I compared it mentally with certain English establishments of a like degree, of which I had lately had observation. In England I should have had a waiter

in an old evening-suit and a white cravat, who would have
treated me to cold meat and bread and cheese. There would
have been a musty little inn parlour and probably a very good
fire in the grate, and the festally-attired waiter would have
been my sole entertainer. At Laon I was in perpetual intercourse with the landlord and his wife, and a large body of
easy-going, confidential domestics. Our intercourse was carried on in an old darksome stone kitchen, with shining copper
vessels hanging all over the walls, in which I was free to
wander about and take down my key in one place and rum-
mage out my candlestick in another, while the domestics sat at
table eating *pot-au-feu*. The landlord cooked the dinner; he
wore a white cap and apron; he brought in the first dish at the
table d'hôte. Of course there was a table d'hôte, with several
lamps and a long array of little dessert-dishes, for the benefit
of two commercial travellers, who tucked their napkins into
their necks, and the writer of these lines. Every country has its
manners. In England the benefits – whatever they are – represented by the evening dress of the waiter would have been
most apparent; in France one was more sensible of the blessings of which the white cap and apron of the host were a
symbol. In England, certainly, one is treated more as a gentleman. It is too often forgotten, however, that even a
gentleman partakes of nourishment. But I am forgetting my
dispenser of vehicles, concerning whom, however, and whose
large red cheeks and crimson cravat, I have left myself room
to say no more than that they were witnesses of a bargain that
I should be driven early on the morrow morning, in an
"Américaine", to the Château de Coucy. The Américaine
proved to be a vehicle of which I should not have been eager
to claim the credit for my native land; but with the aid of a
ragged but resolute little horse, and a driver so susceptible as
regards his beast's appearance that, referring to the exclama-

tion of dismay with which I had greeted it, he turned to me at
the end of each successive kilometre with a rancorous "Now,
do you say he can't go?" – with these accessories, I say, it conveyed me more than twenty miles. It was entertaining to wind
down the hillside from Laon in the early morning of a
splendid autumn day; to dip into the glistening plain, all void
of hedges and fences, and sprinkled with light and dew; to jog
along the straight white roads, between the tall, thin poplars;
to rattle through the half-waked villages and past the orchards
heavy with sour-looking crimson apples. The Château de
Coucy is a well-known monument; it is one of the most considerable ruins in France, and it is in some respects the most
extraordinary. As you come from Laon a turn in the road suddenly, at last, reveals it to you. It is still at a distance; you will
not reach it for half an hour; but its huge white donjon stands
up like some gigantic lighthouse at sea. Coucy is altogether on
a grand scale, but this colossal, shining cylinder is a wonder of
bigness. As M. Viollet-le-Duc says, it seems to have been built
by giants for a race of giants. The very quaint little town of
Coucy-le-Château nestles at the foot of this strange, half-
substantial, half-spectral structure; it was, together with a
goodly part of the neighbouring country, the feudal appanage
of those terrible lords who erected the present indestructible
edifice, and whose "boastful motto" (I quote from Murray) was

> "Roi je ne suis,
> Prince ni comte aussi;
> Je suis le Sire de Coucy."

Coucy is a sleepy little borough, still girdled, with its ancient
wall, entered by its old gateways, and supported on the ver-
durous flanks of a hill-top. I interviewed the host of the
Golden Apple in his kitchen; I breakfasted – *ma foi, fort bien,*

as they would say in the indigenous tongue – in his parlour;
and then I visited the château, which is at five minutes' walk.
This very interesting ruin is the property of the state, and the
state is represented by a very civil and intelligent woman, who
divests the trade of custodian of almost all its grossness. Any
feudal ruin is a charming affair, and Coucy has much of the
sweet melancholy of its class. There are four great towers,
connected by a massive curtain and enclosing the tremendous
donjon of which I just now spoke. All this is very crumbling
and silvery; the enclosure is a tangle of wild verdure, and the
pigeons perch upon the inaccessible battlements exactly where
the sketcher would wish them. But the place lacked, to my
sense, the peculiar softness and venerableness, the ivied mellowness, of a great English ruin. At Coucy there is no ivy to
speak of; the climate has not caressed and embroidered the
rugged masses of stone. This is what I meant by speaking of
the famous donjon as spectral; the term is an odd one to apply
to an edifice whose walls are thirty-four feet thick. Its vast,
pale surface has not a speck nor a stain, not a clinging weed
nor a creeping plant. It looks like a tower of ivory.

I took my way from Coucy to the ancient town of Soissons,
where I found another cathedral, from which, I think, I
extracted all the entertainment it could legitimately yield.
There is little other to be had at Soissons, in spite of the suggestiveness of its name, which is redolent of history and local
colour. The truth is, I suppose, that Soissons looks so new, precisely because she is so old. She is in her second youth; she has
renewed herself. The old city was worn out; it could no longer
serve; it has been succeeded by another. The new one is a
quiet, rather aristocratic-looking little *ville de province* – a collection of well-conditioned, sober-faced abodes of gentility,
with high-walled gardens behind them and very carefully
closed portes-cochère in front. Occasionally a porte-cochère

opens; an elderly lady in black emerges and paces discreetly away. An old gentleman has come to the door with her. He is comfortably corpulent; he wears gold spectacles and embroidered slippers. He looks up and down the dull street, and sees nothing at all; then he retires, closing the porte-cochère very softly and firmly. But he has stood there long enough to give an observant stranger the impression of a cautious provincial bourgeoisie that has a solid fortune well invested, and that marries its daughters only *à bon escient*. This latter ceremony, however, whenever it occurs, probably takes place in the cathedral, and though resting on a prosaic foundation must borrow a certain grace from that charming building. The cathedral of Soissons has a statueless front and only a single tower; but it is full of a certain natural elegance.

V.

CHARTRES.

1876.

The spring, in Paris, since it has fairly begun, has been enchanting. The sun and the moon have been blazing in emulation, and the difference between the blue sky of day and of night has been as slight as possible. There are no clouds in the sky, but there are little thin green clouds, little puffs of raw, tender verdure, entangled among the branches of the trees. All the world is in the streets; the chairs and tables which have stood empty all winter before the doors of the cafés are at a premium; the theatres have become intolerably close; the puppet-shows in the Champs Elysées are the only form of dramatic entertainment which seems consistent with the season. By way of doing honour, at a small cost, to this ethereal mildness, I went out the other day to the ancient town of Chartres, where I spent several hours, which I cannot consent to pass over as if nothing had happened. It is the experience of the writer of these lines, who likes nothing so much as moving about to see the world, that if one has been for a longer time than usual resident and stationary, there is a kind of overgrown entertainment in taking the train, even for a suburban goal; and that if one takes it on a charming April day, when there is a sense, almost an odour, of change in the air, the innocent pleasure is as nearly as possible complete. My accessibility to emotions of this kind amounts to an infirmity, and

the effect of it was to send me down to Chartres in a shame-
lessly optimistic state of mind. I was so prepared to be
entertained and pleased with everything that it is only a mercy
that the cathedral happens really to be a fine building. If it had
not been, I should still have admired it inordinately, at the risk
of falling into heaven knows what æsthetic heresy. But I am
almost ashamed to say how soon my entertainment began. It
began, I think, with my hailing a little open carriage on the
Boulevard and causing myself to be driven to the Gare de
l'Ouest – far away across the river, up the Rue Bonaparte, of
art-student memories, and along the big, straight Rue de
Rennes to the Boulevard Montparnasse. Of course, at this
rate, by the time I reached Chartres – the journey is of a
couple of hours – I had almost drained the cup of pleasure.
But it was replenished at the station, at the buffet, from the
pungent bottle of wine I drank with my breakfast. Here, by
the way, is another excellent excuse for being delighted with
any day's excursion in France – that wherever you are, you
may breakfast to your taste. There may, indeed, if the station
is very small, be no buffet; but if there is a buffet, you may be
sure that civilisation – in the persons of a sympathetic young
woman in a well-made black dress, and a rapid, zealous,
grateful waiter – presides at it. It was quite the least, as the
French say, that after my breakfast I should have thought the
cathedral, as I saw it from the top of the steep hill on which
the town stands, rising high above the clustered houses and
seeming to make of their red-roofed agglomeration a mere
pedestal for its immense beauty, promised remarkably well.
You see it so as you emerge from the station, and then, as you
climb slowly into town, you lose sight of it. You perceive
Chartres to be a rather shabby little *ville de province*, with a
few sunny, empty open places, and crooked shady streets, in
which two or three times you lose your way, until at last, after

more than once catching a glimpse, high above some slit
between the houses, of the clear gray towers shining against
the blue sky, you push forward again, risk another short cut,
turn another interposing corner, and stand before the goal of
your pilgrimage.

I spent a long time looking at this monument. I revolved
around it, like a moth around a candle; I went away and I
came back; I chose twenty different standpoints; I observed it
during the different hours of the day, and saw it in the moonlight as well as the sunshine. I gained, in a word, a certain
sense of familiarity with it; and yet I despair of giving any
coherent account of it. Like most French cathedrals, it rises
straight out of the street, and is destitute of that setting of turf
and trees and deaneries and canonries which contribute so
largely to the impressiveness of the great English churches.
Thirty years ago a row of old houses was glued to its base and
made their back walls of its sculptured sides. These have been
plucked away, and, relatively speaking, the church is fairly isolated. But the little square that surrounds it is deplorably
narrow, and you flatten your back against the opposite houses
in the vain attempt to stand off and survey the towers. The
proper way to look at them would be to go up in a balloon
and hang poised, face to face with them, in the blue air. There
is, however, perhaps an advantage in being forced to stand so
directly under them, for this position gives you an overwhelming impression of their height. I have seen, I suppose,
churches as beautiful as this one, but I do not remember ever
to have been so fascinated by superpositions and vertical
effects. The endless upward reach of the great west front, the
clear, silvery tone of its surface, the way three or four magnificent features are made to occupy its serene expanse, its
simplicity, majesty, and dignity – these things crowd upon
one's sense with a force that makes the act of vision seem for

the moment almost all of life. The impressions produced by architecture lend themselves as little to interpretation by another medium as those produced by music. Certainly there is an inexpressible harmony in the façade of Chartres.

The doors are rather low, as those of the English cathedrals are apt to be, but (standing three together) are set in a deep framework of sculpture – rows of arching grooves, filled with admirable little images, standing with their heels on each other's heads. The church, as it now exists, except the northern tower, dates from the middle of the thirteenth century, and these closely-packed figures are full of the grotesqueness of the period. Above the triple portals is a vast round-topped window, in three divisions, of the grandest dimensions and the stateliest effect. Above this window is a circular aperture, of huge circumference, with a double row of sculptured spokes radiating from its centre and looking on its lofty field of stone, as expansive and symbolic as if it were the wheel of Time itself. Higher still is a little gallery with a delicate balustrade, supported on a beautiful cornice and stretching across the front from tower to tower; and above this is a range of niched statues of kings – fifteen, I believe, in number. Above the statues is a gable, with an image of the Virgin and Child on its front, and another of Christ on its apex. In the relation of all these parts there is such a high felicity that while on the one side the eye rests on a great many large blanks there is no approach on the other to poverty. The little gallery that I have spoken of, beneath the statues of the kings, had for me a peculiar charm. Useless, at its tremendous altitude, for other purposes, it seemed intended for the little images to step down and walk about upon. When the great façade begins to glow in the late afternoon light, you can imagine them strolling up and down their long balcony in couples, pausing with their elbows on the balustrade, resting their stony chins in their hands, and looking out, with their little blank eyes, on the great view of the old French monarchy they once ruled, and which now has passed away. The two great towers of the cathedral are among the noblest of their kind. They rise in solid simplicity to a height as great as the eye often troubles itself to travel, and then suddenly they begin to execute a magnificent series of feats in architectural gymnastics. This is especially true of the northern spire, which is a late creation, dating from the sixteenth century. The other is relatively quiet; but its companion is a sort of tapering bouquet of sculptured stone. Statues and buttresses, gargoyles, arabesques and crockets pile themselves in successive stages, until the eye loses the sense of everything but a sort of architectural lacework. The pride of Chartres, after its front, is the two portals of its transepts – great dusky porches, in three divisions, covered with more images than I have time to talk about. Wherever you look, along the sides of the church, a time-worn image is niched or perched. The face of each flying buttress is garnished with one, with the features quite melted away.

The inside of the cathedral corresponds in vastness and grandeur to the outside – it is the perfection of gothic in its prime. But I looked at it rapidly, the place was so intolerably cold. It seemed to answer one's query of what becomes of the winter when the spring chases it away. The winter hereabouts has sought an asylum in Chartres cathedral, where it has found plenty of room and may reside in a state of excellent preservation until it can safely venture abroad again. I supposed I had been in cold churches before, but the delusion had been an injustice to the temperature of Chartres. The nave was full of the little padded chairs of the local bourgeoisie, whose faith, I hope for their comfort, is of the good old red-hot complexion. In a higher temperature I should have done more justice to the magnificent old glass of the windows – which glowed through the icy dusk like the purple and orange of a winter sunset – and to the immense sculptured external casing of the choir. This latter is an extraordinary piece of work. It is a high gothic screen, shutting in the choir, and covered with elaborate bas-reliefs of the sixteenth and seventeenth centuries, representing scenes from the life of Christ and of the Virgin. Some of the figures are admirable, and the effect of the whole great semicircular wall, chiselled like a silver bowl, is superb. There is also a crypt of high antiquity and, I believe, great interest, to be seen; but my teeth chattered a respectful negative to the sacristan who offered to guide me to it. It was so agreeable to stand in the warm outer air again, that I spent the rest of the day in it.

Although, besides its cathedral, Chartres has no very rare architectural treasures, the place is pictorial, in a shabby, third-rate, poverty-stricken degree, and my observations were not unremunerative. There is a little church of Saint-Aignan, of the sixteenth century, with an elegant, decayed façade, and a small tower beside it, lower than its own roof, to which it is joined, in unequal twinship, by a single long buttress. Standing there with its crumbling Renaissance doorway, in a kind of grass-grown alcove, it reminded me of certain monuments that the tourist encounters in small Italian towns. Most of the streets of Chartres are crooked lanes, winding over the face of the steep hill, the summit of the hill being occupied by half a dozen little open squares, which seem like reservoirs of the dullness and stillness that flow through the place. In the midst of one of them rises an old dirty brick obelisk, commemorating the glories of the young General Marceau, of the first Republic – "Soldier at 16, general at 23, he died at 27." Such memorials, when one comes upon them unexpectedly, produce in the mind a series of circular waves of feeling like a splash in a quiet pond. Chartres gives us an impression of extreme antiquity, but it is an antiquity that has gone down in the world. I saw very few of those stately little hôtels, with pilastered fronts, which look so well in the silent streets of provincial towns. The houses are mostly low, small, and of sordid aspect, and though many of them have overhanging upper stories, and steep, battered gables, they are rather wanting in character. I was struck, as an American always is in small French and English towns, with the immense number of shops, and their brilliant appearance, which seems so out of proportion to any visible body of consumers. At Chartres the shopkeepers must all feed upon each other, for, whoever buys, the whole population sells. This population appeared to consist mainly of several hundred brown old peasant women, in the seventies and eighties, with their faces cross-hatched with wrinkles and their quaint white coifs drawn tightly over their weather-blasted eye-brows. Labour-stricken grandams, all the world over, are the opposite of lovely, for the toil that wrestles for its daily bread, morsel by morsel, is not beautifying; but I thought I had never seen the possibilities of female ugliness so variously embodied as in the crones of Chartres. Some of them were leading small children by the hand – little red-cheeked girls, in the close black caps and black pinafores of humble French infancy – a costume which makes French children always look like orphans. Others were guiding along the flinty lanes the steps of small donkeys, some of them fastened into little carts, some with well-laden backs. These were the only quadrupeds I perceived at Chartres. Neither horse nor carriage did I behold, save at the station the omnibuses of the rival inns – the "Grand Monarque" and the "Duc de Chartres" – which glare at each other across the Grande Place. A friend of mine told me that a few years ago, passing through Chartres, he went by night to call upon a gentleman who lived there. During his visit it came on to rain violently, and when the hour for his departure arrived the rain had made the streets impassable. There was no vehicle to be had, and my friend was resigning himself to a soaking. "You can be taken of course in the sedan-chair," said his host with dignity. The sedan-chair was produced, a couple of serving-men grasped the handles, my friend stepped into it, and went swinging back – through the last century – to the "Grand Monarque". This little anecdote, I imagine, still paints Chartres socially.

Before dinner I took a walk on the planted promenade which encircles the town – the Tour-de-ville it is called – much of which is extremely picturesque. Chartres has lost her walls as a whole, but here and there they survive, and play a desultory part in holding the town together. In one place the rampart is really magnificent – smooth, strong and lofty, curtained with ivy, and supporting on its summit an old convent and its garden. Only one of the city-gates remains – a narrow arch of the fourteenth century, flanked by two admirable round towers, and preceded by a fosse. If you stoop a little, as you stand outside, the arch of this hoary old gate makes a capital setting for the picture of the interior of the town, and, on the inner hill-top, against the sky, the large gray mass of the cathedral. The ditch is full, and to right and to left it flows along the base of the mouldering wall, through which the shabby backs of houses extrude, and which is garnished with little wooden galleries, lavatories of the town's soiled linen. These little galleries are filled with washerwomen, who crane over and dip their many-coloured rags into the yellow stream. The old patched and interrupted wall, the ditch with its weedy edges, the spots of colour, the white-capped laundresses in their little wooden cages – one lingers to look at it all.

VI.

ROUEN.

1876.

It is quite in the nature of things that a Parisian correspondence should have flagged during the last few weeks; for even the most brilliant of capitals, when the summer has fairly begun to be summer, affords few topics to the chronicler. To a chronicle of small beer such a correspondence almost literally finds itself reduced. The correspondent consumes a goodly number of those magnified thimblefuls of this fluid, known in Paris as "bocks," and from the shadiest corner of the coolest café he can discover watches the softened bitumen grow more largely interspaced. There is little to do or to see, and therefore little to write about. There is in fact only one thing to do, namely, to get out of Paris. The lively imagination of the correspondent anticipates his departure and takes flight to one of the innumerable watering-places whose charms at this season are set forth in large yellow and pink placards on all the empty walls. They order this matter, like so many others, much better in France. Here you have not, as in America, to hunt up the "summer retreat" about which you desire information in a dense alphabetical list in the columns of a newspaper; you are familiar with its merits for weeks before you start – you have seen them half a dozen times a day emblazoned on the line of your customary walk, over the hand and seal of the company that runs, as we should say in America, the Casino. If you are

detained in Paris, however, after luckier mortals have departed
– your reflections upon the fate of the luckless mortals who do
not depart at all are quite another question, demanding
another chapter – it does not perhaps make you much happier
to peruse these lyrical advertisements, which seem to flutter
with the breezes of Houlgate and Etretat. You must take your
consolation where you can find it, and it must, be added that
of all great cities Paris is the most tolerable in hot weather. It
is true that the asphalt liquifies, and it is true that the brilliant
limestone of which the city is built reflects the sun with
uncomfortable fierceness. It is also true that of a summer
evening you pay a penalty for living in the best-lighted capital
in the world. The inordinate amount of gas in the streets
makes the atmosphere hot and thick, so that even under the
dim constellations you feel of a July night as if you were in a
big music-hall. If you look down at such a time upon the central portions of Paris from a high window in a remoter
quarter, you see them wrapped in a lurid haze, of the devil's
own brewing. But, on the other hand, there are a hundred
facilities for remaining out of doors. You are not obliged to sit
on a "stoop" or on a curb-stone, as in New-York. The
Boulevards are a long chain of cafés, each one with its little
promontory of chairs and tables projecting into the sea of
asphalt. These promontories are doubtless not exactly islands
of the blessed, peopled though some of them may be with
sirens addicted to beer, but they may help you to pass a hot
evening. Then you may dine in the Champs Elysées, at a table
spread under the trees, beside an ivied wall, and almost believe
you are in the country. This illusion, imperfect as it is, is a
luxury, and must be paid for accordingly; the dinner is not so
good as at a restaurant on the Boulevard, and is considerably
dearer, and there is after all not much difference in sitting with
one's feet in dusty gravel or on a sanded floor. But the whole

situation is more idyllic. I indulged in a cheap idyl the other day by taking the penny steamer down the Seine to Auteuil (a very short sail), and dining at what is called in Parisian parlance a *guingette* on the bank of the stream. It was a very humble style of entertainment, but the most ambitious pursuit of pleasure can do no more than succeed, and this was a success. The Seine at Auteuil is wide, and is spanned by a stately viaduct of two tiers of arches, which stands up against the sky in a picturesque and monumental manner. Your table is spread under a trellis which scratches your headspread chiefly with fried fish – and an old man who looks like a political exile comes and stands before it and sings a doleful ditty on the respect due to white hairs. You testify by the bestowal of copper coin the esteem with which his own inspire you, and he is speedily replaced by a lad with one arm, who treats you to something livelier:

"A la bonne heure; parlez-moi de ça!"

You eventually return to Paris on the top of a tram-car. It is a very different affair to go out and dine at the Bois de Boulogne, at the charming restaurant which is near the cascade and the Longchamp racecourse. Here are no ballad-singers, but stately trees majestically grouped and making long evening shadows on a lawn, and irreproachable tables, and carriages rolling up behind high-stepping horses and depositing all sorts of ladies. The drive back through the wood at night is most charming, and the coolness of the air extreme, however hot you may still be certain to find the city.

The best thing, therefore, is not to go back. I write these lines at an inn at Havre, before a window which frames the picture of the seaward path of the transatlantic steamers. One of the great black ships is at this moment painted on the canvas, very near, and beginning its outward journey. I watch it to the right-hand ledge of the window, which is as far as so poor a sailor need be expected to follow it. The hotel at Havre is called, for mysterious reasons, "Frascati" – reasons which I give up the attempt to fathom, so undiscoverable are its points of analogy with the lovely village of the same name which nestles among the olives of the Roman hills. The locality has its charms, however. It is very agreeable, for instance, at the end of a hot journey, to sit down to dinner in a great open cage, hung over the Atlantic, and, while the sea-breeze cools your wine, watch the swiftly-moving ships pass before you like the figures on the field of a magic lantern. It is pleasant also to open your eyes in the early dawn, before the light is intense, and without moving your head on the pillow, enjoy the same clear vision of the ocean highway. In the vague dusk, with their rapid gliding, the passing vessels look like the ghosts of wrecked ships. Most seaports are picturesque, and Havre is not the least so; but my enjoyment has been not of my goal, but of my journey.

My head is full of the twenty-four hours I have just passed at Rouen, and of the charming sail down the Seine to Honfleur. Rouen is a city of very ancient renown, and yet I confess I was not prepared to find a little town of so much expression. The traveller who treads the Rouen streets at the present day sees but the shadow of their former characteristics; for the besom of M. Haussmann has swept through the city, and a train of "embellishments" has followed in its track. The streets have been widened and straightened, and the old houses – gems of mediæval domestic architecture – which formed the peculiar treasure of the place, have been more than decimated. A great deal remains, however, and American eyes are quick to make discoveries. The cathedral, the churches, the Palais de Justice, are alone a splendid group of monuments, and a stroll through the streets reveals a collection of brown and sculptured façades, of quaintly-timbered gables, of curious turrets and casements, of doorways which still may be called rich. Every now and then a considerable stretch of duskiness and crookedness delights the sentimental tourist who is to pass but a couple of nights at Rouen, and who does not care if his favourite adjective happen to imply another element which also is spelled with a *p*. It is nothing to him that the picturesque is pestiferous. It is everything to him that the great front of the cathedral is magnificently battered, heavy, impressive. It has been defaced immensely, and is now hardly more than a collection of empty niches. I do not mean, of course, that the wanton tourist rejoices in the absence of the statues which once filled them, but up to the present moment, at least, he is not sorry that the façade has not been restored. It consists of a sort of screen, pierced in the centre with a huge wheel-window, crowned with a pyramid of chiselled needles and spires, flanked with two turrets capped with tall empty canopies, and covered, generally, with sculptures – friezes, statues, excrescences. On each side of it rises a great tower; one a rugged mass of early Norman work, with little ornament save its hatcheted closed arches, and its great naked base, as huge and white as the bottom of a chalk-cliff; the other a specimen of sixteenth century gothic, extremely flamboyant and confounding to the eye. The sides of the cathedral are as yet more or less imbedded in certain black and dwarfish old houses, but if you pass around them by a long détour, you arrive at two superb lateral porches. The so-called Portail des Libraires, in especial, on the northern side, is a magnificent affair, sculptured from summit to base (it is now restored), and preceded by a long forecourt, in which the guild of booksellers used to hold its musty traffic. From here you see the immense central tower, perched above the junction of the transepts and

the nave, and crowned with a gigantic iron spire, lately erected
to replace one which was destroyed by lightning in the early
part of the century. This gaunt pyramid has the drawback, to
American eyes, of resembling too much the tall firetowers
which are seen in transatlantic cities, and its dimensions are
such that, viewed from a distance, it fairly makes little Rouen
look top-heavy. Behind the choir, within, is a beautiful lady-
chapel, and in this chapel are two enchanting works of art.
The larger and more striking of these is the tomb of the two
Cardinals d'Amboise, uncle and nephew – the elder, if I mistake not, minister of Louis XII. It consists of a shallow, oblong
recess in the wall, lined with gilded and fretted marble, and
corniced with delicate little statues. Within the recess the
flaures of the two cardinals are kneeling, with folded hands
and ruggedly earnest faces, their long robes spread out behind
them with magnificent amplitude. They are full of life, dignity,
and piety; they look like portraits of Holbein transferred into
marble. The base of the monument is composed of a series of
admirable little images representing the cardinal and other
virtues, and the effect of the whole work is wonderfully grave
and rich. The discreet traveller will never miss an opportunity
to come into a great church at eventide – the hour when his
fellow-travellers, less discreet, are lingering over the table
d'hôte, when the painted windows glow with a deeper splendour, when the long wand of the beadle, slowly tapping the
pavement, or the shuffle of the old sacristan, has a ghostly res-
onance along the empty nave, and three or four work-weary
women, before a dusky chapel, are mumbling for the remis-
sion of unimaginable sins. At this hour, at Rouen, the tomb of
the Duke of Brézé, husband of Diana of Poitiers, placed opposite to the monument I have just described, seemed to me the
most beautiful thing in the world. It is presumably the work of
the delightful Jean Goujon, and it bears the stamp of his

graceful and inventive talent. The deceased is lying on his back, almost naked, with a part of his shroud bound in a knot about his head – a realistic but not a repulsive image of death. At his head kneels the amiable Diana, in sober garments, all decency and devotion; at his feet stands the Virgin, a charming young woman with a charming child. Above, on another tier, the subject of the monument is represented in the fulness of life, dressed as for a tournament, bestriding a high-stepping war-horse, riding forth like a Roland or a Galahad. The architecture of the tomb is exceedingly graceful and the subordinate figures admirable, but the image of the dead Duke is altogether a masterpiece. The other evening, in the solemn stillness and the fading light of the great cathedral, it seemed irresistibly human and touching. The spectator felt a sort of impulse to smooth out the shroud and straighten the helpless hands.

The second church of Rouen, Saint-Ouen, the beautiful and harmonious, has no monuments of this value, but it offers within a higher interest than the Cathedral. Without, it looks like an English abbey, scraped and restored, disencumbered of huddling neighbours and surrounded on three sides by a beautiful garden. Seen to this excellent advantage it is one of the noblest of churches; but within, it is one of the most fascinating. My taste in architecture greatly resembles my opinions in fruit; the particular melon or pear or peach that I am eating appears to me to place either peaches, pears, or melons, beyond all other succulent things. In the same way, in a fine building the present impression is the one that convinces me most. This is deplorable levity; yet I risk the affirmation *à propos* of Saint-Ouen. I can imagine no happier combination of lightness and majesty. Its proportions bring tears to the eyes. I have left myself space only to recommend the sail down the Seine from Rouen to the mouth of the stream; but I recommend it in the highest terms. The heat was extreme and the little steamer most primitive, but the river is as entertaining as one could wish. It makes an infinite number of bends and corners and angles, rounded off by a charming vegetation. Abrupt and rocky hills go with it all the way – hills with cornfields lying in their hollows and deep woods crowning their tops. Out of the woodland peep old manors, and beneath, between the hills and the stream, are high-thatched farmsteads, lying deep in their meadows and orchards, cottages pallisaded with hollyhocks, gray old Norman churches and villas flanked with big horse-chestnuts. It is a land of peace and plenty, and remarkable to Anglo-Saxon eyes for the English-looking details of its scenery. I noticed a hundred places where one might have been in Kent as well as in Normandy. In fact it is almost better than Kent, for Kent has no Seine. At the last the river becomes unmistakably an arm of the sea, and as a river, therefore, less interesting. But crooked little Honfleur, with its miniature port, clinging to the side of a cliff as luxuriant as one of the headlands of the Mediterranean, gratifies in a high degree the tourist with a propensity for sketching.

VII.

ETRETAT.

1876.

The coast of Normandy and Picardy, from Trouville to Boulogne, is a chain of *stations balnéaires*, each with its particular claim to patronage. The grounds of the claim are in some cases not especially obvious; but they are generally found to reside in the fact that if one's spirits, on arriving, are low, so also are the prices. There are the places that are dear and brilliant, like Trouville and Dieppe, and places that are cheap and dreary, like Fécamp and Cabourg. Then there are the places that are both cheap and pleasant. This delightful combination of qualities may be found at the modest *plage* from which I write these lines. At Etretat you may enjoy some of the finest cliff-scenery it has been my fortune to behold, and you may breakfast and dine at the principal hotel for the sum of five and a half francs a day. You may engage a room in the town over the butcher's, the baker's, the cobbler's, at a rate that will depend upon your talent for driving a bargain, but that in no case will be exorbitant. Add to this that there are no other opportunities at Etretat to spend money. You wear old clothes, you walk about in canvas shoes, you deck your head with a fisherman's cap (when made of white flannel these articles may be extolled for their coolness, convenience, and picturesqueness), you lie on the pebbly strand most of the day, watching the cliffs, the waves, and the bathers; in the evening

you converse with your acquaintance on the terrace of the
Casino, and you keep monkish hours. Though Etretat enjoys
great and deserved popularity, I see no symptoms of the
decline of these simple fashions – no menace of the invasion
of luxury. A little more luxury, indeed, might be imported
without doing any harm; though after all we soon learn that it
is an idle enough prejudice that has hitherto prevented us
from keeping our soap in a sugar-dish and regarding a small
rock, placed against a door, as an efficient substitute for a key.
From a Parisian point of view, Etretat is certainly primitive,
but it would be affectation on the part of an American to pretend that he was not agreeably surprised to find a "summer
resort," in which he had been warned that he would have to
rough it, so elaborately appointed and organised. Etretat may
be primitive, but Etretat is French, and therefore Etretat is
"administered".

Like most of the French watering-places, the place has a limited past. Twenty years ago it was but a cluster of fishing-huts.
A group of artists and literary people were its first colonists,
and Alphonse Karr became the mouthpiece of their enthusiasm. In vulgar phrase, he wrote up Etretat, and he lives in
legend, at the present hour, as the *genius loci*. The main street
is named after him; the gable of the chief inn – the classic
Hôtel Blanquet – is adorned with a coloured medallion representing his cropped head and long beard; the shops are
stocked with his photographs and with pictures of his villa.
Like the magician who has evoked the spirit, he has made his
bow and retired; but the artistic fraternity, his disciples, still
haunt the place, and it enjoys also the favour of theatrical
people, three or four of whom, having retired upon their lau-
rels, possess villas here. From my open window, as I write
these lines, I look out beyond a little cluster of clean housetops
at the long green flank of the down, as it slopes to the village

from the summit of the cliff. To the right is the top of an old storm-twisted grove of oaks, in the heart of which stands a brown old farmhouse; then comes the sharp, even outline of the down, with its side spotted with little flat bushes and wrinkled with winding paths, along which here and there I see a bright figure moving; on the left, above the edge of the cliff, stands a bleak little chapel, dedicated to our Lady of the fishing-folk. Just here a provoking chimney starts up and cuts off my view of the downward plunge of the cliff, showing me, with a bar of blue ocean beyond, but a glimpse of its white cheek – its fantastic profile is to the left. But there is not far to go to see without impediments. Three minutes' walk along the Rue Alphonse Karr, where every house is a shop, and every shop has lodgers above it, who scramble bedward by a ladder and trap-door, brings you to the little pebbly bay where the cliffs are perpendicular and the foreign life of Etretat goes forward. At one end are the small fishing-smacks, with their green sides and their black sails, resting crookedly upon the stones; at the other is the Casino, and the two or three tiers of bathing-houses on the slope of the beach in front of it. This beach may be said to be Etretat. It is so steep and stony as to make circulation impossible; one's only course is to plant a camp-chair among the stones or to look for a soft spot in the pebbles, and to abide in the position so chosen. And yet it is the spot in Etretat most sacred to tranquil pleasure.

The French do not treat their beaches as we do ours – as places for a glance, a dip, or a trot, places animated simply during the balneary hours, and wrapped in natural desolation for the rest of the twenty-four. They love them, they adore them, they take possession of them, they live upon them. The people here sit upon the beach from morning to night; whole families come early and establish themselves, with umbrellas and rugs, books and work. The ladies get sunburnt and don't mind it; the gentlemen smoke interminably; the children roll over on the pointed pebbles and stare at the sun like young eagles. (The children's lot I rather commiserate; they have no wooden spades and pails; they have no sand to delve and grub in; they can dig no trenches and canals, nor see the creeping tide flood them.) The great occupation and amusement is the bathing, which has many entertaining features (I allude to it as a spectacle), especially for strangers who keep an eye upon national idiosyncrasies. The French take their bathing very seriously; supplemented by opéra-bouffe in the evening at the Casino it is their most preferred form of communion with nature. The spectators and the bathers commingle in graceful promiscuity; it is the freedom of the golden age. The whole beach becomes a large family party, in which the sweetest familiarities prevail. There is more or less costume, but the minimum rather than the maximum is found the more comfortable. Bathers come out of their dressing-houses wrapped in short white sheets, which they deposit on the stones, taking an air-bath for some minutes before entering the water. Like everything in France, the bathing is excellently managed, and you feel the firm hand of a paternal and overlooking government the moment you issue from your hut. The Government will on no consideration consent to your being rash. There are six or eight worthy old sons of Neptune on the beach – perfect amphibious creatures – who, if you are a new-comer, immediately accost you and demand pledges that you know how to swim. If you do not, they give you much excellent advice, and keep an eye on you while you are in the water. They are moreover obliged to render you any service you may demand – to pour buckets of water over your head, to fetch your bathing-sheet and your slippers, to carry your wife and children into the sea, to dip them, cheer them, sustain them, to teach them how to swim and how to dive, to hover about, in short, like ministering and trickling angels. At a short distance from the shore are two boats, freighted with sundry other marine divinities, who remain there perpetually, taking it as a personal offence if you venture out too far.

The French themselves have every pretext for venturing, being in general excellent swimmers. Every one swims, and swims indefatigably – men, women, and children. I have been especially struck with the prowess of the ladies, who take the neatest possible headers from the two long plunging-boards which are rigged in the water upon high wheels. As you recline upon the beach you may observe Mademoiselle X. issue from her cabin – Mademoiselle X., the actress of the Palais Royal Theatre, whom you have seen and applauded behind the footlights. She wears a bathing-dress in which, as regards the trousers, even what I have called the minimum has been appreciably scanted; but she trips down, surveying her liberated limbs. "*C'est convenable, j'espère, hein?*' says Mademoiselle, and trots up the spring-board which projects over the waves with one end uppermost, like a great see-saw. She balances a moment, and then gives a great aerial dive, executing on the way the most graceful of somersaults. This performance the star of the Palais Royal repeats during the ensuing hour, at intervals of five minutes, and leaves you, as you lie tossing little stones into the water, to consider the curious and delicate question why a lady may go so far as to put herself into a single scant clinging garment and take a straight leap, head downward, before three hundred spectators, without violation of propriety – and why impropriety should begin only when she turns over in the air in such a way that for five seconds her head is upwards. The logic of the matter is mysterious; white and black are divided by a hair. But the fact remains that virtue is on one side of the hair and vice on the other. There are some days here so still and

radiant, however, that it seems as if vice itself, steeped in such
an air and such a sea, might be diluted into innocence. The sea
is as blue as melted sapphires, and the rugged white faces of
the bordering cliffs make a silver frame for the picture. Every
one is idle, amused, good-natured; the bathers take to the
water as easily as mermen and mermaids. The bathing men in
the two *bateaux de surveillance* have in their charge a freight
of rosy children, more or less chubbily naked, and they have
nailed a gay streamer and a rude nosegay to their low mast-
heads. The swimmers dip and rise, circling round the boats
and playing with the children. Every now and then they grasp
the sides of the boats and cling to them in a dozen harmonious
attitudes, making one fancy that Eugène Delacroix's great picture of Dante and Virgil on the Styx, with the damned trying
to scramble into Charon's bark, has been repainted as a scene
on one of the streams of Paradise. The swimmers are not the
damned, but the blessed, and the demonstrative French babies
are the cherubs.

The Casino at Etretat is a modest but respectable establishment, with a sufficiently capacious terrace, directly upon the
beach, a café, a billiard-room, a ballroom – which may also be
used as a theatre, a reading-room, and a *salon de conversation*.
It is in very good taste, without any attempt at gilding or mirrors; the ballroom, in fact, is quite a masterpiece, with its
charm of effect produced simply by unpainted woods and
happy proportions. Three evenings in the week a blond young
man in a white necktie plays waltzes on a grand piano; but the
effect is not that of an American "hop", owing to the young
ladies of France not being permitted to dance in public places.
They may only sit wistfully beside their mammas. Imagne a
"hop" at which sweet seventeen is condemned to immobility.
The burden of the gaiety is sustained by three or four rosy
English maidens and as many of their American sisters. On the

other evenings a weak little operatic troupe gives light specimens of the lyric drama, the privilege of enjoying which is
covered by your subscription to the Casino. The French hurry
in joyously (four times a week in July and August!) at the
sound of the bell, but I can give no report of the perfor-
mances. Sometimes I look through the lighted windows and
see, on the diminutive stage, a short-skirted young woman
with one hand on her heart and the other persuasively
extended. Through the hot unpleasant air comes a little ghost
of a roulade. I turn away and walk on the terrace and listen to
the ocean vocalising to the stars.

But there are (by daylight) other walks at Etretat than the
terrace, and no account of the place is complete without some
commemoration of the admirable cliffs. They are the finest I
have seen; their fantastic needles and buttresses, at either end
of the little bay, give to careless Etretat an extreme distinction.
In spite of there being no sands, a persistent admirer of nature
will walk a long distance upon the tiresome sea-margin of
pebbles for the sake of being under them and visiting some of
their quiet caves and embrowned recesses, varnished by the
ocean into splendid tones. Seen in this way from directly
below, they look stupendous; they hold up their heads with
attitudes quite Alpine. They are marvellously white and
straight and smooth; they have the tint and something of the
surface of time-yellowed marble, and here and there, at their
summits, they break into quaint little pinnacles and turrets.
But to be on the top of them is even better; here you may walk
over miles of grassy, breezy down, with the woods, contorted
and seastunted, of old farmsteads on your land-side (the farmhouses here have all a charming way of being buried in a
wood, like the castle of the Sleeping Beauty), coming every
little while upon a weather-blackened old shepherd and his
flock (their conversation – the shepherds' – is delightful), or

on some little seaward-plunging valley, holding in its green hollow a diminutive agricultural village, curtained round from the sea-winds by a dense stockade of trees. So you may go southward or northward, without impediment, to Havre or to Dieppe.

VIII.

FROM NORMANDY TO
THE PYRENEES.

1876.

The other day, before the first fire of winter, when the deep-ening dusk had compelled me to close my book and wheel my chair closer, I indulged in a retrospect. The objects of it were not far distant, and yet they were already interfused with the mellow tints of the past. In the crackling flame the last rem-nant of the summer appeared to shrink up and vanish. But the flicker of its destruction made a sort of fantastic imagery, and in the midst of the winter fire the summer sunshine seemed to glow. It lit up a series of visible memories.

I.

One of the first was that of a perfect day on the coast of Normandy – a warm, still Sunday in the early part of August. From my pillow, on waking, I could look at a strip of blue sea and a great cube of white cliff. I observed that the sea had never been so brilliant, and that the cliff was shining as if it had been painted in the night. I rose and came forth with the sense that it was the finest day of summer, and that one ought to do something uncommon by way of keeping it. At Etretat it was uncommon to take a walk; the custom of the country is to lie all day upon the pebbly strand, watching, as we should say in America, one's fellow-boarders. Your leisurely stroll, in a scanty sheet, from your bathing-cabin into the water, and your trickling progress from the water back into your cabin, form, as a general thing, the sum total of your pedestrianism. For the rest you remain horizontal, contemplating the horizon. To mark the day with a white stone, therefore, it was quite sufficient to stretch my legs. So I climbed the huge grassy cliff which shuts in the little bay on the right (as you lie on the beach, head upward), and gained the bleak white chapel of Notre Dame de la Garde, which a lady told me she was sure was the original of Matthew Arnold's "little gray church on the windy shore." This is very likely; but the little church to-day was not gray, neither was the shore windy.

I had occasion, by the time I reached the summit, to wish it had been. Deep, silent sunshine filled the air, and the long grass of the downs stood up in the light without a tremor. The downs at Etretat are magnificent, and the way they stretched off toward Dieppe, with their shining levels and their faintly-shaded dells, was in itself an irresistible invitation. On the land-side they have been somewhat narrowed by cultivation; the woods, and farms, and grain-fields here and there creep close enough to the edge of the cliff almost to see the shifting of the tides at its base. But cultivation in Normandy is itself picturesque, and the pedestrian rarely needs resent its encroachments. Neither walls nor hedges nor fences are any-where visible; the whole land lies open to the breezes and to his curious footsteps. This universal absence of barriers gives an air of vastness to the landscape, so that really, in a little French province, you have more of the feeling of being in a big country than on our own huge continent, which bristles so incongruously with defensive palings and dykes. Norman farmhouses, too, with their mossy roofs and their visible beams making all kinds of triangles upon the ancient plaster of their walls, are very delightful things. Hereabouts they have always a dark little wood close beside them; often a *chénaie*, as the term is – a fantastic little grove of tempest-tossed oaks. The trees look as if, some night, when the sea-blasts were howling their loudest and their boughs were tossing most wildly, the tumult had suddenly been stilled and they had stopped short, each in the attitude into which the storm was twisting it. The only thing the storm can do with them now is to blow them straight. The long, indented coast-line had never seemed to me so charming. It stretched away into the light haze of the horizon, with such lovely violet spots in its caves and hollows, and such soft white gleams on its short headlands – such exquisite gradations of distance and such capricious interruptions of perspective – that one could only say that the land was really trying to smile as intensely as the sea. The smile of the sea was a positive simper. Such a glittering and twinkling, such a softness and blueness, such tiny little pin-points of foam, and such delicate little wrinkles of waves – all this made the ocean look like a flattered portrait.

The day I speak of was a Sunday, and there were to be races at Fécamp, ten miles away. The agreeable thing was, of course, to walk to Fécamp over the grassy downs. I walked and walked, over the levels and the dells, having land and ocean quite to myself. Here and there I met a shepherd lying flat on his stomach in the sun, while his sheep, in extreme dishabille (shearing-time being recent), went huddling in front of me as I approached. Far below, on the blue ocean, like a fly on a table of lapis, crawled a little steamer, carrying people from Etretat to the races. I seemed to go much faster, yet the steamer got to Fécamp before me. But I stopped to gossip with a shepherd on a grassy hillside, and to admire certain little villages which are niched in small, transverse, seaward-sloping valleys. The shepherd told me that he had been farm-servant to the same master for five-and-thirty years – ever since the age of ten; and that for thirty-five summers he had fed his flock upon those downs. I don't know whether his sheep were tired of their diet, but he professed himself very tired of his life. I remarked that in fine weather it must be charming, and he observed, with humility, that to thirty-five summers there went a certain number of rainy days.

The walk to Fécamp would be quite satisfactory if it were not for the *fonds*. The *fonds* are the transverse valleys just mentioned – the channels, for the most part, of small water-courses which discharge themselves into the sea. The downs subside, precipitately, to the level of the beach, and then slowly lift their grassy shoulders on the other side of the gully. As the cliffs are of immense height, these indentations are pro-found, and drain off a little of the exhilaration of the too elastic pedestrian. The first *fond* strikes him as delightfully pic-turesque, and he is down the long slope on one side and up the gigantic hump on the other before he has time to feel hot. But the second is greeted with that tempered *empressement* with which you bow in the street to an acquaintance whom you have met half an hour before; the third is a stale repeti-tion; the fourth is decidedly one too many, and the fifth is sensibly exasperating. The *fonds*, in a word are very tiresome. It was, if I remember rightly, in the bottom of the last and widest of the series that I discovered the little town of Yport. Every little fishing-village on the Norman coast has, within the last ten years, set up in business as a watering-place; and, though one might fancy that nature had condemned Yport to modest obscurity, it is plain she has no idea of being out of the fashion. But she is a miniature imitation of her rivals. She has a meagre little wood behind her and an evil-smelling beach, on which bathing is possible only at the highest tide. At the scorching midday hour at which I inspected her she seemed

absolutely empty, and the ocean, beyond acres of slippery sea-
weed, looked very far away. She has everything that a properly
appointed *station de bains* should have, but everything is on a
Lilliputian scale. The whole place looked like a huge
Nüremburg toy. There is a diminutive hotel, in which, properly, the head-waiter should be a pigmy and the chambermaid
a sprite, and beside it there is a Casino on the smallest possible
scale. Everything about the Casino is so consistently micro-
scopic, that it seems a matter of course that the newspapers in
the reading-room should be printed in the very finest type. Of
course there is a reading-room, and a dancing-room, and a
café and a billiard-room, with a bagatelle-board instead of a
table, and a little terrace on which you may walk up and down
with very short steps. I hope the prices are as tiny as everything else, and I suspect, indeed, that Yport honestly claims,
not that she is attractive, but that she is cheap.

I toiled up the perpendicular cliff again, and took my way
over the grass, for another hour, to Fécamp, where I found the
peculiarities of Yport directly reversed. The place is a huge,
straggling village, seated along a wide, shallow bay, and
adorned, of course, with the classic Casino and the row of
hotels. But all this is on a very brave scale, though it is not
manifest that the bravery at Fécamp has won a victory; and,
indeed, the local attractions did not strike me as irresistible. A
pebbly beach of immense length, fenced off from the town by
a grassy embankment; a Casino of a bald and unsociable
aspect; a principal inn, with an interminable brown façade,
suggestive somehow of an asylum or an almshouse – such are
the most striking features of this particular watering-place.
There are magnificent cliffs on each side of the bay, but, as the
French say, without impropriety, it is the devil to get to them.
There was no one in the hotel, in the Casino, or on the beach;
the whole town being in the act of climbing the farther cliff,

to reach the downs on which the races were to be held. The green hillside was black with trudging spectators and the long sky-line was fretted with them. When I say there was no one at the inn, I forget the gentleman at the door, who informed me positively that he would give me no breakfast; he seemed to have stayed at home from the races expressly to give himself this pleasure. But I went farther and fared better, obtaining a meal of homely succulence in an unfashionable tavern, in a back street, where the wine was sound, the cutlets were tender, and the serving-maid was rosy. Then I walked along for a mile, it seemed – through a dreary, gray *grand'-rue*, where the sunshine was hot, the odours were portentous, and the doorsteps garnished with aged fishwives, retired from business, whose plaited linen coifs gave a value, as the painters say, to the brown umber of their cheeks. I inspected the harbour and its goodly basin – with nothing in it – and certain pink and blue houses which surround it, and then, joining the last stragglers, I clambered up the side of the cliff to the downs.

The races had already begun, and the ring of spectators was dense. I picked out some of the smallest people, looked over their heads, and saw several young farmers, in parti-coloured jackets and very red in the face, bouncing up and down on handsome cart-horses. Satiated at last with this diversion, I turned away and wandered down the hill again; and after strolling through the streets of Fécamp, and gathering not a little of the wayside entertainment that a seaport and fishing-town always yields, I repaired to the Abbey-church, a monument of some importance, and almost as great an object of pride in the town as the Casino. The Abbey of Fécamp was once a very rich and powerful establishment, but nothing remains of it now save its church and its *trappistine*. The church, which is for the most part early gothic, is very stately and interesting, and the *trappistine*, a distilled liquor of the Chartreuse family, is much prized by people who take a little glass after their coffee. By the time I had done with the Abbey the townsfolk had slid *en masse* down the cliff again, the yellow afternoon had come, and the holiday-takers, before the wine shops, made long and lively shadows. I hired a sort of two-wheeled gig, without a hood, and drove back to Etretat in the rosy stage of evening. The gig dandled me up and down in a fashion of which I had been unconscious since I left off baby-clothes; but the drive, through the charming Norman country, over roads which lay among the peaceful meadows like paths across a park, was altogether delightful. The sunset gave a deeper mellowness to the standing crops, and in the grassiest corner of the wayside villages the young men and maidens were dancing like the figures in vignette-illustrations of classic poets.

II.

It was another picked day – you see how freely I pick them – when I went to breakfast at Saint-Jouin, chez la belle Ernestine. The beautiful Ernestine is as hospitable as she is fair, and to contemplate her charms you have only to order breakfast. They shine forth the more brilliantly in proportion as your order is liberal, and Ernestine is beautiful according as your bill is large. In this case she comes and smiles, really very handsomely, round your table, and you feel some hesitation in accusing so well-favoured a person of extortion. She keeps an inn at the end of a lane which diverges from the high road between Etretat and Havre, and it is an indispensable feature of your "station" at the former place that you choose some fine morning and seek her hospitality. She has been a celebrity these twenty years, and is no longer a simple maiden in her flower; but twenty years, if they have diminished her early bloom, have richly augmented her *musée*. This is a collection of all the verses and sketches, the autographs, photographs, monographs, trinkets, presented to the amiable hostess by admiring tourists. It covers the walls of her sitting-room and fills half a dozen big albums which you look at while breakfast is being prepared, just as if you were awaiting dinner in genteel society. Most Frenchmen of the day whom one has heard of appear to have called at Saint-Jouin, and to have left their *homages*. Each of them has turned a compliment with pen or pencil, and you may see in a glass case on the parlour wall what Alexandre Dumas *fils* thought of the landlady's nose, and how several painters measured her ankles.

Of course you must make this excursion in good company, and I affirm that I was in the very best. The company prefers, equally of course, to have its breakfast in the orchard in front of the house; which, if the repast is good, will make it seem better still, and if it is poor, will carry off its poorness. Clever innkeepers should always make their victims (in tolerable weather) eat in the garden. I forget whether Ernestine's breakfast was intrinsically good or bad, but I distinctly remember enjoying it, and making everything welcome. Everything, that is, save the party at the other table – the Paris actresses and the American gentlemen. The combination of these two classes of persons, individually so delightful, results in certain phenomena which seem less in harmony with appleboughs and summer breezes than with the gas-lamps and thick perfumes of a *cabinet particulier*; and yet it was characteristic of this odd mixture of things that Mademoiselle Ernestine, coming to chat with her customers, should bear a beautiful infant on her arm, and smile with artless pride on being assured of its filial resemblance to herself. She looked handsomer than ever as she caressed this startling attribute of presumptive spinsterhood.

Saint-Jouin is close to the sea and to the finest cliffs in the world. One of my companions, who had laden the carriage with the implements of a painter, went off into a sunny meadow to take the portrait of a windmill, and I, choosing the better portion, wandered through a little green valley with the other. Ten minutes brought us to the edge of the cliffs, which at this point of the coast are simply sublime. I had supposed the white seawalls of Etretat the finest thing possible in this way, but the huge red porphyritic-looking masses of Saint-Jouin have an even grander character. I have rarely seen a landscape more "plastic". They are strange, fantastic, out of keeping with the country, and for some rather arbitrary reason suggested to me a Spanish or even an African prospect. Certain sun-scorched precipices in Spanish sierras must have very much the same warmth of tone and desolation of attitude. The great distinction of the cliffs of Saint-Jouin is their extraordinary doubleness. Falling to an immense depth, they encounter a certain outward ledge, or terrace, where they pause and play a dozen fantastic tricks, such as piling up rocks into the likeness of needles and watch-towers; then they plunge again, and in another splendid sweep descend to the beach. There was something very impressive in the way their evil brows, looking as if they were stained with blood and rust, were bent upon the indifferent – the sleeping – sea.

III.

In a month of beautiful weather at Etretat, every day was not an excursion, but every day seemed indeed a picked day. For that matter, as I lay on the beach watching the procession of the easy-going hours, I took a good many mental excursions. The one, perhaps, on which I oftenest embarked, was a comparison between French manners, French habits, French types, and those of my native land. These comparisons are not invidious; I do not conclude against one party and in favour of the other; as the French say, *je constate* simply. The French people about me were "spending the summer", just as I had so often seen my fellow-countrymen spend it, and it seemed to me, as it had seemed to me at home, that this operation places men and women under a sort of monstrous magnifying-glass. The human figure has a higher relief in the country than in town, and I know of no place where psychological studies prosper so much as at the seaside. I shall not pretend to relate my observations in the order in which they occurred to me (or indeed to relate them in full at all); but I may say that one of the foremost was to this effect – that the summer-question, for every one, had been more easily settled than it usually is in America. The solution of the problem of where to go had not been a thin-petalled rose, plucked from among particularly sharp-pointed thorns. People presented themselves with a calmness and freshness very different from the haggardness of aspect which announces that the American citizen and his family have "secured accommodations". This impression, with me, rests perhaps on the fact that most Frenchwomen turned of thirty – the average wives and mothers – are so comfortably endowed with flesh. I have never seen such richness of contour as among the mature *baigneuses* of Etretat. The lean and desiccated person into whom a dozen years of matrimony so often converts the blooming American girl is not emulated in France. A majestic plumpness flourished all around me – the plumpness of triple chins and deeply dimpled hands. I mused upon it, and I discovered that it was the result of the best breakfasts and dinners in the world. It was the corpulence of ladies who are thoroughly well fed, and who never walk a step that they can spare. The assiduity with which the women of America measure the length of our democratic pavements is doubtless a factor in their frequent absence of redundancy of outline. As a "regular boarder" at the Hôtel Blanquet – pronounced by Anglo-Saxon visitors Blanket – I found myself initiated into the mysteries of the French dietary system. I assent to the common tradition that the French are a temperate people, so long as it is understood in this sense – that they eat no more than they want to. But their wants are very comprehensive. Their capacity strikes me as enormous, and we ourselves, if we are less regulated, are certainly much more slender consumers.

The American breakfast has, I believe, long been a subject of irony to the foreign observer; but the American breakfast is an ascetic meal compared with the French *déjeûner-à-la-fourchette*. The latter, indeed, is simply a dinner without soup; it differs neither generically nor specifically from the evening repast. If it excludes soup, it includes eggs, prepared in a hundred forms; and if it proscribes champagne, it admits beer in foaming pitchers, so that the balance is fairly preserved. I think that an American will often suffer vicariously from the reflection that a French family which sits down at half-past eleven to fish and entrees and roasts, to asparagus and beans, to salad and dessert, and cheese and coffee, proposes to do exactly the same thing at half-past six. But we may be sure at any rate that the dinner will be as good as the breakfast, and that the breakfast has nothing to fear from prospective comparison with the dinner; and we may further reflect that in a country where the pleasures of the table are thoroughly organised, it is natural that they should be prolonged and reiterated. Nothing is more noticeable among the French than their superior intelligence in dietary matters; every one seems naturally a judge, a dilettante. They have analysed tastes and savours to a finer point than we; they are aware of differences and relations of which we take no heed.

Observe a Frenchman of any age and of any condition (I have been quite as much struck with it in the very young men as in the old), as he orders his breakfast or his dinner at a Parisian restaurant, and you will perceive that the operation is much more solemn than it is apt to be in New York or in London. Monsieur has, in a word, a certain ideal for a particular repast, and it will make a difference in his happiness whether the kidneys, for instance, of a certain style, are chopped to the ultimate or only to the penultimate smallness. His directions and admonitions to the waiter are therefore minute and exquisite, and eloquently accentuated by the pressure of thumb and forefinger and it must be added that the imagination of the waiter is usually quite worthy of the refined communion opened to it.

This subtler sense of quality is observable even among those classes in which in other countries it is generally forestalled by a depressing consciousness on the subject of quantity. Observe your concierge and his wife at their mid-day meal, as you pass up and down stairs. They are not satisfying nature upon green tea and potatoes; they are seated before a repast which has been reasoned out, which, on its modest scale, is served in courses, and has a beginning, a middle, an end. I will not say that the French sense of comfort is confined to the philosophy of nutrition, but it is certainly here that it is most highly evolved. French people must have a good dinner and a good bed; but they are willing that the bed should be stationed and the dinner be eaten in the most insufferable corners. Your porter and his wife dine with a certain distinction, and sleep soft in their lodge; but their lodge is in all probability a fetid black hole, five feet square, in which, in England or in America, people of their talents would never consent to live. The French are willing to abide in the dark, to huddle together, to forgo privacy, to let bad smells grow great among them. They have an accursed passion for coquettish furniture; for cold, brittle chairs, for tables with scalloped edges, for ottomans without backs, for fireplaces muffled in plush and fringe. A French bedroom is a bitter mockery – a ghastly attempt to serve two masters which succeeds in being agreeable to neither. It is a thing of traps and delusions, constructed on the assumption that it is inelegant to be known to wash or to sleep, and yet pervaded with suggestions of uncleanness compared with which the matutinal "tub", well *en évidence*, is a delightful symbol of purity. This comes of course from that supreme French quality, the source of half the charm of the French mind as well as of all its dryness, the genius for economy. It is wasting a room to let it be a bedroom alone; so it must be tricked out ingeniously as a sitting-room, and ends by being (in many cases) insufferable both by night and by day. But allowing all weight to these latter reflections, it is still very possible that the French have the better part. If you are well fed, you can perhaps afford to be ill lodged; whereas enjoyment of the most commodious apartments is incompatible with inanition and dyspepsia.

If I had not cut short my mild retrospect by these possibly milder generalisations, I should have touched lightly upon some of the social phenomena of which the little beach at Etretat was the scene. I should have narrated that the French, at the seaside, are not "sociable" as Americans affect to be in a similar situation, and I should subjoin that at Etretat it was very well on the whole that they should not have been. The immeasurably greater simplicity of composition of American society makes sociability with us a comparatively untaxed virtue; but anything like an equal exercise of it in France would be attended with alarming drawbacks. Sociability (in the American sense of the word) in any aristocratic country would indeed be very much like an attempt to establish visiting relations between birds and fishes. At Etretat no making of acquaintance was to be perceived; people went about in compact, cohesive groups, of natural formation, governed doubtless, internally, by humane regulations, but presenting to the world an impenetrable defensive front. The groups usually formed a solid phalanx around two or three young girls, compressed into the centre, the preservation of whose innocence was their chief solicitude. These groups were doubtless wisely constituted, for with half a dozen *cocottes*, in scarlet petticoats, scattered over the sunny, harmless-looking beach, what were mammas and duennas to do? I used to pity the young ladies at first, for this perpetual application of the leading-string; but a little reflection showed me that the French have ordered this as well as they have ordered everything else. The case is not nearly so hard as it would be with us, for there is this immense difference between the lot of the *jeune fille* and her American sister, that the former may as a general thing be said to be certain to marry. "Alas, to marry badly," the Anglo-Saxon objector may reply. But the objection is precipitate; for if French marriages are almost always arranged, it must be added that they are in the majority of cases arranged successfully. Therefore, if a *jeune fille* is for three or four years tied with a very short rope and compelled to browse exclusively upon the meagre herbage which sprouts in the maternal shadow, she has at least the comfort of reflecting that, according to the native phrase, *on s'occupe de la marier* – that measures are being carefully taken to promote her to a condition of unbounded liberty. Whatever, to her imagination, marriage may fail to mean, it at least means freedom and consideration. It does not mean, as it so often means in America, being socially shelved – and it is not too much to say, in certain circles, degraded; it means being socially launched and consecrated. It means becoming that exalted personage, a *mère de famille*. To be a *mère de famille* is to occupy not simply (as is mostly the case with us) a sentimental, but really an official position. The consideration, the authority, the domestic pomp and circumstance allotted to a French mamma are in striking contrast with the amiable tolerance which in our own social order is so often the most liberal measure that the female parent may venture to expect at her children's hands, and which, on the part of the young lady of eighteen who represents the family in society, is not unfrequently tempered by a conscientious severity. All this is worth waiting for, especially if you have not to wait very long. Mademoiselle is married certainly, and married early, and she is sufficiently well informed to know, and to be sustained by the knowledge, that the sentimental expansion which may not take place at present will have an open field after her marriage. That it should precede her marriage seems to her as unnatural as that she should put on her shoes before her stockings. And besides all this, to browse in the maternal shadow is not considered in the least a hardship. A young French girl who is *bien-élevée* – an expression which means so much – will be sure to consider her mother's company the most delightful in the world, and to think that the herbage which sprouts about this lady's petticoats is peculiarly tender and succulent. It may be fanciful, but it often seems to me that the tone with which such a young girl says *Ma mère* has a peculiar intensity of meaning. I am at least not wrong in affirming that in the accent with which the mamma – especially if she be of the well-rounded order alluded to above – speaks of *Ma fille* there is a kind of sacerdotal dignity.

IV.

After this came two or three pictures of quite another complexion – pictures of which a long green valley, almost in the centre of France, makes the general setting. The valley itself, indeed, forms one delightful picture, although the country which surrounds it is by no means one of the regions that place themselves on exhibition. It is the old territory of the Gâtinais, which has much history, but no renown of beauty. It is very quiet, deliciously rural, immitigably French; the typical, average, "pleasant" France of history, literature, and art – of art, of landscape-art, perhaps, especially. Wherever I look I seem to see one of the familiar pictures on a dealer's wall – a Lambinet, a Troyon, a Daubigny, a Diaz. The Lambinets perhaps are in the majority; the mood of the landscape usually expresses itself in silvery lights and vivid greens. The history of this part of France is the history of the monarchy, and its language is, I won't say absolutely the classic tongue, but a nearer approach to it than any local patois. The peasants deliver themselves with rather a drawl, but their French is as consecutive as that of Ollendorf.

Each side of the long valley is a continuous ridge, which offers it a high, wooded horizon, and through the middle of it there flows a charming stream, wandering, winding and doubling, smothered here and there in rushes and spreading into lily-coated reaches, beneath the clear shadow of tall, straight light-leaved trees. On each side of the stream the meadows stretch away flat, clean, magnificent, lozenged across with rows of lateral foliage, under which a cow-maiden sits on the grass, hooting now and then, nasally, to the large-uddered browsers in front of her. There are no hedges nor palings nor walls; it is all a single estate. Occasionally in the meadows there rises a cluster of red-roofed hovels – each a diminutive village. At other points, at about half an hour's walk apart, are three charming old houses. The châteaux are extremely different, but, both as pictures and as dwellings, each has its points. They are very intimate with each other, so that these points may be amicably discussed. The points in one case, however, are remarkably strong. The little old *castel* I mention stands directly in the attenuated river, on an island just great enough to hold it, and the garden-flowers grow upon the farther bank. This, of course, is a most delightful affair. But I found something very agreeable in the aspect of one of the others, when I made it the croal of certain of those walks before breakfast, which of cool mornings, in the late summer, do not fall into the category of ascetic pleasures. (In France, indeed, if one did not do a great many things before breakfast, the work of life would be but meagrely performed.)

The dwelling in question stands on the top of the long ridge which encloses the comfortable valley to the south, being by its position quite in the midst of its appurtenant acres. It is not particularly "kept up," but its quiet rustiness and untrimmedness only help it to be familiar. A grassy plateau approaches it from the edge of the hill, bordered on one side by a short avenue of horse-chestnuts, and on the other by a dusky wood. Beyond the chestnuts are the steep-roofed, yellow-walled farm-buildings, and under cover of the wood a stretch of beaten turf, where, on Sundays and holidays, the farm-servants play at bowls. Directly before the house is a little square garden, enclosed by a low parapet, which is interrupted by a high gateway of mossy pillars and iron arabesques, the whole of it muffled in creeping plants. The house, with its yellow walls and russet roof, is ample and substantial; it is a very proper *gentilhommière*. In a corner of the garden, at the angle of the parapet, rises that classic emblem of rural gentility, the *pigeonnier*, the old stone dovecot. It is a great round tower, as broad of base as a lighthouse, with its roof shaped like an extinguisher, and a hole in its upper portion, in and out of which a dove is always fluttering.

You see all this from the windows of the drawing-room. Be

sure that the drawing-room is panelled in white and gray, with old rococo mouldings over the doorways and mantelpiece. The open gateway of the garden, with its tangled creepers, makes a frame for the picture that lies beyond the grassy esplanade where the thistles have been suffered to grow round a disused stone well, placed in odd remoteness from the house (if, indeed, it be not a relic of an earlier habitation): a picture of a wide green country, rising beyond the unseen valley and stretching away to a far horizon in deep blue lines of wood. Behind, through other windows, you look out on the gardens proper. There are places that take one's fancy by some accident of expression, some mystery of accident. This one is high and breezy, both genial and reserved, plain yet picturesque, extremely cheerful and a little melancholy. It has what in the arts is called "style", and so I have attempted to commemorate it.

Going to call on the peasants was as charming an affair as a chapter in one of George Sand's rural tales. I went one Sunday morning with my hostess, who knew them well and enjoyed their most garrulous confidence. I don't mean that they told her all their secrets, but they told her a good many; if the French peasant is a simpleton, he is a very shrewd simpleton. At any rate, of a Sunday morning in August, when he is stopping at home from work and has put on his best jacket and trousers, and is loafing at the door of his neighbour's cabin, he is a very charming person. The peasantry in the region I speak of had admirably good manners. The curé gave me a low account of their morals, by which he meant, on the whole, I suspect, that they were moderate church-goers. But they have the instinct of civility and a talent for conversation; they know how to play the host and the entertainer. By "he", just now, I meant she quite as much; it is rare that, in speaking superlatively of the French, in any connection, one does not think of

the women even more than of the men. They constantly strike
the foreigner as a stronger expression of the qualities of the
race. On the occasion I speak of the first room in the very
humble cabins I successively visited – in some cases, evidently,
it was the only room – had been set into irreproachable order
for the day. It had usually a fine brownness of tone, generated
by the high chimney-place, with its swinging pots, the important bed, in its dusky niche, with its flowered curtains, the
bi-bellied earthenware in the cupboard, the long-legged clock
in the corner, the thick, quiet light of the small, deeply-set
window, the mixture, on all things, of smoke-stain and the
polish of horny hands. Into the midst of this "la Rabillon" or
"la mère Léger" brings forward her chairs and begs us to be
seated, and, seating herself, with crossed hands, smiles expres-
sively and answers abundantly every inquiry about her cow,
her husband, her bees, her eggs, her baby. The men linger half
outside and half in, with their shoulders against dressers and
door-posts; every one smiles with that simple, clear-eyed smile
of the gratified peasant; they talk much more like George
Sand's Berrichons than might be supposed. And if they receive
us without gross awkwardness, they speed us on our way with
proportionate urbanity. I go to six or eight little hovels, all of
them dirty outside and clean within; I am entertained everywhere with the bonhomie, the quaintness, the good faces and
good manners of their occupants, and I finish my tour with an
esteem for my new acquaintance which is not diminished by
learning that several of them have thirty or forty thousand
francs carefully put away.

And yet, as I say, M. le Curé thinks they are in a bad way,
and he knows something about them. M. le Curé, too, is not
a dealer in scandal; there is something delightfully quaint in
the way in which he deprecates an un-Christian construction
of his words. There is more than one curé in the valley whose

charms I celebrate; but the worthy priest of whom I speak is the pearl of the local priesthood. He has been accused, I believe, of pretensions to *illuminisme*; but even in his most illuminated moments it can never occur to him that he has been chronicled in an American magazine, and therefore it is not indiscreet to say that he is the curé, not of Gy, but of the village nearest to Gy. I write this sentence half for the pleasure of putting down that briefest of village-names and seeing how it looks in print. But it may be elongated at will, and yet be only improved. If you wish to be very specific, you may call it Gy-les-Nonnains – Gy of the Little Nuns. I went with my hostess, another morning to call upon M. le Curé, who himself opened his garden door to us (there was a crooked little black cross perched upon it), and, lifting his rusty *calotte*, stood there a moment in the sunshine, smiling a greeting more benignant than his words.

A rural *presbytère* is not a very sumptuous dwelling, and M. le Curé's little drawing-room reminded me of a Yankee parlour (*minus* the subscription-books from Hartford on the centre-table) in some out-of-the-way corner of New England. But he took us into his very diminutive garden, and showed us an ornament that would not have flourished in the shadow of a Yankee parlour – a rude stone image of the Virgin, which he had become possessed of I know not how, and for which he was building a sort of niche in the wall. The work was going on slowly, for he must take the labour as he could get it; but he appealed to his visitors, with a smile of indulgent irony, for an assurance that his little structure would not make too bad a figure. One of them told him that she would send him some white flowers to set out round the statue; whereupon he clasped his hands together over his snuff-box and expressed cheerful views of the world we live in. A couple of days afterward he came to breakfast, and of course arrived early, in his new cassock and band. I found him in the billiard-room, walking up and down alone and reading his breviary. The combination of the locality, the personage and the occupation, made me smile; and I smiled again when, after breakfast, I found him strolling about the garden, puffing a cigarette. Of course he had an excellent appetite; but there is something rather cruel in those alternations of diet to which the French parish priest is subjected. At home he lives like a peasant – a fact which, in itself is not particularly cruel, inasmuch as he has usually – or in many cases – been brought up to that life. But his fellow-peasants don't breakfast at the château and gaze down the savoury vistas opened by cutlets à la Soubise. They have not the acute pain of relapsing into the stale atmosphere of bread and beans. Of course it is by no means every day, or every week even, that M. le Curé breakfasts at the château; but there must nevertheless be a certain uncomfortable crookedness in his position. He lives like a labourer, yet he is treated like a gentleman. The latter character must seem to him sometimes to have rather a point of irony. But to the ideal curé, of course, all characters are equal; he thinks neither too ill of his bad breakfasts nor too well of his good ones. I won't say that the excellent man I speak of is the ideal curé, but I suspect he is an approach to it; he has a grain of the epicurean to an ounce of stoicism. In the garden-path, beside the moat, while he puffed his cigarette, he told me how he had held up his head to the Prussians; for, hard as it seemed to believe it, that pastoral valley had been occupied by ravaging Teutons. According to this recital, he had spoken his mind civilly, but very distinctly, to the group of officers who had made themselves at home in his dwelling – had informed them that it grieved him profoundly that he was obliged to meet them standing there in his *soutane*, and not out in the fields with a musket in his hands and a dozen congenial spirits at his side.

The scene must have been dramatic. The first of the officers got up from table and asked for the privilege of shaking his hand. "M. le Curé," he said, "j'estime hautement votre caractère."

Six miles away – or nearer, by a charming shaded walk along a canal – was an ancient town with a legend – a legend which, as a child, I read in my lesson-book at school, marvelling at the woodcut above it, in which a ferocious dog was tearing a strange man to pieces, while the king and his courtiers sat by as if they were at the circus. I allude to it chiefly in order to mention the name of one of its promenades, which is the stateliest, beyond all comparison, in the world; the name, I mean, not the street. The latter is called the Promenade des Belles Manières. Could anything be finer than that? With what a sweep gentlemen must once have taken off their hats there; how ladies must once have curtsied, regardless of gutters, and how people must have turned out their toes as they walked!

V.

My next impressions were gathered on the margin of a southern sea – if the Bay of Biscay indeed deserve so sympathetic a name. We generally have a mental image beforehand of a place on which we may intend to project ourself, and I supposed I had a tolerably vivid prevision of Biarritz. I don't know why, but I had a singular sense of having been there; the name always seemed to me expressive. I saw the way it lay along its gleaming beach; I had taken in imagination long walks toward Spain over the low cliffs, with the blue sea always to my right and the blue Pyrenees always before me. My only fear was that my mental picture had not been brilliant enough; but this could easily be touched up on the spot.

In truth, however, on the spot I was exclusively occupied in toning it down. Biarritz seemed to be decidedly below its reputation; I am at a loss to see how its reputation was made. There is a partial explanation that is obvious enough. There is a low, square, bare brick mansion seated on the sands, under shelter of a cliff; it is one of the first objects to attract the attention of an arriving stranger. It is not picturesque, it is not romantic, and even in the days of its prosperity it never can have been impressive. It is called the Villa Eugénie, and it explains in a great measure, as I say, the Biarritz which the arriving stranger, with some dismay, perceives about him. It has the aspect of one of the "cottages" of Newport during the winter season, but is surrounded by a vegetation much less dense than the prodigies of arborescence now so frequent at Newport. It was what the newspapers call the "favourite resort" of the ex-Empress of the French, who might have been seen at her imperial avocations with a good glass, at any time, from the Casino. The Casino, I hasten to add, has quite the air of an establishment frequented by gentlemen who look at ladies' windows with telescopes. There are Casinos and Casinos, and that of Biarritz is, in the summary French phrase, "impossible". Except for its view, it is moreover very unattractive. Perched on the top of a cliff which has just space enough to hold its immense brick foundations, it has no garden, no promenade, no shade, no place of out-of-door reunion – the most indispensable feature of a Casino. It turns its back to the Pyrenees and to Spain, and looks out prettily enough over a blue ocean to an arm of the low French coast.

Biarritz, for the rest, scrambles over two or three steep hills, directly above the sea, in a promiscuous, many-coloured, noisy fashion. It is a watering place pure and simple; every house has an expensive little shop in the basement and a still more expensive set of rooms to let above stairs. The houses are blue and pink and green; they stick to the hillsides as they can, and being near Spain, you try to fancy they look Spanish. You succeed, perhaps, even a little, and are rewarded for your zeal by finding, when you cross the border a few days afterward, that the houses at San Sebastian look strikingly French. Biarritz is bright, crowded, irregular, filled with many sounds, and not without a certain second-rate pictorial quality; but it struck me as common and cockneyfied, and my vision travelled back to modest little Etretat, by its northern sea, as to a very much more downy couch. The south-western coast of France has little of the exquisite charm of the Mediterranean shore. It has of course a southern expression which in itself is always delightful. You see a brilliant, yellow sun, with a pink-faced, red-tiled house staring up at it. You can see here and there a trellis and an orange-tree, a peasant-woman in a gold necklace, driving a donkey, a lame beggar adorned with ear-rings, a glimpse of blue sea between white garden-walls. But the superabundant detail of the French Riviera is wanting; the softness, luxuriousness, enchantment.

The most pictorial thing at Biarritz is the Basque population, which overflows from the adjacent Spanish provinces and swarms in the crooked streets. It lounges all day in the public places, sprawls upon the curbstones, clings to the face of the cliffs, and vociferates continually a shrill, strange tongue, which has no discoverable affinity with any other. The Basques look like hardier and thriftier Neapolitan lazzaroni; if the superficial resemblance is striking, the difference is very much in their favour. Although those specimens which I observed at Biarritz appeared to enjoy an excess of leisure, they had nothing of a shiftless or beggarly air, and seemed as little disposed to ask favours as to confer them. The roads leading into Spain were dotted with them, and here they were coming and going as if on important business – the business of the abominable Don Carlos himself. They struck me as a very handsome race. The men are invariably clean-shaven; smooth chins seem a positively religious observance. They wear little round maroon-coloured caps, like those of sailor-boys, dark stuff shirts, and curious white shoes, made of strips of rope laid together – an article of toilet which makes them look like honorary members of base-ball clubs. They sling their jackets cavalier-fashion, over one shoulder, hold their heads very high, swing their arms very bravely, step out very lightly, and, when you meet them in the country at eventide, charging down a hillside in companies of half a dozen, make altogether a most impressive appearance. With their smooth chins and childish caps, they may be taken, in the distance, for a lot of very naughty little boys; for they have always a cigarette in their teeth.

The best thing at Biarritz is your opportunity for driving over into Spain. Coming speedily to a consciousness of this fact, I found a charm in sitting in a landau and rolling away to San Sebastian behind a coachman in a high glazed hat with long streamers, a jacket of scarlet and silver and a pair of yellow breeches and jack-boots. If it has been the desire of one's heart and the dream of one's life to visit the land of Cervantes, even grazing it so lightly as by a day's excursion from Biarritz is a matter to encourage visions. Everything helping – the admirable scenery, the charming day, the operatic coachman, the smooth-rolling carriage – I am afraid I became more visionary than it is decent to tell of. You move toward the magnificent undulations of the Pyrenees, as if you were going to plunge straight into them; but in reality you travel beneath them and beside them, pass between their expiring spurs and the sea. It is on proceeding beyond San Sebastian that you seriously attack them. But they are already extremely vivid – none the less so that in this region they abound in suggestions of the recent Carlist war. Their far-away peaks and ridges are crowned with lonely Spanish watch-towers, and their lower slopes are dotted with demolished dwellings. It was hereabouts that the fighting was most constant. But the healing powers of nature are as remarkable as the destructive powers of man, and the rich September landscape appeared already to have forgotten the injuries of yesterday. Everything seemed to me a small foretaste of Spain; I discovered an unreasonable amount of local colour. I discovered it at Saint-Jean-de-Luz, the last French town, in a great brown church, filled with galleries and boxes, like a play-house – the altar and choir, indeed, looked very much like a proscenium; at Bohébie, on the Bidassoa, the small yellow stream which divides France from Spain, and which at this point offers to view the celebrated Isle of Pheasants, a little bushy strip of earth adorned with a decayed commemorative monument, on which, in the seventeenth century, the affairs of Louis XIV and the Iberian monarch were discussed in ornamental conference; at Fuentarabia (glorious name), a mouldering relic of Spanish stateliness; at Hendaye, at Irun, at Renteria, and finally at San Sebastian. At all of these wayside towns the houses show marks of Alphonsist bullets (the region was strongly Carlist); but to be riddled and battered seems to carry out the meaning of the pompous old escutcheons carven above the doorways, some of them covering almost half the house. It struck me, in fact, that the narrower and shabbier was the poor little dusky dwelling, the grander and more elaborate was this noble advertisement. But it represented knightly prowess, and pitiless time had taken up the challenge. I found it a luxury to ramble through the narrow single street of Irun and Renteria, between the strange-coloured houses, the striped awnings, the universal balconies and the heraldic doorways.

San Sebastian is a lively watering-place, and is set down in the guide-books as the Biarritz or the Brighton of Spain. It has of course a new quarter in the provincial-elegant style (fresh stucco cafés, barber-shops, and apartments to let), looking out upon a planted promenade and a charming bay, locked in fortified heights, with a narrow portal to the ocean. I walked about for two or three hours and devoted most of my attention to the old quarter, the town proper, which has a great frowning gate upon the harbour, through which you look along a vista of gaudy house-fronts, balconies, awnings, surmounted by a narrow strip of sky. Here the local colour was richer, the manners more naïf. Here too was a church with a flamboyant Jesuit façade and an interior redolent of Spanish Catholicism. There was a life-sized effigy of the Virgin perched upon a table beside the great altar (she appeared to have been walking abroad in a procession), which I looked at with extreme interest. She seemed to me a heroine, a solid Spanish person, as perfect a reality as Don Quixote or Saint Theresa. She was dressed in an extraordinary splendour of laces, brocades and jewels, her coiffure and complexion were of the finest, and she evidently would answer to her name if you should speak to her. Mustering up the stateliest title I could think of, I addressed her as Doña Maria of the Holy Office; whereupon she looked round the great dusky, perfumed church, to see whether we were alone, and then she dropped her fringed eyelids and held out her hand to be kissed. She was the sentiment of Spanish catholicism; gloomy, yet bedizened, emotional as a woman and mechanical as a doll. After a moment I grew afraid of her, and went slinking away. After this I didn't really recover my spirits until I had the satisfaction of hearing myself addressed as "Caballero". I was hailed with this epithet by a ragged infant, with sickly eyes and a cigarette in his lips, who invited me to cast a copper into the sea, that he might dive for it; and even with these limitations, the sensation seemed worth the cost of my excursion. It appeared kinder, to my gratitude, to make the infant dive upon the pavement.

A few days later I went back to San Sebastian, to be present at a bull-fight; but I suppose my right to descant upon this entertainment should be measured less by the gratification it afforded me than by the question whether there is room in literature for another chapter on this subject. I incline to think there is not; the national pastime of Spain is the best-described thing in the world. Besides, there are other reasons for not describing it. It is extremely disgusting, and one should not describe disgusting things – except (according to the new school) in novels, where they have not really occurred, and are invented on purpose. Description apart, one has taken a certain sort of pleasure in the bull-fight, and yet how is one to state gracefully that one has taken pleasure in a disgusting thing? It is a hard case. If you record your pleasure, you seem to exaggerate it and to calumniate your delicacy; and if you record nothing but your displeasure, you feel as if you were wanting in suppleness. Thus much I can say, at any rate, that as there had been no bull-fights in that part of the country during the Carlist war, the native dilettanti (and every man, woman, and child of them comes under this denomination) returned to their precious pastime with peculiar zest. The spectacle, therefore, had an unusual splendour. Under these circumstances it is highly effective. The weather was beautiful; the near mountains peeped over the top of the vast open arena, as if they too were curious; weary of disembowelled horses and posturing *espadas*, the spectator (in the boxes) might turn away and look through an unglazed window at the empty town and the cloud-shadowed sea. But few of the native spectators availed themselves of this privilege. Beside me sat a blooming matron, in a white lace mantilla, with three very juvenile daughters; and if these ladies sometimes yawned they never shuddered. For myself, I confess that if I sometimes shuddered I never yawned. A long list of bulls was sacrificed, each of whom had pretensions to originality. The *banderillos*, in their silk stockings and embroidered satin costumes, skipped about with a great deal of attitude; the *espada* folded his arms within six inches of the bull's nose and stared him out of countenance; yet I thought the bull, in any case, a finer fellow than any of his tormentors, and I thought his tormentors finer fellows than the spectators. In truth, we were all, for the time, rather sorry fellows together. A bull-fight will, to a certain extent, bear looking at, but it will not bear thinking of. There was a more innocent effect in what I saw afterward, when we all came away, in the late afternoon, as the shadows were at their longest: the bright-coloured southern crowd, spreading itself over the grass, and the women, with mantillas and fans, and the Andalusian gait, strolling up and down before the mountains and the sea.

IX.

AN ENGLISH EASTER.

1877.

I.

It may be said of the English, as is said of the council of war in Sheridan's farce of *The Critic* by one of the spectators of the rehearsal, that when they do agree, their unanimity is wonderful. They differ among themselves greatly just now as regards the machinations of Russia, the derelictions of Turkey, the merits of the Reverend Arthur Tooth, the genius of Mr. Henry Irving, and a good many other matters; but neither just now nor at any other time do they fail to conform to those social observances on which respectability has set her seal. England is a country of curious anomalies, and this has much to do with her being so interesting to foreign observers. The English individual character is very positive, very independent, very much made up according to its own sentiment of things, very prone to startling eccentricities; and yet at the same time it has beyond any other this peculiar gift of squaring itself with fashion and custom. In no other country, I imagine, are so many people to be found doing the same thing, in the same way, at the same time – using the same slang, wearing the same hats and neckties, collecting the same china-plates, playing the same game of lawn-tennis or of polo, admiring the same professional beauty. The monotony of such a spectacle would soon become oppressive if the foreign observer were not conscious of this latent capacity in the performers for great freedom of action; he finds a good deal of entertainment in wondering how they reconcile the traditional insularity of the individual with this perpetual tribute to usage. Of course, in all civilised societies, the tribute to usage is constantly paid; if it is less apparent in America than elsewhere the reason is not, I think, because individual independence is greater, but because usage is more sparsely established. Where custom can be ascertained people certainly follow it; but for one definite precedent in American life there are fifty in English. I am very far from having discovered the secret; I have not in the least learned what becomes of that explosive personal force in the English character which is compressed and corked down by social conformity. I look with a certain awe at some of the manifestations of the conforming spirit, but the fermenting idiosyncrasies beneath it are hidden from my vision. The most striking example, to foreign eyes, of the power of custom in England is, of course, the universal church-going. In the sight of the English people getting up from its tea and toast of a Sunday morning and brushing its hat, and drawing on its gloves, and taking its wife on its arm, and making its offspring march before, and so, for decency's, respectability's, propriety's sake, taking its way to a place of worship appointed by the State, in which it repeats the formulas of a creed to which it attaches no positive sense, and listens to a sermon over the length of which it explicitly haggles and grumbles – in this exhibition there is something very striking to a stranger, something which he hardly knows whether to regard as a great force or as a great infirmity. He inclines, on the whole, to pronounce the spectacle sublime, because it gives him the feeling that whenever it may become necessary for a people trained in these manoeuvres to move all together under a common direction, they will have it in them to do so with tremendous weight and cohesiveness. We hear a good deal about the effect of the Prussian military system in consolidating the German people and making them available for a particular purpose; but I really think it not fanciful to say that the military punctuality which characterises the English observance of Sunday ought to be appreciated in the same fashion. A nation which has passed through the mill will certainly have been stamped by it. And here, as in the German military service, it is really the whole nation. When I spoke just now of paterfamilias and his *entourage* I did not mean to limit the statement to him. The young unmarried men go to church, the gay bachelors, the irresponsible members of society. (That last epithet must be taken with a grain of allowance. No one in England is literally irresponsible; that perhaps is the shortest way of describing the nation. Every one is free and every one is responsible. To say what it is people are responsible to is of course a great extension of the question: briefly, to social expectation, to propriety, to morality, to "position", to the classic English conscience, which is, after all, such a powerful factor. With us there is infinitely less responsibility; but there is also, I think, less freedom.)

The way in which the example of the more luxurious classes imposes itself upon the less luxurious may of course be noticed in smaller matters than church-going; in a great many matters which it may seem trivial to mention. If one is bent upon observation, nothing, however, is trivial. So I may cite the practice of banishing the servants from the room at breakfast. It is the fashion, and accordingly, through the length and breadth of England, every one who has the slightest pretension to standing high enough to feel the way the social breeze is blowing conforms to it. It is awkward, unnatural, troublesome for those at table, it involves a vast amount of leaning and stretching, of waiting and perambulating, and it has just that vice against which, in English history, all great movements have been made – it is arbitrary. But it flourishes for all that, and all genteel people, looking into each other's eyes with the desperation of gentility, agree to endure it for gentility's sake. My instance may seem feeble, and I speak honestly when I say I might give others, forming part of an immense body of pre-scriptive usage, to which a society possessing in the largest manner, both by temperament and education, the sense of the "inalienable" rights and comforts of the individual, contrives to accommodate itself. I do not mean to say that usage in England is always uncomfortable and arbitrary. On the con-trary, few strangers can be unfamiliar with that sensation (a most agreeable one) which consists in perceiving in the rigidity of a tradition which has struck one at first as mechanical, a reason existing in the historic "good sense" of the English race. The sensation is frequent, though in saying so I do not mean to imply that even superficially the presumption is against the usages of English society. It is not, for instance, necessarily against the custom of which I had it more espe-cially in mind to speak in writing these lines. The stranger in London is forewarned that at Easter all the world goes out of town, and that if he have no mind to be left as lonely as Marius on the ruins of Carthage, he, too, had better make arrangements for a temporary absence. It must be admitted that there is a sort of unexpectedness in this prompt re-emigration of a body of people who, but a week before, were apparently devoting much energy to settling down for the season. Half of them have but lately come back from the country, where they have been spending the winter, and they have just had time, it may be supposed, to collect the scattered threads of town-life. Presently, however, the threads are dropped and society is dispersed, as if it had taken a false start. It departs as Holy Week draws to a close, and remains absent for the following ten days. Where it goes is its own affair; a good deal of it goes to Paris. Spending last winter in that city, I remember how, when I woke up on Easter Monday and looked out of my window, I found the street covered, overnight, with a sort of snow-fall of disembarked Britons. They made, for other people, an uncomfortable week of it. One's customary table at the restaurant, one's habitual stall at the Théâtre Français, one's usual fiacre on the cab-stand, were very apt to have suffered pre-emption. I believe that the pilgrimage to Paris was this year of the usual proportions and you maybe sure that people who did not cross the Channel were not without invitations to quiet old places in the country, where the pale, fresh primroses were beginning to light up the dark turf and the purple bloom of the bare tree-masses to be freckled here and there with verdure. In England country-life is the obverse of the medal, town-life the reverse, and when an occasion comes for quitting London there are few members of what the French call the "easy class" who have not a collection of dull, moist, verdant resorts to choose from. Dull I call them, and I fancy not without reason, though at the moment I speak of, their dulness must have been mitigated by the unintermittent presence of the keenest and liveliest of east winds. Even in mellow English country homes Easter-tide is a period of rawness and atmospheric acridity – the moment at which the frank hostility of winter, which has at last to give up the game, turns to peevishness and spite. This is what makes it arbitrary, as I said just now, for "easy" people to go forth to the wind-swept lawns and the shivering parks. But nothing is more striking to an American than the frequency of English holidays and the large way in which occasions for "a little change" are made use of. All this speaks to Americans of three things which they are accustomed to see allotted in scantier measure. The English have more time than we, they have more money, and they have a much higher relish for active leisure. Leisure, fortune, and the love of sport – these things are implied in English society at every turn. It was a very small number of weeks before Easter that Parliament met, and yet a ten days' recess was already, from the luxurious Parliamentary point of view, a necessity. A short time hence we shall be having the Whitsuntide holidays, which I am told are even more of a season of revelry than Easter, and from this point to mid-summer, when everything stops, it is an easy journey. The men of business and the professional men partake in equal measure of these agreeable diversions, and I was interested in hearing a lady whose husband was an active member of the bar say that, though he was leaving town with her for ten days, and though Easter was a very nice "little break", they really amused themselves more during the later festival, which would come on toward the end of May. I thought this highly probable, and admired so dramatic an interfusion of work and play. If my phrase has a slightly ironical sound, this is purely accidental. A large appetite for holidays, the ability not only to take them but to know what to do with them when taken, is the sign of a robust people, and judged by this measure we Americans are rather incompetent. Such holidays as we take are taken very often in Europe, where it is sometimes noticeable that our privilege is rather heavy on our hands. Acknowledgment made of English industry, however (our own stands in no need of compliments), it must be added that for those same easy classes I just spoke of things are very easy indeed. The number of persons obtainable for purely social purposes at all times and seasons is infinitely greater than among ourselves; and the ingenuity of the arrangements permanently going forward to disembarrass them of their superfluous leisure is as yet in America an undeveloped branch of civilisation. The young men who are preparing for the stern realities of life among the gray-green cloisters of Oxford are obliged to keep their terms but half the year, and the rosy little cricketers of Eton and Harrow are let loose upon the parental home for an embarrassing number of months. Happily the parental home is apt to be an affair of gardens, lawns, and parks.

II.

Passion Week, in London, is distinctly an ascetic period; there is really an approach to sackcloth and ashes. Private dissipation is suspended; most of the theatres and music-halls are closed; the huge dusky city seems to take on a still sadder colouring and a sort of hush steals over its mighty uproar. At such a time, for a stranger, London is not cheerful. Arriving there, during the past winter, about Christmas-time, I encountered three British Sundays in a row – a spectacle to strike terror into the stoutest heart. A Sunday and a "bank-holiday", if I remember aright, had joined hands with a Christmas-day, and produced the portentous phenomenon to which I allude. I betrayed, I suppose, some apprehension of its oppressive character, for I remember being told in a consolatory way that I needn't fear; it would not come round again for another year. This information was given me on the occasion of that surprising interruption of one's relations with the laundress which is apparently characteristic of the period. I was told that all the washerwomen were intoxicated, and that, as it would take them some time to revive, I must not count upon a relay of "fresh things". I shall not forget the impression made upon me by this statement; I had just come from Paris and it almost sent me spinning back. One of the incidental *agréments* of life in the latter city had been the knock at my door on Saturday evenings of a charming young woman with a large basket covered with a snowy napkin on her arm, and on her head a

frilled and fluted muslin cap, which was an irresistible advertisement of her art. To say that my admirable *blanchisseuse*
was not in liquor is altogether too gross a compliment; but I
was always grateful to her for her russet cheek, her frank,
expressive eye, her talkative smile, for the way her charming
cap was poised upon her crisp, dense hair, and her well-made
dress was fitted to her well-made waist. I talked with her; I
could talk with her; and as she talked she moved about and
laid out her linen with a delightful modest ease. Then her light
step carried her off again, talking, to the door, and with a
brighter smile and an "Adieu, monsieur!" she closed it behind
her, leaving one to think how stupid is prejudice and how
poetic a creature a washerwoman may be. London, in
December, was livid with sleet and fog, and against this dismal
background was offered me the vision of a horrible old
woman in a smoky bonnet, lying prone in a puddle of whisky!
She seemed to assume a kind of symbolic significance, and she
almost frightened me away.

I mention this trifle, which is doubtless not creditable to my
fortitude, because I found that the information given me was
not strictly accurate, and that at the end of three months I had
another array of London Sundays to face. On this occasion,
however, nothing occurred to suggest again the dreadful
image I have just sketched, though I devoted a good deal of
time to observing the manners of the lower orders. From
Good Friday to Easter Monday, inclusive, they were very
much *en évidence*, and it was an excellent occasion for getting
an impression of the British populace. Gentility had retired to
the background, and in the West End all the blinds were low-
ered; the streets were void of carriages, and well-dressed
pedestrians were rare; but the "masses" were all abroad and
making the most of their holiday, and I strolled about and
watched them at their gambols. The heavens were most

unfavourable, but in an English "outing" there is always a margin left for a drenching, and throughout the vast smoky city, beneath the shifting gloom of the sky, the grimy crowds trooped about with a kind of weatherproof stolidity. The parks were full of them, the railway stations overflowed, and the Thames embankment was covered. The "masses", I think, are usually an entertaining spectacle, even when observed through the distorting medium of London bad weather. There are indeed few things in their way more impressive than a dusky London holiday; it suggests a variety of reflections. Even looked at superficially, the British capital is one of the most interesting of cities, and it is perhaps on such occasions as this that I have most felt its interest. London is ugly, dusky, dreary, more destitute than any European city of graceful and decorative incident; and though on festal days, like those I speak of, the populace is massed in large numbers at certain points, many of the streets are empty enough of human life to enable you to perceive their intrinsic want of charm. A Christmas-day or a Good Friday uncovers the ugliness of London. As you walk along the streets, having no fellow-pedestrians to look at, you look up at the brown brick house-walls, corroded with soot and fog, pierced with their straight stiff window-slits, and finished, by way of a cornice, with a little black line resembling a slice of curbstone. There is not an accessory, not a touch of architectural fancy, not the narrowest concession to beauty. If I were a foreigner it would make me rabid; being an Anglo-Saxon I find in it what Thackeray found in Baker Street – a delightful proof of English domestic virtue, of the sanctity of the British home. There are miles and miles of these edifying monuments, and it would seem that a city made up of them should have no claim to that larger effectiveness of which I just now spoke. London, however, is not made up of them; there are architectural combinations of a statelier kind, and the impression moreover does not rest on details. London is pictorial in spite of details – from its dark-green, misty parks, the way the light comes down leaking and filtering from its cloud-ceiling, and the softness and richness of tone which objects put on in such an atmosphere as soon as they begin to recede. Nowhere is there such a play of light and shade, such a struggle of sun and smoke, such aërial gradations and confusions. To eyes addicted to such contemplations this is a constant diversion, and yet this is only part of it. What completes the effect of the place is its appeal to the feelings, made in so many ways, but made above all by agglomerated immensity. At any given point London looks huge; even in narrow corners you have a sense of its hugeness, and petty places acquire a certain interest from their being parts of so mighty a whole. Nowhere else is so much human life gathered together, and nowhere does it press upon you with so many suggestions. These are not all of an exhilarating kind; far from it. But they are of every possible kind, and that is the interest of London. Those that were most forcible during the showery Easter season were certain of the more perplexing and depressing ones; but even with these was mingled a brighter strain.

I walked down to Westminster Abbey on Good Friday afternoon – walked from Piccadilly across the Green Park and through that of St. James. The parks were densely filled with the populace – the elder people shuffling about the walks and the poor little smutty-faced children sprawling over the dark damp turf. When I reached the Abbey I found a dense group of people about the entrance, but I squeezed my way through them and succeeded in reaching the threshold. Beyond this it was impossible to advance, and I may add that it was not desirable. I put my nose into the church and promptly withdrew it. The crowd was terribly compact, and beneath the gothic arches the odour was not that of incense. I slowly eliminated myself, with that very modified sense of disappointment that one feels in London at being crowded out of a place. This is a frequent disappointment, for you very soon find out that there are, selfishly speaking, too many people. Human life is cheap; your fellow-mortals are too numerous. Wherever you go you make the observation. Go to the theatre, to a concert, to an exhibition, to a reception; you always find that, before you arrive, there are people enough in the field. You are a tight fit in your place, wherever you find it; you have too many companions and competitors. You feel yourself at times in danger of thinking meanly of the human personality; numerosity, as it were, swallows up quality, and perpetual association is rather irritating. This is the reason why the perfection of luxury in England is to own a "park" – an artificial solitude. To get one's self into the middle of a few hundred acres of oak-studded turf and to keep off the crowd by the breadth, at least, of this grassy cincture, is to enjoy a comfort which circumstances make peculiarly precious. But I walked back through the profane pleasure-grounds of London, in the midst of "superfluous herds", and I found that entertainment which I never fail to derive from a great English assemblage. The English are, to my eyes, so much the handsomest people in Europe that, it takes some effort of the imagination to believe that the fact requires proof. I never see a large number of them without feeling this impression confirmed; though I hasten to add that I have sometimes felt it to be rather shaken in the presence of a limited group. I suspect that a great English crowd would yield a larger percentage of handsome faces and figures than any other. With regard to the upper class I suppose this is generally granted; but I should extend it to the whole people. Certainly, if the English populace strike the observer by their good looks, they must be very good-looking indeed. They are

as ill-dressed as their betters are well-dressed, and their garments have that sooty-looking surface which has nothing in
common with some of the more romantic forms of poverty. It
is the hard prose of misery – an ugly and hopeless imitation of
respectable attire. This is especially noticeable in the battered
and bedraggled bonnets of the women, which look as if their
husbands had stamped on them in hobnailed boots, as a hint
of what is in store for their wearers. Then it is not too much
to say that two-thirds of the London faces, among the
"masses", bear in some degree or other the traces of alcoholic
action. The proportion of flushed, empurpled, eruptive coun-
tenances is very striking; and the ugliness of the sight is not
diminished by the fact that many of the faces thus disfigured
were evidently meant to please. A very large allowance is to be
made, too, for the people who bear the distinctive stamp of
that physical and mental degradation which comes from the
slums and purlieus of this dusky Babylon – the pallid, stunted,
misbegotten, and in every way miserable figures. These people
swarm in every London crowd, and I know of none in any
other place that suggest an equal degree of misery. But when
these abatements are made, the observer is still liable to be
struck by the frequency of well-moulded faces and bodies well
put together; of strong, straight brows and handsome mouths
and noses, of rounded, finished chins and well-poised heads,
of admirable complexions and well-disposed limbs.

The capacity of an Englishwoman for being handsome
strikes me as absolutely unlimited, and even if (I repeat) it is
in the luxurious class that it is most freely exercised, yet
among the daughters of the people one sees a great many fine
points. Among the men fine points are strikingly numerous –
especially among the younger ones. Here the same distinction
is to be made – the gentlemen are certainly handsomer than
the vulgarians. But taking one young Englishman with

another, they are physically very well turned out. Their features are finished, composed, as it were, more harmoniously than those of many of their nearer and remoter neighbours, and their figures are apt to be both powerful and compact. They present to view very much fewer accidental noses and inexpressive mouths, fewer sloping shoulders and ill-planted heads of hair, than their American kinsmen. Speaking always from the sidewalk, it may be said that as the spring increases in London and the symptoms of the season multiply, the beautiful young men who adorn the West End pavements, and who advance before you in couples, arm-in-arm, fair-haired, gray-eyed, athletic, slow-strolling, ambrosial, are among the most brilliant features of the brilliant period. I have it at heart to add that if the English are handsomer than ourselves, they are also very much uglier. Indeed I think that all the European peoples are uglier than the American; we are far from producing those magnificent types of facial eccentricity which flourish among older civilisations. American ugliness is on the side of physical poverty and meanness; English on that of redundancy and monstrosity. In America there are few grotesques; in England there are many – and some of them have a high pictorial value.

III.

The element of the grotesque was very noticeable to me in the most striking collection of the shabbier English types that I had seen since I came to London. The occasion of my seeing them was the funeral of Mr. George Odger, which befell some four or five weeks before the Easter period. Mr. George Odger, it will be remembered, was an English radical agitator of humble origin, who had distinguished himself by a perverse desire to get into Parliament. He exercised, I believe, the

useful profession of shoemaker, and he knocked in vain at the
door that opens but to the refined. But he was a useful and
honourable man, and his own people gave him an honourable
burial. I emerged accidentally into Piccadilly at the moment
they were so engaged, and the spectacle was one I should have
been sorry to miss. The crowd was enormous, but I managed
to squeeze through it and to get into a hansom cab that was
drawn up beside the pavement, and here I looked on as from
a box at the play. Though it was a funeral that was going on I
will not call it a tragedy; but it was a very serious comedy. The
day happened to be magnificent – the finest of the year. The
funeral had been taken in hand by the classes who are socially
unrepresented in Parliament, and it had the character of a
great popular "manifestation". The hearse was followed by
very few carriages, but the *cortége* of pedestrians stretched
away in the sunshine, up and down the classic gentility of
Piccadilly, on a scale that was highly impressive. Here and
there the line was broken by a small brass band – apparently
one of those bands of itinerant Germans that play for coppers
beneath lodging-house windows; but for the rest it was com-
pactly made up of what the newspapers call the dregs of the
population. It was the London rabble, the metropolitan mob,
men and women, boys and girls, the decent poor and the inde-
cent, who had scrambled into the ranks as they gathered them
up on their passage, and were making a sort of solemn "lark",
of it. Very solemn it all was – perfectly proper and undemon-
strative. They shuffled along in an interminable line, and as I
looked at them out of the front of my hansom I seemed to be
having a sort of panoramic view of the under side, the wrong
side, of the London world. The procession was filled with figures which seemed never to have "shown out", as the English
say, before; of strange, pale, mouldy paupers who blinked and
stumbled in the Piccadilly sunshine. I have no space to

describe them more minutely, but I found the whole affair rather suggestive. My impression rose not simply from the radical, or, as I may say for the sake of colour, the revolutionary, emanation of this dingy concourse, lighted up by the ironical sky; but from the same causes that I had observed a short time before, on the day the Queen went to open Parliament, when in Trafalgar Square, looking straight down into Westminster and over the royal procession, were gathered a group of banners and festoons inscribed in big staring letters with mottoes and sentiments which a sensitive police department might easily have found seditious. They were mostly in allusion to the Tichborne claimant, whose release from his dungeon they peremptorily demanded, and whose cruel fate was taken as a pretext for several sweeping reflections on the social arrangements of the time and country. These impertinent standards were allowed to sun themselves as freely as if they had been the manifestoes of the Irish Giant or the Oriental Dwarf at a fair. I had lately come from Paris, where the police-department is more sensitive, and where revolutionary placards are not observed to adorn the base of the obelisk in the Place de la Concorde. I was, therefore, the more struck on both of the occasions I speak of with the admirable English practice of letting people alone – with the good sense and the good humour and even the good taste of it. It was this that I found impressive, as I watched the "manifestation" of Mr. Odger's underfed partisans – the fact that the mighty mob could march along and do its errand, while the excellent quiet policemen stood by simply to see that the channel was kept clear and comfortable.

When Easter Monday came it was obvious that every one (save Mr. Odger's friends – three or four million or so) had gone out of town. There was hardly a pair of shutters in the West End that was not closed; there was not a bell that it was

any use to pull. The weather was detestable, the rain inces-
sant, and the fact that all one's friends were away gave one
plenty of leisure to reflect that the country must be the
reverse of enlivening. But all one's friends had gone thither
(this is the unanimity I began by talking about), and to restrict
as much as possible the proportions of that game of hide-and-
seek of which, at the best, so much of London social life
consists, it seemed wise to bring within the limits of the dull
season any such excursion as one might have projected in
commemoration of the first days of spring. After due cogita-
tion I paid a little visit to Canterbury and Dover, taking
Rochester by the way, and it was of this momentous journey
that I proposed, in beginning these remarks, to give an
account. But I have dallied so much by the way that I have
come almost to my rope's end without reaching my first
stage. I should have begun, artistically, by relating that I put
myself in the humour for remote adventure by going down
the Thames on a penny steamboat to – the Tower. This was
on the Saturday before Easter, and the City was as silent as
the grave. The Tower was a memory of my childhood, and
having a theory that from such memories the dust of the ages
had better not be shaken, I had not retraced my steps to its
venerable walls. But the Tower is very good – much less cockneyfied than I supposed it would seem to my maturer vision;
very gray and historical, with the look that vivifies – rather
lividly indeed – the past. I could not get into it, as it had been
closed for Passion Week, but I was consequently relieved
from the obligation to march about with a dozen fellow-
starers in the train of a didactic beef-eater, and I strolled at
will through the courts and the garden, sharing them only
with the lounging soldiers of the garrison, who seemed to
connect the place with important events.

IV.

At Rochester I stopped for the sake of its castle, which I espied from the railway-train, perched on a grassy bank beside the widening Medway. There were other reasons as well; the place has a small cathedral, and one has read about it in Dickens, whose house of Gadshill was a couple of miles from the town. All this Kentish country, between London and Dover, figures indeed repeatedly in Dickens; he is to a certain extent, for our own time, the spirit of the land. I found this to be quite the case at Rochester. I had occasion to go into a little shop kept by a talkative old woman who had a photograph of Gadshill lying on her counter. This led to my asking her whether the illustrious master of the house often made his appearance in the town. "Oh, bless you, sir," she said, "we every one of us knew him to speak to. He was in this very shop on the Tuesday with a party of foreigners – as he was dead in his bed on the Friday." (I should remark that I probably do not repeat the days of the week as she gave them.) "He 'ad on his black velvet suit, and it always made him look so 'andsome. I said to my husband, 'I *do* think Charles Dickens looks so nice in that black velvet suit.' But he said he couldn't see as he looked any way particular. He was in this very shop on the Tuesday, with a party of foreigners." Rochester consists of little more than one long street, stretching away from the castle and the river toward neighbouring Chatham, and edged with low brick houses, of intensely provincial aspect, most of which have some small, dull quaintness of gable or window. Nearly opposite to the shop of the old lady with the dissentient husband is a little dwelling with an inscribed slab set into its face, which must often have provoked a smile in the great master of laughter. The slab relates that in the year 1579 Richard Watts here established a charity which should furnish "six poor trav-

ellers, not rogues or proctors," one night's lodging and entertainment gratis, and four pence in the morning to go on their
way withal, and that in memory of his "munificence " the
stone has lately been renewed. The inn at Rochester was poor,
and I felt strongly tempted to knock at the door of Mr. Watts's
asylum, under plea of being neither a rogue nor a proctor. The
poor traveller who avails himself of the testamentary fourpence may easily resume his journey as far as Chatham
without breaking his treasure. Is not this the place where little
Davy Copperfield slept under a cannon on his journey from
London to Dover to join his aunt, Miss Trotwood? The two
towns are really but one, which forms an interminable
crooked thoroughfare, lighted up in the dusk, as I measured it
up and down, with the red coats of the vespertinal soldier
quartered at the various barracks of Chatham.

The cathedral of Rochester is small and plain, hidden away
in rather an awkward corner, without a verdant close to set it
off. It is dwarfed and effaced by the great square Norman keep
of the adjacent castle. But within it is very charming, especially
beyond the detestable wall, the vice of almost all the English
cathedrals, which shuts in the choir and breaks the sacred perspective of the aisle. Here, as at Canterbury, you ascend a high
range of steps, to pass through the small door in this wall.
When I speak slightingly, by the way, of the outside of
Rochester cathedral, I intend my faint praise in a relative
sense. If we were so happy as to possess this inferior edifice in
America, we should go barefoot to see it; but here it stands in
the great shadow of Canterbury, and that makes it humble. I
remember, however, an old priory gateway which leads you to
the church, out of the main street; I remember a kind of
haunted-looking deanery, if that be the technical name, at the
base of the eastern walls; I remember a fluted tower that took
the afternoon light and let the rooks and the swallows come

circling and clamouring around it. Better than these things, however, I remember the ivy-draped mass of the castle – a very noble and imposing ruin. The old walled precinct has been converted into a little public garden, with flowers and benches, and a pavilion for a band, and the place was not empty, as such places in England never are. The result is agreeable, but I believe the process was barbarous, involving the destruction and dispersion of many interesting portions of the ruin. I sat there for a long time, however, looking in the fading light at what was left. This rugged pile of Norman masonry will be left when a great many solid things have departed; it is a sort of satire on destruction or decay. Its walls are fantastically thick; their great time-bleached expanses and all their rounded roughnesses, their strange mixture of softness and grimness, have an undefinable fascination for the eye. English ruins always come out peculiarly when the day begins to fail. Weather-bleached, as I say they are, they turn even paler in the twilight and grow consciously solemn and spectral. I have seen many a mouldering castle, but I remember in no single mass of ruin more of the helpless, amputated look.

It is not the absence of a close that damages Canterbury; the cathedral stands amid grass and trees, with a cultivated margin all round it, and is placed in such a way that, as you pass out from under the gate-house, you appreciate immediately its grand feature – its extraordinary and magnificent length. None of the English cathedrals seems more beautifully isolated, more shut up to itself. It is a long walk, beneath the walls, from the gateway of the close to the farther end of the last chapel. Of all that there is to observe in this upward-gazing stroll I can give no detailed account; I can speak only of the general impression. This is altogether delightful. None of the rivals of Canterbury has a more complicated and elaborate architecture, a more perplexing intermixture of periods, a

more charming jumble of Norman arches and English points
and perpendiculars. What makes the side-view superb, moreover, is the double transepts, which produce a fine
agglomeration of gables and buttresses. It is as if two great
churches had joined forces toward the middle – one giving its
nave and the other its choir, and each keeping its own great
cross-aisles. Astride of the roof, between them, sits a huge
gothic tower, which is one of the latest portions of the
building, though it looks like one of the earliest, so crumbled
and blunted and suffused is it by time and weather. Like the
rest of the structure it has a magnificent colour – a sort of rich
dull yellow, a something that is neither brown nor gray. This
is particularly appreciable from the cloisters on the farther
side of the church – the side, I mean, away from the town and
the open garden-sweep I spoke of; the side that looks toward
a damp old clerical house, lurking behind a brown archway,
through which you see young ladies in Gainsborough hats
playing something on a patch of velvet turf; the side, in short,
that is somehow intermingled with a green quadrangle – a
quadrangle serving as a playground to a King's School, and
adorned externally with a very precious and picturesque old
fragment of Norman staircase. This cloisters is not "kept up";
it is very dusky and mouldy and dilapidated, and of course
very sketchable. The old black arches and capitals are various
and handsome, and in the centre are tumbled together a group
of crooked gravestones, themselves almost buried in the deep
soft grass. Out of the cloisters opens the chapter-house, which
is not kept up either, but which is none the less a magnificent
structure; a noble, lofty hall, with a beautiful wooden roof,
simply arched like that of a tunnel, without columns or
brackets. The place is now given up to dust and echoes; but it
looks more like a banqueting-hall than a council-room of
priests, and as you sit on the old wooden bench, which, raised

on two or three steps, runs round the base of the four walls, you may gaze up and make out the faint ghostly traces of decorative paint and gold upon the brown ceiling. A little patch of this has been restored, "to give an idea." From one of the angles of the cloisters you are recommended by the verger to take a view of the great tower, which indeed detaches itself with tremendous effect. You see it base itself upon the roof as broadly as if it were striking roots in earth, and then pile itself away to a height which seems to make the very swallows dizzy, as they drop from the topmost shelf. Within the cathedral you hear a great deal, of course, about poor Thomas A'Becket, and the great sensation of the place is to stand on the particular spot where he was murdered and look down at a small fragmentary slab which the verger points out to you as a bit of the pavement that caught the blood-drops of the struggle. It was late in the afternoon when I first entered the church; there had been a service in the choir, but that was well over, and I had the place to myself. The verger, who had some pushing-about of benches to attend to, turned me into the locked gates and left me to wander through the side-aisles of the choir and into the great chapel beyond it. I say I had the place to myself; but it would be more decent to affirm that I shared it, in particular, with another gentleman. This personage was stretched upon a couch of stone, beneath a quaint old canopy of wood; his hands were crossed upon his breast, and his pointed toes rested upon a little griffin or leopard. He was a very handsome fellow and the image of a gallant knight. His name was Edward Plantagenet, and his sobriquet was the Black Prince. "*De la mort ne pensai-je mye,*" he says in the beautiful inscription embossed upon the bronze base of his image; and I too, as I stood there, lost the sense of death in a momentary impression of personal nearness to him. One had been farther off, after all, from other famous knights. In this same chapel for many a year stood the shrine of St. Thomas of Canterbury, one of the richest and most potent in Christendom. The pavement which lay before it has kept its place, but Henry VIII swept away everything else in his famous short cut to reform. Becket was originally buried in the crypt of the church; his ashes lay there for fifty years, and it was only little by little that his martyrdom was, as the French say, "exploited". Then he was transplanted into the Lady Chapel; every grain of his dust became a priceless relic, and the pavement was hollowed by the knees of pilgrims. It was on this errand of course that Chaucer's story-telling cavalcade came to Canterbury. I made my way down into the crypt, which is a magnificent maze of low, dark arches and pillars, and groped about till I found the place where the frightened monks had first shuffled the inanimate victim of Moreville and Fitzurse out of the reach of further desecration. While I stood there a violent thunderstorm broke over the cathedral; great rumbling gusts and rain-drifts came sweeping through the open sides of the crypt, and, mingling with the darkness which seemed to deepen and flash in corners, and with the potent mouldy smell, made me feel as if I had descended into the very bowels of history. I emerged again, but the rain had settled down and spoiled the evening, and I splashed back to my inn and sat in an uncomfortable chair by the coffee-room fire, reading Dean Stanley's agreeable *Memorials of Canterbury*, and wondering over the musty appointments and meagre resources of English hostels. This establishment had entitled itself (in compliment to the Black Prince, I suppose) the " Fleur-de-Lis". The name was very pretty (I had been foolish enough to let it attract me to the inn), but the lily was sadly deflowered.

X.

LONDON AT MIDSUMMER.

1877.

I believe it is supposed to require a good deal of courage to confess that one has spent the month of August in London; and I will therefore, taking the bull by the horns, plead guilty at the very outset to this dishonourable weakness. I might attempt some ingenious extenuation of it. I might say that my remaining in town had been the most unexpected necessity or the merest inadvertence; I might pretend I liked it – that I had done it, in fact, for the love of the thing; I might claim that you don't really know the charms of London until on one of the dog-days you have imprinted your boot-sole in the slumbering dust of Belgravia, or, gazing along the empty vista of the Drive, in Hyde Park, have beheld, for almost the first time in England, a landscape without figures. But little would remain of these specious apologies save the naked fact that I had distinctly failed to retire from the metropolis – either on the first of August with the ladies and children, or on the thirteenth with the members of Parliament, or on the twelfth when the grouse-shooting began. (I am not sure that I have got my dates right to a day, but these were about the proper opportunities.) I have, in fact, survived the departure of everything genteel, and the three millions of persons who remained behind with me have been witnesses of my shame.

I cannot pretend, on the other hand, that, having lingered

in town, I have found it a very odious or painful experience. Being a stranger, I have not felt it necessary to incarcerate myself during the day and steal abroad only under cover of the darkness – a line of conduct imposed by public opinion, if I am to trust the social criticism of the weekly papers (which I am far from doing), upon the native residents who allow themselves to be overtaken by the unfashionable season. I have indeed always had a theory that few things are pleasanter than during the hot weather to have a great city, and a large house within it, quite to one's self.

These majestic conditions have not been combined in my own metropolitan sojourn, and I have received an impression that in London it would be rather difficult for a person not having the command of a good deal of powerful machinery to find them united. English summer weather is rarely hot enough to make it necessary to darken one's house and disrobe. The present year has indeed in this respect been "exceptional", as any year is, for that matter, that one spends anywhere. But the manners of the people are, to American eyes, a sufficient indication that at the best (or the worst) even the highest flights of the thermometer in the British Islands betray a broken wing. People live with closed windows in August, very much as they do in January, and there is to the eye no appreciable difference in the character of their apparel. A "bath" in England, for the most part all the year round, means a little portable tin tub and a sponge. Peaches and pears, grapes and melons, are not a more obvious ornament of the market at midsummer than at Christmas. This matter of peaches and melons, by the way, offers one of the best examples of that fact to which a foreign commentator on English manners finds himself constantly recurring, and to which he grows at last almost ashamed of alluding – the fact that the beauty and luxury of the country – that elaborate system known and revered all over the world as "English comfort" is a limited and restricted, an essentially private, affair. I am not one of those irreverent strangers who talk of English fruit as a rather audacious *plaisanterie*, though I could see very well what was meant a short time since by an anecdote related to me in a tone of contemptuous generalisation by a couple of my fellow-countrywomen. They had arrived in London in the dog-days, and, lunching at their hotel, had asked to be served with some fruit. The hotel was of the stateliest pattern, and they were waited upon by a functionary whose grandeur was proportionate. This gentleman bowed and retired, and, after a long delay reappearing, placed before them, with an inimitable gesture, a dish of gooseberries and currants. It appeared upon investigation that these acrid vegetables were the only things of succulence that the establishment could undertake to supply; and it seemed to increase the irony of the situation that the establishment was as near as possible to Buckingham Palace. I say that the heroines of my anecdote seemed disposed to generalise: this was sufficiently the case, I mean, to give me a pretext for assuring them that on a thousand charming estates the most beautiful peaches and melons were at that moment ripening under glass. My auditors tossed their heads, of course, at the beautiful estates and the glass; and indeed at their ascetic hostelry close to Buckingham Palace such a piece of knowledge was but scantily consoling.

It is to a more public fund of entertainment that the desultory stranger in any country chiefly appeals, especially in summer weather; and as I have implied that there is little encouragement in England to such an appeal, it may appear remarkable that I should not have found London, at this season, at least as uncongenial as orthodoxy pronounces it. But one's liking for London – a stranger's liking at least – is at the best an anomalous and illogical sentiment of which he may feel it hardly less difficult to give a categorical account at one time than at another. I am far from meaning by this that there are not in this mighty metropolis a thousand sources of interest, entertainment, and delight: what I mean is, that for one reason and another, with all its social resources, the place lies heavy on the foreign consciousness. It seems grim and dusky, fierce and unmerciful. And yet the foreign consciousness accepts it at last with an active satisfaction, and finds something warm and comfortable, something that if removed would be greatly missed, in its tremendous pressure. It must be admitted, however, that, granting that every one is out of town, your choice of pastimes is not embarrassing. If it has been your fortune to spend a certain amount of time in foreign cities, London will seem to you but slenderly provided with innocent diversions. This, indeed, brings us back simply to that question of the absence of a "public fund" of amusement to which reference was just now made. You must give up the idea of going to sit somewhere in the open air, to eat an ice and listen to a band of music. You will find neither the seat, the ice, nor the band; but, on the other hand, faithful to your profession of observant foreigner, you may supply the place of these delights by a little private meditation upon the deep-lying causes of the English indifference to them. In such reflections nothing is idle – every grain of testimony counts; and one need therefore not be accused of jumping too suddenly from small things to great if one traces a connection between the absence of ices and music and the aristocratic constitution of English society. This aristocratic constitution of English society is the great and ever-present fact to the mind of a stranger: there is hardly a detail of English life that does not appear in some degree to point to it. It is really only in a country in which a good deal of democratic feeling prevails that people of "refinement", as we say in America, will be willing to sit at little round tables, on a pavement or a gravel-walk, at the door of a café. The upper classes are too refined, and the lower classes are too miserable. One must hasten to add too, in justice, that the upper classes are, as a general thing, quite too well furnished with entertainments of their own; they have those special resources to which I alluded a moment since. They are people of fortune, and are naturally independent of communistic pleasures. If you can sit on a terrace in a high-walled garden and have your *café noir* handed to you in Pompadour cups by servants in powder and plush, you have hardly a decent pretext for going to a public-house. In France and Italy, in Germany and Spain, the count and countess will sally forth and encamp for the evening, under a row of coloured lamps, upon the paving-stones, but it is ten to one that the count and countess live on a single floor, up several pair of stairs. They are, however, I think, not appreciably affected by considerations which operate potently in England. An Englishman who should propose to sit down at a café-door would find himself remembering that he is exposing himself to the danger of meeting his social inferiors. The danger is great, because his social inferiors are so numerous; and I suspect that if we could look straight into the English consciousness we should be interested to find how serious a danger it appears, and how good – given the texture of English life – are some of his reasons for wishing not to expose himself.

The consideration of these reasons, however, would lead us very far from the potential little tables for ices in – where shall I say? – in Oxford Street; but, after all, there is no reason why our imagination should hover about these articles of furniture. I am afraid they would not strike us as happily situated. In such matters everything hangs together, and I am certain that the customs of the Boulevard des Italiens and the Piazza Colonna would not harmonise with the scenery of the great

London thoroughfare. A gin-palace right and left and a
detachment of the London rabble in an admiring semicircle –
these, I confess, strike me as some of the more obvious features of the affair. Yet at the season of which I write, one's
social studies must at the least be studies of low life, for wherever one may go for a stroll or to spend the summer
afternoon, the unfashionable side of things is uppermost.
There is no one in the parks save the rough characters who are
lying on their faces in the sheep-polluted grass. These people
are always tolerably numerous in the Green Park, through
which I frequently pass, and I never fail to drop a wondering
glance upon them. But your wonder will go far if it begins to
bestir itself on behalf of the recumbent British tramp. You perceive among them some rich possibilities. Their velveteen legs
and their colossal high-lows, their purple necks and ear-tips,
their knotted sticks and little greasy hats, make them look like
stage-villains in a realistic melodrama. I may do them great
injustice, but I always assume that they have had a taste of
penal servitude – that they have paid the penalty of stamping
on some weaker human head with those huge square heels
that are turned up to the summer sky. But, actually, they are
innocent enough, for they are sleeping as peacefully as the
most accomplished philanthropist, and it is their look of
having walked over half England, and of being confoundedly
hungry and thirsty, that constitutes their romantic attractive-
ness. These six square feet of brown grass are their present
sufficiency; but how long will they sleep, whither will they go
next, and whence did they come last? You permit yourself to
wish that they might sleep for ever and go nowhere else at all.

   The month of August is so uncountenanced in London that
going a few days since to Greenwich, that famous resort, I
found it possible to get but half a dinner. The celebrated hotel
had put out its stoves and locked up its pantry. But for this dis-

covery I should have mentioned the little expedition to Greenwich as a charming relief to the monotony of a London August. Greenwich and Richmond are, classically, the two suburban dining-places. I know not how it may be at this time with Richmond, but the Greenwich incident brings me back (I hope not once too often) to the element of what has lately been called "particularism" in English pleasures. It was in obedience to a perfectly logical argument that the Greenwich hotel had, as I say, locked up its pantry. All well-bred people leave London after the first week in August, *ergo* those who remain behind are not well-bred, and cannot therefore rise to the conception of a "fish dinner". Why, then, should we have anything ready? I had other impressions, fortunately, of this interesting suburb, and I hasten to declare that during the period of good-breeding the dinner at Greenwich is the most amusing of all dinners. It begins with fish and it continues with fish: what it ends with – except songs and speeches and affectionate partings – I hesitate to affirm. It is a kind of mermaid reversed; for I do know, in a vague way, that the tail of the creature is elaborately and interminably fleshy. If it were not grossly indiscreet, I should risk an allusion to the particular banquet which was the occasion of my becoming acquainted with the Greenwich *cuisine*. I would affirm that it is very pleasant to sit in a company of clever and distinguished men, before the large windows that look out upon the broad brown Thames. The ships swim by confidently, as if they were part of the entertainment and put down in the bill; the light of the afternoon fades ever so slowly. We eat all the fish of the sea, and wash them down with liquids that bear no resemblance to salt water. We partake of any number of those sauces with which, according to the French adage, one could swallow one's grandmother with a good conscience. To speak of the particular merits of my companions would indeed be indis-

creet, but there is nothing indelicate in expressing a high
appreciation of the frankness and robustness of English con-
viviality. The stranger – the American at least – who finds
himself in the company of a number of Englishmen assembled
for a convivial purpose becomes conscious of a certain indefinable and delectable something which, for want of a better
name, he will call their superior richness of temperament. He
takes note of the liberal share of the individual in the magnificent temperament of the people. This seems to him one of the
finest things in the world, and his satisfaction will take a
keener edge from such an incident as the single one I may
permit myself to mention. It was one of those little incidents
which can occur only in an old society – a society in which
every one that a newly-arrived observer meets strikes him as
having in some degree or other a sort of historic identity, being
connected with some one or something that he has heard of.
If they are not the rose, they have lived more or less near it.
There is an old English song-writer whom we all know and
admire – whose songs are sung wherever the language is
spoken. Of course, according to the law I just hinted at, one
of the gentlemen sitting opposite must needs be his great-
grandson. After dinner there are songs, and the gentleman
trolls out one of his ancestral ditties with the most charming
voice and the most finished art.

I have still other memories of Greenwich, where there is a
charming old park, on a summit of one of whose grassy undulations the famous observatory is perched. To do the thing
completely, you must take passage upon one of the little grimy
sixpenny steamers that ply upon the Thames, perform the
journey by water, and then, disembarking, take a stroll in the
park to get up an appetite for dinner. I find an irresistible
charm in any sort of river navigation, but I am rather at a loss
how to speak of the little voyage from Westminster Bridge to

Greenwich. It is in truth the most prosaic possible form of being afloat, and to be recommended rather to the inquiring than to the fastidious mind. It initiates you into the duskiness, the blackness, the crowdedness, the intensely commercial character of London. Few European cities have a finer river than the Thames, but none certainly has expended more ingenuity in producing an ugly river-front. For miles and miles you see nothing but the sooty backs of warehouses, or perhaps they are the sooty fronts: in buildings so very expressionless it is impossible to distinguish. They stand massed together on the banks of the wide, turbid stream, which is fortunately of too opaque a quality to reflect the dismal image. A damp-looking dirty blackness is the universal tone. The river is almost black, and is covered with black barges; above the black housetops, from among the far-stretching docks and basins, rises a dusky wilderness of masts. The little puffing steamer is dingy and gritty – it belches a sable cloud that keeps you company as you go. In this carboniferous shower your companions, who belong chiefly, indeed, to the less brilliant classes, assume an harmonious grayness; and the whole picture, glazed over with the glutinous London mist, becomes a masterly composition. But it is very impressive in spite of its want of lightness and brightness, and though it is ugly it is not insignificant. Like so many of the aspects of English civilisation that are untouched by elegance or grace, it has the merit of expressing something very serious. Viewed in this intellectual light, the polluted river, the sprawling barges, the dead-faced warehouses, the frowsy people, the atmospheric impurities, become richly suggestive. It sounds rather absurd to say so, but all this sordid detail reminds me of nothing less than the wealth and power of the British empire at large; so that a kind of metaphysical magnificence hovers over the scene, and supplies what may be literally wanting. I don't exactly understand the association, but I know that when I look off to the left at the East India Docks, or pass under the dark, hugely-piled bridges, where the railway trains and the human processions are for ever moving, I feel a kind of imaginative thrill. The tremendous piers of the bridges, in especial, seem the very pillars of the British empire aforesaid.

It is doubtless owing to this habit of obtrusive and unprofitable reverie that the sentimental tourist thinks it very fine to see the Greenwich observatory lifting its two modest little brick towers. The sight of this useful edifice gave me an amount of pleasure which may at first seem unreasonable. The reason was, simply, that I used to see it as a child, in woodcuts, in school-geographies, and in the corners of large maps which had a glazed, sallow surface, and which were suspended in unexpected places, in dark halls and behind doors. The maps were hung so high that my eyes could reach only to the lower corners, and these corners usually contained a print of a strange-looking house, standing among trees upon a grassy bank that swept down before it with the most engaging steepness. I used always to think that it must be an immense pleasure to hurl one's self down this curving precipice. Close at hand was usually something printed about something being at such and such a number of degrees "east of Greenwich." Why east of Greenwich? The vague wonder that the childish mind felt on this point gave the place a mysterious importance, and seemed to put it into relation with the difficult and fascinating parts of geography – the countries of unintentional outline and the lonely-looking pages of the atlas. Yet there it stood the other day, the precise point from which the great globe is measured; there was the plain little façade, with the old-fashioned cupolas; there was the bank on which it would be so delightful not to be able to stop running. It made me feel terribly old to find that I was not even tempted to begin.

There are indeed a great many steep banks in Greenwich Park, which tumbles up and down in the most picturesque fashion. It is a charming place, rather shabby and footworn, as befits a strictly popular resort, but with a character all its own. It is filled with magnificent foreign-looking trees, of which I know nothing but that they have a vain appearance of being chestnuts, planted in long, convergent avenues, with trunks of extraordinary girth and limbs that fling a dusky shadow far over the grass; there are plenty of benches, and there are deer as tame as sleepy children; and from the tops of the bosky hillocks there are views of the widening Thames, and the moving ships, and the two classic inns by the waterside, and the great pompous buildings, designed by Inigo Jones, of the old Hospital, which have been despoiled of their ancient pensioners and converted into a kind of naval academy.

Taking note of all this, I arrived at a far-away angle in the wall of the park, where a little postern door stood ajar. I pushed the door open, and found myself, by a picturesque transition, upon Blackheath Common. One had often heard of Blackheath: well, here it was – a great green, breezy place, where various lads in corduroys were playing cricket. I always admire an English common; it may be curtailed and cockneyfied, as this one was – which had lamp-posts stuck about on its turf and a fresh-painted banister all around – but it is sure to be one of the places that remind you vividly that you are in England. Even if the turf is too much trodden, there is, to foreign eyes, an English greenness about it, and there is something peculiarly insular in the way the high-piled, weather-bearing clouds hang over it and drizzle down their gray light. Still further to identify this spot, here was the British soldier emerging from two or three of the roads, with his cap upon his ear, his white gloves in one hand and his foppish little cane in the other. He wore the uniform of the artillery, and I asked him where he had come from. I learned that he had walked over from Woolwich, and that this feat might be accomplished in half an hour. Inspired again by vague associations, I proceeded to accomplish its equivalent. I bent my steps to Woolwich, a place which I knew, in a general way, to be a nursery of British valour. At the end of my half hour I emerged upon another common, where local colour was still more intense. The scene was very entertaining. The open grassy expanse was immense, and, the evening being beautiful, it was dotted with strolling soldiers and townsfolk. There were half a dozen cricket matches, both civil and military. At one end of this peaceful *campus martius*, which stretches over a hilltop, rises an interminable façade – one of the fronts of the artillery barracks. It has a very honourable air, and more windows and doors, I imagine, than any building in Britain. There is a great clean parade before it, and there are many sentinels pacing in front of neatly-kept places of ingress to officers' quarters. Everything it looks out upon is military – the distinguished college (where the poor young man whom it would perhaps be premature to call the last of the Bonapartes lately studied the art of war) on one side; a sort of model camp – a collection of the tidiest plank huts – on the other; a hospital, on a well-ventilated site, at the remoter end. And then in the town below there are a great many more military matters – barracks on an immense scale; a dockyard that presents an interminable dead wall to the street; an arsenal which the gatekeeper (who refused to admit me) declared to be "five miles" in circumference; and, lastly, grogshops enough to inflame the most craven spirit. These latter institutions I glanced at on my way to the railway station at the bottom of the hill; but before departing I had spent half an hour in strolling about the common in vague consciousness of certain emotions that are called into play (I speak but for

myself) by almost any glimpse of the imperial machinery of
this great country. The glimpse may be of the slightest; it stirs
a peculiar sentiment. I know not what to call this sentiment
unless it be simply an admiration for the greatness of England.
The greatness of England; that is a very off-hand phrase, and
of course I don't pretend to use it analytically. I use it sentimentally – as it sounds in the ears of any American who finds
in English history the sacred source of his own national affection. I think of the great part that England has played in
human affairs, the great space she has occupied, her tremendous might, her far-stretching sway. That these
clumsily-general ideas should be suggested by the sight of
some infinitesimal fraction of the English administrative
system may seem to indicate a cast of fancy too hysterical; but
if so, I must plead guilty to the weakness. Why should a
sentry-box more or less set one thinking of the glory of this
little island, which has found in her bosom the means of so
vast a dominion? This is more than I can say; and all I shall
attempt to say is, that in the difficult days that are now
elapsing a sympathetic stranger finds his meditations singularly quickened. It is the dramatic element in English history
that he has, chiefly cared for, and he finds himself wondering
whether the dramatic epoch is completely closed. It is a
moment when all the nations of Europe seem to be doing
something, and he waits to see, what England, who has done
so much, will do. He has been meeting of late a good many of
his country-people – Americans who live on the Continent
and pretend to speak with assurance of continental ways of
feeling. These people have been passing through London, and
many of them are in that irritated condition of mind which
appears to be the portion of the American sojourner in the
British metropolis when he is not given up to the delights of
the historic sentiment. They have affirmed with emphasis that

the continental nations have ceased to care a straw for what England thinks, that her traditional prestige is completely extinct, and that the affairs of Europe will be settled quite independently of the power whose capital is on the Thames. England will do nothing, will risk nothing; there is no cause bad enough for her not to find a selfish interest in it – there is no cause good enough for her to fight about it. Poor old England is exploded; it is about time she should haul in her nets. To all this the sympathetic stranger replies that, in the first place, he doesn't believe a word of it; and, in the second place, he doesn't care a fig for it – care, that is, what the continental nations think. If the greatness of England were really waning it would be to him as a personal grief; and as he strolls about the breezy common of Woolwich, with all those mementoes of British dominion around him, he is quite too keenly exhilarated to be distracted by such vapours.

He wishes, nevertheless, as I said before, that England would do something – something striking and powerful, which should be at once characteristic and unexpected. He asks himself what she can do, and he remembers that this greatness of England which he so much admires was formerly much exemplified in her "taking" something. Can't she "take" something now? There is the *Spectator*, who wants her to occupy Egypt: can't she occupy Egypt? The *Spectator* considers this her moral duty – inquires even whether she has a right not to bestow the blessings of her beneficent rule upon the down-trodden Fellaheen. I found myself in company with an acute young Frenchman a day or two after this eloquent plea for a partial annexation of the Nile had appeared in the most ingenious of journals. Some allusion was made to it, and my companion proceeded to pronounce it a finished example of British hypocrisy. I don't know how powerful a defence I made of it, but while I read it I certainly had been carried away by it. I recalled it while I pursued my contemplations, but I recalled at the same time that sadly prosaic speech of Mr. Gladstone's to which it had been a reply. Mr. Gladstone had said that England had much more urgent duties than the occupation of Egypt: she had to attend to the great questions of – What were the great questions? Those of local taxation and the liquor-laws! Local taxation and the liquor-laws! The phrase, to my ears, just then made a painful discord. These were not the things I had been thinking of; it was not as she should bend anxiously over these doubtless interesting subjects that the sympathetic stranger would seem to see England in his favourite posture – that, as Macaulay says, of hurling defiance at her foes. Of course, Mr. Gladstone was probably right, but Mr. Gladstone was not a sympathetic stranger.

XI.

TWO EXCURSIONS.

1877.

I.

They differed greatly from each other, but each had an interest of its own. There seemed (as regards the first) a general consensus of opinion as to its being a great pity that a stranger in England should miss the Derby day. Every one assured me that this was the great festival of the English people, and the most characteristic of national holidays. So much, since it had to do with horse-flesh, I could readily believe. Had not the newspapers been filled for weeks with recurrent dissertations upon the animals concerned in the ceremony? and was not the event, to the nation at large, only imperceptibly less momentous than the other great question of the day – the fate of empires and the reapportionment of the East? The space allotted to sporting intelligence in a compact, eclectic, "intellectual" journal like the *Pall Mall Gazette*, had seemed to me for some time past a measure of the hold of such questions upon the British mind. These things, however, are very natural in a country in which in "society" you are liable to make the acquaintance of some such syllogism as the following. You are seated at dinner next a foreign lady, who has on her other hand a native gentleman, by whom she is being instructed in the art of getting the right point-of-view for looking at English life. I profit by their conversation, and I learn that this point-of-view is apparently the saddle. "You see, English life," says the gentleman, "is really English country life. It's the country that is the basis of English society. And you see, country life is – well, it's the *hunting*. It's the hunting that is at the bottom of it all." In other words, "the hunting" is the basis of English society. Duly initiated into this interpretation of things, the American observer is prepared for the colossal proportions of the annual pilgrimage to Epsom. This pilgrimage, however, I was assured, though still well worth taking part in, is by no means so characteristic as in former days. It is now performed in a large measure by rail, and the spectacle on the road has lost its ancient brilliancy. The road has been given up more and more to the populace and the strangers, and has ceased to be graced by the presence of ladies. Nevertheless, as a man and a stranger, I was strongly recommended to take it; for the return from the Derby is still, with all its abatements, a classic spectacle.

I mounted upon a four-horse coach, a charming coach, with a yellow body, and handsome, clean-flanked leaders; placing myself beside the coachman, as I had been told this was the point of vantage. The coach was one of the vehicles of the new fashion – the fashion of public conveyances driven for the entertainment of themselves and of the public, by gentlemen of leisure. On the Derby day all the coaches that start from the classic headquarters – the "White Horse", in Piccadilly – and stretch away from London toward a dozen different and well-selected goals, had been dedicated to the Epsom road. The body of the vehicle is empty, as no one thinks of occupying any but one of the thirteen places on the top. On the Derby day, however, a properly laden coach carries a company of hampers and champagne-baskets in its inside places. I must add that on this occasion my companion was by exception a professional whip, who proved an entertaining cicerone.

Other companions there were, perched in the twelve places behind me, whose social quality I made less of a point of testing – though in the course of the expedition their various characteristics, under the influence of champagne, expanded so freely as greatly to facilitate the operation. We were a society of exotics – Spaniards, Frenchmen, Germans. There were only two Britons, and these, according to my theory, were Australians – an antipodal bride and groom, on a centripetal wedding-tour.

The drive to Epsom, when you get well out of London, is sufficiently pretty; but the part of it which most took my fancy was a suburban district – the classic neighbourhood of Clapham. The vision of Clapham had been a part of the furniture of my imagination – the vision of its respectable common, its evangelical society, and its goodly brick mansions of the era. I now beheld these objects for the first time, and I thought them very charming. This epithet, indeed, scarcely applies to the evangelical society, which naturally, on the morning of the Derby day, and during the desecrating progress of the Epsom revellers, was not much in the foreground. But all around the verdant, if cockneyfied common, are ranged commodious houses of a sober red complexion, from under whose neoclassic pediments you expect to see a mild-faced lady emerge – a lady in a cottage-bonnet and mittens, distributing tracts from a little satchel. It would take an energetic piety, however, to stem the current of heterogeneous vehicles which at about this point takes up its metropolitan affluents and bears them in its rumbling, rattling, tide. The concourse of wheeled conveyances of every possible order here, becomes dense, and the spectacle from the top of the coach proportionately absorbing. You begin to perceive that the brilliancy of the road has in truth departed, and that well-appointed elegance is not the prevailing characteristic.

But when once you have grasped this fact your entertainment is continuous. You perceive that you are "in", as the phrase is, for something, vulgar, something colossally, unimaginably, heroically vulgar; all that is necessary is to accept this situation and look out for illustrations. Beside you, before you, behind you, is the mighty London populace, taking its *ébats*. You get for the first time a notion of the London population at large. It has piled itself into carts, into omnibuses, into every possible and impossible species of "trap". A large proportion of it is of course on foot, trudging along the perilous margin of the middle way, in such comfort as may be gathered from fifteen miles' dodging of broken shins. The smaller the vehicle, the more rat-like the animal that drags it, the more numerous and ponderous its human freight; and as every one is nursing in his lap a parcel of provender as big as himself, wrapped in ragged newspapers, it is not surprising that roadside halts are frequent, and that the taverns all the way to Epsom (it is wonderful how many there are) are encompassed by dense groups of dusty pilgrims, indulging liberally in refreshment for man and beast. And when I say man I must by no means be understood to exclude woman. The female contingent on the Derby day is not the least remarkable part of the London multitude. Every one is prepared for an "outing", but the women are even more brilliantly and resolutely prepared than the men; it is the best possible chance to observe the various types of the British female of the lower orders. The lady in question is usually not ornamental. She is useful, robust, prolific, excellently fitted to play the somewhat arduous part allotted to her in the great scheme of English civilisation. But she has not those graces which enable her to become easily and harmoniously festal. On smaller holidays – or on simple working-days – in London crowds, I have often thought her handsome; thought, that is, that she has handsome points, and

that it was not impossible to see how it is that she helps to
make the English race, on the whole, the comeliest in the
world. But at Epsom she is too stout, too hot, too red, too
thirsty, too boisterous, too strangely accoutred. And yet I wish
to do her justice; so I must add that if there is something to
which an American cannot refuse a tribute of admiration in
the gross plebeian jollity of the Derby day, it is not evident
why these lusty she-revellers should not get part of the credit
of it. The striking thing, the interesting thing, both on the outward drive and on the return, was that the holiday was so
frankly, heartily, good-humouredly taken. The people that of
all peoples is habitually the most governed by decencies, proprieties, rigidities of conduct, was, for one happy day,
unbuttoning its respectable straight-jacket and letting its powerful, carnal, healthy temperament take the air. In such a
spectacle there was inevitably much that was unlucky and
unprofitable; these things came uppermost chiefly on the
return, when demoralisation was supreme, when the temperament in question had quite taken what the French call the key
of the fields, and seemed in no mood to come back and give
an account of itself. For the rest, to be dressed with a kind of
brutal gaudiness, to be very thirsty and violently flushed, to
laugh perpetually at everything and at nothing, thoroughly to
enjoy, in short, a momentous occasion – all this is not, in
simple persons of the more susceptible sex, an unpardonable
crime.

The course at Epsom is in itself very pretty, and disposed by
nature herself in sympathetic prevision of the sporting passion. It is something like the crater of a volcano, without the
mountain. The outer rim is the course proper; the space
within it is a vast, shallow, grassy concavity in which vehicles
are drawn up and beasts tethered, and in which the greater
part of the multitude – the mountebanks, the betting-men, and

the myriad hangers-on of the scene – are congregated. The
outer margin of the uplifted rim in question is occupied by the
grand stand, the small stands, the paddock. The day was
exceptionally beautiful; the charming sky was spotted over
with little idle-looking, loafing, irresponsible clouds; the
Epsom Downs went swelling away as greenly as in a coloured
sporting-print, and the wooded uplands, in the middle distance, looked as innocent and pastoral as if they had never
seen a policeman or a rowdy. The crowd that spread itself over
this immense expanse was the richest representation of human
life that I have ever looked upon. One's first fate after
arriving, if one is perched upon a coach, is to see the coach
guided, by means best known to the coachman himself,
through the tremendous press of vehicles and pedestrians,
introduced into a precinct roped off and guarded from intru-
sion save under payment of a fee, and then drawn up
alongside of the course, as nearly as possible opposite the
grand stand and the winning post. Here you have only to
stand up in your place – on tiptoe, it is true, and with a good
deal of stretching – to see the race fairly well. But I hasten to
add that seeing the race is indifferent entertainment. If I might
be Irish on the occasion of a frolic, I would say that in the first
place you do not see it at all, and in the second place you perceive it to be not much worth the seeing. It may be very fine
in quality, but in quantity it is inappreciable. The horses and
their jockeys first go dandling and cantering along the course
to the starting-point, looking as insubstantial as sifted sunbeams.
Then there is a long wait, during which, of the sixty thousand
people present (my figures are imaginary) thirty thousand
affirm positively that they have started, and thirty thousand as
positively deny it. Then the whole sixty thousand are suddenly
resolved into unanimity by the sight of a dozen small jockey-
heads whizzing along a very distant sky-line. In a shorter space

of time than it takes me to write it, the whole thing is before
you, and for the instant it is anything but beautiful. A dozen
furiously revolving arms – pink, green, orange, scarlet, white
– whacking the flanks of as many straining steeds; a glimpse of
this, and the spectacle is over. The spectacle, however, is of
course an infinitesimally small part of the purpose of Epsom
and the interest of the Derby. The interest is in having money
in the affair, and doubtless those most interested do not
trouble themselves particularly to watch the race. They learn
soon enough whether they are, in the English phrase, to the
good or to the bad.

When the Derby stakes had been carried off by a horse of
which I confess I am barbarous enough to have forgotten the
name, I turned my back to the running, for all the world as if
I too were largely "interested", and sought entertainment in
looking at the crowd. The crowd was very animated; that is
the most succinct description I can give of it. The horses of
course had been removed from the vehicles, so that the pedestrians were free to surge against the wheels and even to a
certain extent to scale and overrun the carriages. This tendency became most pronounced when, as the mid-period of
the day was reached, the process of lunching began to unfold
itself and every coach-top to become the scene of a picnic.
From this moment, at the Derby, demoralisation begins. I was
in a position to observe it, all around me, in the most characteristic forms. The whole affair, as regards the conventional
rigidities I spoke of a while since, becomes a real dégringolade.
The shabbier pedestrians bustle about the vehicles, staring up
at the lucky mortals who are perched in a kind of tormentingly
near empyrean – a region in which dishes of lobster-salad are
passed about and champagne-corks cleave the air like celestial
meteors. There are nigger-minstrels and beggars and mountebanks and spangled persons on stilts, and gipsy matrons, as

genuine as possible, with glowing Oriental eyes and dropping their *h*'s; these last offer you for sixpence the promise of everything genteel in life except the aspirate. On a coach drawn up beside the one on which I had a place, a party of opulent young men were passing from one stage of exhilaration to another with a punctuality which excited my admiration. They were accompanied by two or three young ladies of the kind that usually shares the choicest pleasures of youthful British opulence – young ladies in whom nothing has been neglected that can make a complexion Titianesque. The whole party had been drinking deep, and one of the young men, a pretty lad of twenty, had in an indiscreet moment staggered down as best he could to the ground. Here his cups proved too many for him, and he collapsed and rolled over. In plain English, he was beastly drunk. It was the scene that followed that arrested my observation. His companions on the top of the coach called down to the people herding under the wheels to pick him up and put him away inside. These people were the grimiest of the rabble, and a couple of men who looked like coal-heavers out of work undertook to handle this hapless youth. But their task was difficult; it was impossible to imagine a young man more drunk. He was a mere bag of liquor – at once too ponderous and too flaccid to be lifted. He lay in a helpless heap under the feet of the crowd – the best intoxicated young man in England. His extemporised chamberlains took him first in one way and then in another; but he was like water in a sieve. The crowd hustled over him; every one wanted to see; he was pulled and shoved and fumbled. The spectacle had a grotesque side, and this it was that seemed to strike the fancy of the young man's comrades. They had not done lunching, so they were unable to bestow upon the incident the whole of that consideration which its high comicality deserved. But they did what they could. They looked down very often, glass in hand, during the half-hour that it went on, and they stinted neither their generous, joyous laughter, nor their appreciative comments. Women are said to have no sense of humour; but the Titianesque young ladies did liberal justice to the pleasantry of the scene. Toward the last, indeed, their attention rather flagged; for even the best joke suffers by reiteration, and when you have seen a stupefied young man, infinitely bedusted, slip out of the embrace of a couple of clumsy paupers for the twentieth time, you may very properly suppose that you have arrived at the farthest limits of the ludicrous.

After the great race had been run I quitted my perch and spent the rest of the afternoon in wandering about that grassy concave I have mentioned. It was amusing and picturesque; it was like a huge Bohemian encampment. Here also a great number of carriages were stationed, freighted in like manner with free-handed youths and young ladies with gilded tresses. These young ladies were almost the only representatives of their sex with pretensions to elegance; they were often pretty and always exhilarated. Gentlemen in pairs, mounted on stools, habited in fantastic sporting garments, and offering bets to whomsoever listed, were a conspicuous feature of the scene. It was equally striking that they were not preaching in the desert and that they found plenty of patrons among the baser sort. I returned to my place in time to assist at the rather complicated operation of starting for the drive back to London. Putting in horses and getting vehicles into line seemed in the midst of the general crush and entanglement a process not to be facilitated even by the most liberal swearing on the part of those engaged in it. But little by little we came to the end of it; and as by this time a kind of mellow cheerfulness pervaded the upper atmosphere – the region of the perpendicular whip – even those interruptions most trying to

patience were somehow made to minister to jollity. It was for
people below to not get trampled to death or crunched
between opposing wheel-hubs, if they could manage it. Above,
the carnival of "chaff" had set in, and it deepened as the lock
of vehicles grew denser. As they were all locked together (with
a comfortable padding of pedestrians at points of acutest contact), they contrived somehow to move together; so that we
gradually got away and into the road. The four or five hours
consumed on the road were simply as I say, a carnival of
"chaff", the profusely good-humoured savour of which, on
the whole, was certainly striking. The chaff was not brilliant
nor subtle nor especially graceful; and here and there it was
quite too tipsy to be even articulate. But as an expression of
that unbuttoning of the popular straight-jacket of which I
spoke awhile since, it had its wholesome and even innocent
side. It took, indeed, frequently an importunate physical form;
it sought emphasis in the use of pea-shooters and water-
squirts. At its best, too, it was extremely low and rowdyish.
But a stranger even of the most refined tastes might be glad to
have a glimpse of this popular revel, for it would make him
feel that he was learning something more about the English
people. It would give a meaning to the old words "merry
England". It would remind him that the natives of that country
are subject to some of the most frolicsome of the human
passions, and that the decent, dusky vistas of the London residential streets those discreet creations of which Thackeray's
"Baker Street" is the type – are not a complete symbol of the
complicated race that erected them.

II.

It seemed to me such a piece of good fortune to have been
asked down to Oxford at Commemoration by a gentleman

implicated in the remarkable ceremony which goes on under
that name, who kindly offered me the hospitality of his college, that I scarcely waited even to thank him, I simply took
the first train. I had had a glimpse of Oxford in former years,
but I had never slept in a low-browed room looking out on a
grassy quadrangle, opposite a mediæval clock-tower. This satisfaction was vouchsafed me on the night of my arrival; I was
inducted into the rooms of an absent undergraduate. I sat in
his deep arm-chairs; I burned his candles and read his books.
I hereby thank him as tenderly as possible. Before going to bed
I took a turn through the streets and renewed in the silent
darkness that impression of the charm imparted to them by
the quiet college-fronts, which I had gathered in former years.
The college-fronts were now quieter than ever, the streets
were empty, and the old scholastic city was sleeping in the
warm starlight. The undergraduates had retired in large numbers, encouraged in this impulse by the collegiate authorities,
who deprecate their presence at Commemoration. However
many young gownsmen may be sent away, there always
remain enough to make a noise. There can be no better indication of the resources of Oxford in a spectacular way than
this fact that the first step toward preparing an impressive ceremony is to get rid of the undergraduates.

In the morning I breakfasted with a young American who,
in common with a number of his countrymen, had come
hither to seek stimulus for a finer quality of study. I know not
whether he would have reckoned as such stimulus the conversation of a couple of those ingenuous youths of Britain whose
society I always find charming; but it added, from my own
point of view, to the local colour of the entertainment. After
this was over I repaired, in company with a crowd of ladies
and elderly people, interspersed with gownsmen, to the hoary
rotunda of the Sheldonian theatre, which every visitor to

Oxford will remember, with its curious cincture of clumsily-carven heads of warriors and sages perched upon stone posts. The interior of this edifice is the scene of the classic hooting, stamping, and cat-calling by which the undergraduates confer the last consecration upon the distinguished gentlemen who come up for the honorary degree of D.C.L. It is with the design of attenuating as much as possible this incongruous chorus, that the heads of colleges, on the close of the term, a few days before Commemoration, speed their too demonstrative disciples upon the homeward way. As I have already hinted, however, the contingent of irreverent lads was on this occasion quite large enough to produce a very handsome specimen of the traditional rumpus. This made the scene a very singular one. An American of course, with his fondness for antiquity, his relish for picturesqueness, his "emotional" attitude at historic shrines, takes Oxford much more seriously than its customary denizens can be expected to do. These people are not always upon the high horse; they are not always in an acutely sentient condition. Nevertheless, there is a certain maximum of disaccord with their beautiful circumstances which the ecstatic Occidental vaguely expects them not to transcend. No effort of the intellect beforehand would enable him to imagine one of those silver-gray temples of learning converted into a semblance of the Bowery Theatre when the Bowery Theatre is being trifled with.

The Sheldonian edifice, like everything at Oxford, is more or less monumental. There is a double tier of galleries, with sculptured pulpits protruding from them; there are full-length portraits of kings and worthies; there is a general air of antiquity and dignity, which, on the occasion of which I speak, was enhanced by the presence of certain ancient scholars, seated in crimson robes in high-backed chairs. Formerly, I believe, the undergraduates were placed apart – packed together in a corner of one of the galleries. But now they are scattered among the general spectators, a large number of whom are ladies. They muster in especial force, however, on the floor of the theatre, which has been cleared of its benches. Here the dense mass is at last severed in twain by the entrance of the prospective D.C.L.'s walking in single file, clad in crimson gowns, preceded by mace-bearers and accompanied by the Regius professor of Civil Law, who presents them individually to the Vice-Chancellor of the university, in a Latin speech which is of course a glowing eulogy. The five gentlemen to whom this distinction had been offered in 1877 were not among those whom fame has trumpeted most loudly; but there was something very pretty in their standing in their honourable robes, with heads modestly bent, while the orator, equally brilliant in aspect, recited their titles sonorously to the venerable dignitary in the high-backed chair. Each of them, when the little speech is ended, ascends the steps leading to the chair; the Vice-Chancellor bends forward and shakes his hand, and the new D.C.L. goes and sits in the blushing row of his fellow-doctors. The impressiveness of all this is much diminished by the boisterous conduct of the collegians, who super-abound in extravagant applause, in impertinent interrogation, and in lively disparagement of the orator's Latinity. Of the scene that precedes the episode I have just described I have given no account; vivid portrayal of it is not easy. Like the return from the Derby, it is a carnival of "chaff"; and it is a singular fact that the scholastic festival should have forcibly reminded me of the great popular "lark". In each case it is the same race enjoying a certain definitely chartered license; in the young votaries of a liberal education and the London rabble on the Epsom road it is the same perfect good-humour, the same muscular jocosity.

After the presentation of the doctors came a series of those collegiate exercises which have a generic resemblance all the world over: a reading of Latin verses and English essays, a spouting of prize poems and Greek paraphrases. The prize poem alone was somewhat attentively listened to; the other things were received with an infinite variety of critical ejaculation. But after all, I reflected, as the ceremony drew to a close, this discordant racket is more characteristic than it seems; it is at bottom only another expression of the venerable and historic, side of Oxford. It is tolerated because it is traditional; it is possible, because it is classical. Looking at it in this light, one might manage at last to find it impressive and romantic.

I was not obliged to find ingenious pretexts for thinking well of another ceremony of which I was witness after we adjourned from the Sheldonian theatre. This was a lunch-party at the particular college in which I should find it the highest privilege to reside. I may not further specify it. Perhaps, indeed, I may go so far as to say that the reason for my dreaming of this privilege is that it is deemed by persons of a reforming turn the best-appointed abuse in a nest of abuses. A commission for the expurgation of the universities has lately been appointed by Parliament to look into it – a commission armed with a gigantic broom, which is to sweep away all the fine old ivied and cobwebbed improprieties. Pending these righteous changes, one would like while one is about it – about, that is, this business of admiring Oxford – to attach one's self to the abuse, to bury one's nostrils in the rose before it is plucked. At the college in question there are no undergraduates. I found it agreeable to reflect that those gray-green cloisters had sent no delegates to the slangy congregation I had just quitted. This delightful spot exists for the satisfaction of a small society of Fellows who, having no dreary instruction to administer, no noisy hobbledehoys to govern, no obligations but toward their own culture, no care, save for learning as learning and truth as truth, are presumably the happiest and most charming people in the world. The party invited to lunch assembled first, in the library of the college, a cool, gray hall, of very great length and height, with vast wall-spaces of rich-looking book-titles and statues of noble scholars set in the midst. Had the charming Fellows ever anything more disagreeable to do than to finger these precious volumes and then to stroll about together in the grassy courts, in learned comradeship, discussing their precious contents? Nothing, apparently, unless it were to give a lunch at Commemoration in the dining-hall of the college. When lunch was ready there was a very pretty procession to go to it. Learned gentlemen in crimson gowns, ladies in brilliant toilets, paired slowly off and marched in a stately diagonal across the fine, smooth lawn of the quadrangle, in a corner of which they passed through a hospitable door. But here we cross the threshold of privacy; I remained on the farther side of it during the rest of the day. But I brought back with me certain memories of which, if I were not at the end of my space, I should attempt a discreet adumbration: memories of a *fête champêtre* in the beautiful gardens of one of the other colleges – charming lawns and spreading trees, music of Grenadier Guards, ices in striped marquees, mild flirtation of youthful gownsmen and bemuslined maidens; memories, too, of quiet dinner in common-room, a decorous, excellent repast; old portraits on the walls and great windows open upon the ancient court, where the afternoon light was fading in the stillness; superior talk upon current topics, and over all the peculiar air of Oxford – the air of liberty to care for intellectual things, assured and secured by machinery which is in itself a satisfaction to sense.

XII.

IN WARWICKSHIRE.

1877.

There is no better way for the stranger who wishes to know something of England, to plunge in *medias res*, than to spend a fortnight in Warwickshire. It is the core and centre of the English world; midmost England, unmitigated England. The place has taught me a great many English secrets; I have interviewed the genius of pastoral Britain. From a charming lawn – a lawn delicious to one's sentient boot-sole – I looked without obstruction at a sombre, soft, romantic mass, whose outline was blurred by mantling ivy. It made a perfect picture; and in the foreground the great trees overarched their boughs from right and left, so as to give it a majestic frame. This interesting object was the castle of Kenilworth. It was within distance of an easy walk, but one hardly thought of walking to it, any more than one would have thought of walking to a purple-shadowed tower in the background of a Berghem or a Claude. Here there were purple shadows, and slowly-shifting lights, and a soft-hued, bosky country in the middle distance.

Of course, however, I did walk over to the castle; and of course the walk led me through leafy lanes, and beside the hedgerows that make a tangled screen for lawn-like meadows. Of course too, I am bound to add, there was a row of ancient pedlars outside the castle-wall, hawking twopenny pamphlets and photographs. Of course, equally, at the foot of the grassy

mound on which the ruin stands, there were half a dozen public
houses; and, always of course, there were half a dozen
beery vagrants sprawling on the grass in the moist sunshine.
There was the usual respectable young woman to open the
castle-gate and to receive the usual sixpenny fee. And there
were the usual squares of printed cardboard, suspended upon
venerable surfaces, with further enumeration of twopence,
threepence, fourpence. I do not allude to these things queru-
lously, for Kenilworth is a very tame lion – a lion that, in
former years, I had stroked more than once. I remember perfectly my first visit to this romantic spot; how I chanced upon
a picnic; how I stumbled over beer-bottles; how the very
echoes of the beautiful ruin seemed to have dropped all their
h's. That was a sultry afternoon; I allowed my spirits to sink,
and I came away hanging my head. This was a beautiful fresh
morning, and in the interval I had grown philosophic. I had
learned that, with regard to most romantic sites in England,
there is a sort of average cockneyfication with which you must
make your account. There are always people on the field
before you, and there is generally something being drunk on
the premises.

I hoped, on the occasion of which I am now speaking, that
the average would be low; and indeed, for the first five minutes I flattered myself that this was the case. In the beautiful
grassy court of the castle, on my entrance, there were not
more than eight or ten fellow-intruders. There were a couple
of old ladies on a bench, eating something out of a newspaper;
there was a dissenting minister, also on a bench, reading the
guide-book aloud to his wife and sister-in-law; there were
three or four children pushing each other up and down the
turfy hillocks. This was sweet seclusion indeed; and I got a
capital start with the various noble square-windowed frag-
ments of the stately pile. They are extremely majestic, with

their even, pale-red colour, their deep-green drapery, their princely vastness of scale. But presently the tranquil ruin began to swarm like a startled hive. There were plenty of people, if they chose to show themselves. They emerged from crumbling doorways and gaping chambers, with the best conscience in the world; but I know not, after all, why I should bear them a grudge, for they gave me a pretext for wandering about in search of a quiet point of view. I cannot say that I found my point of view, but in looking for it I saw the castle, which is certainly an admirable ruin. And when the respectable young woman had let me out of the gate again, and I had shaken my head at the civil-spoken pedlars who form a little avenue for the arriving and departing visitor, I found it in my good-nature to linger a moment on the trodden, grassy slope, and to think that in spite of the hawkers, the paupers, and the beer-shops, there was still a good deal of old England in the scene. I say in spite of these things, but it may have been, in some degree, because of them. Who shall resolve into its component parts any impression of this richly complex English world, where the present is always seen, as it were, in profile, and the past presents a full face? At all events the solid red castle rose behind me, towering above its small old ladies and its investigating parsons; before me, across the patch of common, was a row of ancient cottages, black-timbered, red-gabled, pictorial, which evidently had a memory of the castle in its better days. A quaintish village straggled away on the right, and on the left the dark, fat meadows were lighted up with misty sun-spots and browsing sheep. I looked about for the village stocks; I was ready to take the modern vagrants for Shakespearean clowns; and I was on the point of going into one of the ale-houses to ask Mrs. Quickly for a cup of sack.

I began these remarks, however, with no intention of

talking about the celebrated curiosities in which this region abounds, but with a design, rather, of noting a few impressions of some of the shyer and more elusive ornaments of the show. Stratford, of course, is a very sacred place, but I prefer to say a word, for instance, about a charming old rectory, a good many miles distant, and to mention the pleasant picture it made of a summer afternoon, during a domestic festival. These are the happiest of a stranger's memories of English life, and he feels that he need make no apology for lifting the corner of the curtain. I drove through the leafy lanes I spoke of just now, and peeped over the hedges into fields where the yellow harvest stood waiting. In some places they were already shorn, and while the light began to redden in the west and to make a horizontal glow behind the dense wayside foliage, the gleaners, here and there, came brushing through gaps in the hedges with enormous sheaves upon their shoulders. The rectory was an ancient, gabled building, of pale red brick, with facings of white stone and creepers that wrapped it up. It dates, I imagine, from the early Hanoverian time; and as it stood there upon its cushiony lawn, among its ordered gardens, cheek to cheek with its little Norman church, it seemed to me the model of a quiet, spacious, easy English home. The cushiony lawn, as I have called it, stretched away to the edge of a brook, and afforded to a number of very amiable people an opportunity of playing lawn-tennis. There were half a dozen games going forward at once, and at each of them a great many "nice girls", as they say in England, were distinguishing themselves. These young ladies kept the ball going with an agility worthy of the sisters and sweethearts of a race of cricketers, and gave me a chance to admire their flexibility of figure and their freedom of action. When they came back to the house, after the games, flushed a little and a little dishevelled, they might have passed for the attendant nymphs of Diana, flocking in from the chase. There had, indeed, been a chance for them to wear the quiver, a target for archery being erected on the lawn. I remembered George Eliot's Gwendolen, and waited to see her step out of the muslin groups; but she was not forthcoming, and it was plain that if lawn-tennis had been invented in Gwendolen's day, this young lady would have captivated Mr. Grandcourt by her exploits with the racket. She certainly would have been a mistress of the game; and, if the suggestion is not too gross, the alertness that she would have learned from it might have proved an inducement to her boxing the ears of the insupportable Deronda.

After a while it grew too dark for lawn-tennis; but while the twilight was still mildly brilliant I wandered away, out of the grounds of the charming parsonage, and turned into the little churchyard beside it. The small weather-worn, rust-coloured church had an appearance of high antiquity; there were some curious Norman windows in the apse. Unfortunately I could not get inside; I could only glance into the open door across the interval of an old-timbered, heavy-hooded, padlocked porch. But the sweetest evening stillness hung over the place, and the sunset was red behind a dark row of rook-haunted elms. The stillness seemed the greater because three or four rustic children were playing, with little soft cries, among the crooked, deep-buried grave-stones. One poor little girl, who seemed deformed, had climbed some steps that served as a pedestal for a tall, mediæval-looking cross. She sat perched there, staring at me through the gloaming. This was the heart of England, unmistakably; it might have been the very pivot of the wheel on which her fortune revolves. One need not be a rabid Anglican to be extremely sensible of the charm of an English country church – and indeed of some of the features of an English rural Sunday. In London there is a certain flat-

ness in the observance of this festival; but in the country some
of the ceremonies that accompany it have an indefinable harmony with an ancient, pastoral landscape. I made this
reflection on an occasion that is still very fresh in my memory.
I said to myself that the walk to church from a beautiful
country-house, of a lovely summer afternoon, may be the
prettiest possible adventure. The house stands perched upon a
pedestal of rock, and looks down from its windows and terraces upon a shadier spot in the wooded meadows, of which
the blunted tip of a spire explains the character. A little company of people, whose costume denotes the highest pitch of
civilisation, winds down through the blooming gardens, passes
out of a couple of small gates, and reaches the footpath in the
fields. This is especially what takes the fancy of the sympathetic stranger; the level, deep-green meadows, studded here
and there with a sturdy oak; the denser grassiness of the footpath, the lily-sheeted pool beside which it passes, the rustic
stiles, where he stops and looks back at the great house and its
wooded background. It is in the highest degree probable that
he has the privilege of walking with a very pretty girl, and it is
morally certain that he thinks a pretty English girl the prettiest
creature in the world. He knows that she doesn't know how
lovely is this walk of theirs; she has been taking it – or taking
another quite as good – any time these twenty years. But her
quiet-eyed unsuspectingness only makes her the more a part of
his delicate entertainment. The latter continues unbroken
while they reach the little churchyard, and pass up to the
ancient porch, round which the rosy rustics are standing,
decently and deferentially, to watch the arrival of the smarter
contingent. This party takes its place in a great square pew, as
large as a small room, and with seats all round, and while he
listens to the respectable intonings the sympathetic stranger
reads over the inscriptions on the mural tablets before him, all

to the honour of the earlier bearers of a name which is, for himself, a symbol of hospitality.

When I came back to the parsonage the entertainment had been transferred to the interior, and I had occasion to admire the maidenly vigour of those charming young girls who, after playing lawn-tennis all the afternoon, were modestly expecting to dance all the evening. And in regard to this it is not impertinent to say that from almost any group of English maidens – though preferably from such as have passed their lives in quiet country homes – an American observer receives a delightful impression of something that he can best describe as an intimate salubrity. He notices face after face in which this rosy absence of a morbid strain – this simple, natural, affectionate development – amounts to positive beauty. If the young lady have no other beauty, the look I speak of is a sufficient charm; but when it is united, as it so often is, to real perfection of feature and colour, the result is the most delightful thing in nature. It makes the highest type of English beauty, and to my sense there is nothing so high as that. Not long since I heard a clever foreigner indulge, in conversation with an English lady – a very wise and liberal woman – in a little lightly restrictive criticism of her countrywomen. "It is possible," she answered, in regard to one of his objections; "but such as they are, they are inexpressibly dear to their husbands." This is doubtless true of good wives all over the world; but I felt, as I listened to these words of my friend, that there is often something in an English girl-face which gives it an extra touch of *justesse*. Such as the woman is, she has here, more than elsewhere, the look of being completely and profoundly at the service of the man she loves. This look, after one has been a while in England, comes to seem so much a proper and indispensable part of a "nice" face, that the absence of it appears a sign of irritability or of shallowness.

Depth of tenderness as regards a masculine counterpart – that is what it means; and I confess that seems to me a very agreeable meaning.

As for the prettiness, I cannot forbear, in the face of a fresh reminiscence, to give it another word. And yet in regard to prettiness, what do words avail? This was what I asked myself the other day as I looked at a young girl who stood in an old oaken parlour, the rugged panels of which made a background for her lovely head, in simple conversation with a handsome lad. I said to myself that the faces of English young people had often a singular charm, but that this same charm is too soft and shy a thing to talk about. The face of this fair creature had a pure oval, and her clear brown eyes a quiet warmth. Her complexion was as bright as a sunbeam after rain, and she smiled in a way that made any other way of smiling than that seem a shallow grimace – a mere creaking of the facial muscles. The young man stood facing her, slowly scratching his thigh and shifting from one foot to the other. He was tall and very well made, and so sun-burned that his fair hair was lighter than his complexion. He had honest, stupid blue eyes, and a simple smile that showed his handsome teeth. He was very well dressed. Presently I heard what they were saying. "I suppose it's pretty big," said the beautiful young girl. "Yes; it's pretty big," said the handsome young man. "It's nicer when they are big," said his interlocutress. The young man looked at her, and at everything in general, with his slowly-apprehending blue eye, and for some time no further remark was made. "It draws ten feet of water," he at last went on. "How much water is there?" said the young girl. She spoke in a charming voice. "There are thirty feet of water," said the young man. "Oh, that's enough," rejoined the damsel. I had had an idea they were flirting, and perhaps indeed that is the way it is done. It was an ancient room and extremely delightful; everything was polished over with the brownness of centuries. The chimney-piece was carved a foot thick, and the windows bore, in coloured glass, the quarterings of ancestral couples. These had stopped two hundred years before; there was nothing newer than that date. Outside the windows was a deep, broad moat, which washed the base of gray walls – gray walls spotted over with the most delicate yellow lichens.

In such a region as this mellow, conservative Warwickshire an appreciative American finds the small things quite as suggestive as the great. Everything, indeed, is suggestive, and impressions are constantly melting into each other and doing their work before he has had time to ask them whence they came. He cannot go into a cottage muffled in plants, to see a genial gentlewoman and a "nice girl", without being reminded forsooth of "The Small House at Allington". Why of "The Small House at Allington"? There is a larger house at which the ladies come up to dine; but that is surely an insufficient reason. That the ladies are charming – even that is not reason enough; for there have been other nice girls in the world than Lily Dale, and other mellow matrons than her mamma. Reminded, however, he is especially when he goes out upon the lawn. Of course there is lawn-tennis, and it seems all ready for Mr. Crosbie to come and play. This is a small example of the way in which in the presence of English life the imagination must be constantly at play, on the part of members of a race in whom it has necessarily been trained to do extra service. In driving and walking, in looking and listening, everything seemed to me in some degree or other characteristic of a rich, powerful, old-fashioned society. One had no need of being told that this is a conservative county; the fact seemed written in the hedgerows and in the verdant acres behind them. Of course the owners of these things were conservative; of course they were stubbornly unwilling to see the harmonious edifice of Church and State the least bit shaken. I had a feeling, as I went about, that I should find some very ancient and curious opinions still comfortably domiciled in the fine old houses whose clustered gables and chimneys appeared here and there, at a distance, above their ornamental woods. Self-complacent British Toryism, viewed in this vague and conjectural fashion – across the fields and behind the oaks and beeches – is by no means a thing the irresponsible stranger would wish away; it deepens the local colour; it may be said to enhance the landscape. I got a sort of constructive sense of its presence in the picturesque old towns of Coventry and Warwick, which appear to be filled with those institutions – chiefly of an eleemosynary order – that Toryism takes a genial comfort in. There are ancient charities in these places – hospitals, almshouses, asylums, infant-schools – so quaint and venerable that they almost make the existence of poverty a delectable and satisfying thought. In Coventry in especial, I believe, these pious foundations are so numerous as almost to place a premium upon misery. Invidious reflections apart, however, there are few things that speak more quaintly and suggestively of the old England that an American loves than these clumsy little monuments of ancient benevolence. Such an institution as Leicester's Hospital at Warwick seems indeed to exist primarily for the sake of its spectacular effect upon the American tourists, who, with the dozen rheumatic old soldiers maintained in affluence there, constitute its principal *clientèle*.

The American tourist usually comes straight to this quarter of England – chiefly for the purpose of paying his respects to the birthplace of Shakespeare. Being here, he comes to Warwick to see the castle; and being at Warwick, he comes to see the odd little theatrical-looking refuge for superannuated warriors which lurks in the shadow of one of the old gate-towers. Every

one will remember Hawthorne's account of the place, which
he left no touch of charming taste to be added to any reference to it. The hospital struck me as a little museum kept up
for the amusement and confusion of those inquiring
Occidentals who are used to seeing charity more dryly and
practically administered. The old hospitallers – I am not sure,
after all, whether they are necessarily soldiers, but some of
them happen to be – are at once the curiosities and the
keepers. They sit on benches outside of their door, at the
receipt of custom, all neatly brushed and darned, and ready,
like Mr. Cook, to conduct you personally. They are only
twelve in number, but their picturesque dwelling, perched
upon the old city rampart, and full of dusky little courts, cross-
timbered gable-ends and deeply sunken lattices, seems a
wonderfully elaborate piece of machinery for its humble purpose. Each of the old gentlemen must be provided with a wife
or "housekeeper"; each of them has a dusky parlour of his
own; and they pass their latter days in their scoured and polished little refuge as softly and honourably as a company of
retired lawgivers or pensioned soothsayers.

At Coventry I went to see a couple of old charities of a similar pattern – places with black-timbered fronts, little
clean-swept courts and Elizabethan windows. One of them
was a romantic residence for a handful of old women, who
sat, each of them, in a cosy little bower, in a sort of mediæval
darkness; the other was a school for little boys of humble
origin, and this last establishment was charming. I found the
little boys playing at "top" in a gravelled court, in front of the
prettiest old building of tender-coloured stucco and painted
timber, ornamented with two delicate little galleries and a fantastic porch. They were dressed in small blue tunics and odd
caps, like those worn by sailors, but, if I remember rightly,
with little yellow tags affixed to them. I was free, apparently,

to wander all over the establishment; there was no sign of pastor or master anywhere; nothing but the little yellow-headed boys playing before the ancient house, and practising most correctly the Warwickshire accent. I went indoors and looked at a fine old oaken staircase; I even ascended it, and walked along a gallery and peeped into a dormitory at a row of very short beds; and then I came down and sat for five minutes on a bench hardly wider than the top rail of a fence, in a little, cold, dim refectory, where there was not at crumb to be seen nor any lingering odour of bygone repasts to be perceived. And yet I wondered how it was that the sense of many generations of boyish feeders seemed to abide there. It came, I suppose, from the very bareness and, if I may be allowed the expression, the clean-licked aspect of the place, which wore the appearance of the famous platter of Jack Sprat and his wife.

Inevitably, of course, the sentimental tourist has a great deal to say to himself about this being Shakespeare's county – about these densely verdant meadows and parks having been, to his musing eyes, the normal landscape. In Shakespeare's day, doubtless, the coat of nature was far from being so prettily trimmed as it is now; but there is one place, nevertheless, which, as he passes it in the summer twilight, the traveller does his best to believe unaltered. I allude, of course, to Charlecote park, whose venerable verdure seems a survival from an earlier England, and whose innumerable acres, stretching away in the early evening, to vaguely seen Tudor walls, lie there like the backward years receding to the age of Elizabeth. It was however, no part of my design in these remarks to pause before so thickly besieged a shrine as this; and if I were to allude to Stratford, it would not be in connection with the fact that Shakespeare came into the world there. It would be rather to speak of a delightful old house near the Avon which struck me as the ideal home for a Shakespearean scholar, or indeed for any passionate lover of the poet. Here, with books, and memories, and the recurring reflection that he had taken his daily walk across the bridge, at which you look from your windows straight down an avenue of fine old trees, with an ever-closed gate at the end of them and a carpet of turf stretched over the decent drive – here, I say, with old brown wainscotted chambers to live in, old polished doorsteps to lead you from one to the other, deep window-seats to sit in, with a play in your lap – here a person for whom the cares of life should have resolved themselves into a care for the greatest genius who has represented and ornamented life, might find a very congruous asylum. Or, speaking a little wider of the mark, the charming, rambling, low-gabled, many-staired, much-panelled mansion would be a very agreeable home for any person of taste who should prefer an old house to a new. I find I am talking about it quite like an auctioneer; but what I chiefly had at heart was to commemorate the fact that I had lunched there, and while I lunched kept saying to myself that there is nothing in the world so delightful as the happy accidents of old English houses.

And yet that same day, on the edge of the Avon, I found it in me to say that a new house too may be a very charming affair. But I must add that the new house I speak of had really such exceptional advantages that it could not fairly be placed in the scale. Besides, was it new after all? I suppose that it was, and yet one's impression there was all of a kind of silvery antiquity. The place stood upon a decent Stratford street, from which it looked usual enough; but when, after sitting a while in a charming modern drawing-room, one stepped thoughtlessly through an open window upon a verandah, one found that the horizon of the morning-call had been wonderfully widened. I will not pretend to relate all that I saw after I stepped off the verandah; suffice it that the spire and chancel of the beautiful old church in which Shakespeare is buried, with the Avon sweeping its base, were one of the elements of the vision. Then there were the smoothest lawns in the world stretching down to the edge of this lovely stream, and making, where the water touched them, a line as even as the rim of a champagne-glass – a verge near which you inevitably lingered to see the spire and the chancel – the church was close at hand – among the well-grouped trees, and look for their reflection in the river. The place was a garden of delight; it was a stage set for one of Shakespeare's comedies – for *Twelfth Night* or *Much Ado*. Just across the river was a level meadow, which rivalled the lawn on which I stood, and this meadow seemed only the more essentially a part of the scene by reason of the voluminous sheep that were grazing on it. These sheep were by no means mere edible mutton; they were poetic, historic, romantic sheep; they were there to be picturesque, and they knew it. And yet, knowing as they were, I doubt whether the wisest old ram of the flock could have told me how to explain why it was that this happy mixture of lawn and river and mirrored spire and blooming garden seemed to me for a quarter of an hour the prettiest corner of England.

If Warwickshire is Shakespeare's country, I found myself remembering that it is also George Eliot's. The author of *Adam Bede* and *Middlemarch* has called the rural background of those admirable fictions by another name, but I believe it long ago ceased to be a secret that her native Warwickshire had been in her intention. The stranger who wanders over its velvety surface recognises at every turn the elements of George Eliot's novels – especially when he carries himself back in imagination to the Warwickshire of forty years ago. He says to himself that it would be impossible to conceive anything more conservatively bucolic, more respectably pastoral. It was in one of the old nestling farmhouses, beyond a hundred hedgerows, that Hetty Sorrel smiled into her milk-pans, as if she were looking for a reflection of her pretty face; it was at the end of one of the leafy-pillared avenues that poor Mrs. Casaubon paced up and down in fervid disappointment. The country suggests, in especial, both the social and the natural scenery of *Middlemarch*. There must be many a genially per-verse old Mr. Brooke there yet, and whether there are many Dorotheas or not, there must be many a well-featured and well-acred young country gentleman, of the pattern of Sir James Chettam, who, as he rides along the leafy lanes, softly cudgels his brain to know why a clever girl shouldn't wish to marry him. But I doubt whether there are many Dorotheas, and I suspect that the Sir James Chettams of the county are not often pushed to that intensity of meditation. You feel, how-ever, that George Eliot could not have placed her heroine in a local medium better fitted to throw her fine impatience into relief – a community more likely to be startled and perplexed by a questioning attitude on the part of a well-housed and well-fed young gentlewoman.

Among the edifying days that I spent in these neighbour-hoods there is one in especial of which I should like to give a detailed account. But I find on consulting my memory that the details have melted away into the single deep impression of a perfect ripeness of civilisation. It was a long excursion, by rail and by carriage, for the purpose of seeing three extremely interesting old country-houses. Our errand led us, in the first place, into Oxfordshire, through the ancient market-town of Banbury, where of course we made a point of looking out for the Cross referred to in the famous nursery-rhyme. It stood there in the most natural manner – though I am afraid it has been "done up" – with various antique gables around it, from one of whose exiguous windows the young person appealed to in the rhyme may have looked at the old woman as she rode and heard the music of her bells. The houses we went to see have not a national reputation; they are simply interwoven figures in the rich pattern of the Midlands. They have, indeed, a local renown, but they are not thought to be very exceptionally curious or beautiful, and the stranger has a feeling that his surprises and ecstasies are held to betray a meagre bringing-up. Such places, to a Warwickshire mind of good habits, must appear to be the pillars and props of a heaven-appointed order of things; and accordingly, in a land on which heaven smiles, they are as natural as the geology of the county or the supply of mutton. But nothing could well give a stranger a stronger impression of the wealth of England in such matters – of the interminable list of her territorial homes – than this fact that the enchanting old mansions I speak of should have but a limited fame – should not be lions of the first magnitude. Of one of them, the finest in the group, one of my companions, who lived but twenty miles away, had never even heard. Such a place was not thought a matter to boast about. Its peers and its mates are scattered all over the country; half of them are not even mentioned in the county guidebooks. You stumble upon them in a drive or a walk. You catch a glimpse of an ivied front at the midmost point of a great estate, and taking your way, by leave of a serious old woman at a lodge-gate, along an overarching avenue, you find yourself introduced to an edifice so human-looking in its beauty, that it seems for the occasion to reconcile art and morality.

To Broughton Castle, the first seen in this beautiful group, I must do no more than allude; but this is not because I failed to think it, as I think every house I see, the most delightful residence in England. It lies rather low, and its woods and pastures slope down to it; it has a deep, clear moat all around it, spanned by a bridge that passes under a charming old gate-tower, and nothing can be prettier than to see its clustered walls of yellow-brown stone so sharply islanded, while its gardens bloom on the other side of the water. Like several other houses in this part of the country, Broughton Castle played a part (on the Parliamentary side) in the civil wars, and not the least interesting features of its beautiful interior are the several mementoes of Cromwell's station there. It was within a moderate drive of this place that in 1642 the battle of Edgehill was fought – the first great battle of the war – and gained by neither party. We went to see the battlefield, where an ancient tower and an artificial ruin (of all things in the world) have been erected for the entertainment of convivial visitors. These ornaments are perched upon the edge of a slope which commands a view of the exact scene of the contest, upwards of a mile away. I looked in the direction indicated, and saw misty meadows, a little greener perhaps than usual, and colonnades of elms, a trifle denser. After this we paid our respects to another old house which is full of memories and suggestions of that most dramatic period of English history. But of Compton Wyniates (the name of this enchanting domicile), I despair of giving any coherent or adequate account. It belongs to the Marquis of Northampton, and it stands empty all the year round. It sits on the grass at the bottom of a wooded hollow, and the glades of a superb old park go wandering upward, away from it. When I came out in front of the house from a short and steep but stately avenue, I said to myself that here surely we had arrived at the farthest limits of what ivy-smothered brick-work and weather-beaten gables, conscious old windows and clustered mossy roofs, can accomplish for the eye. It is impossible to imagine a more perfect picture. And its air of solitude and delicate decay – of having been dropped into its grassy hollow as an ancient jewel is deposited upon a cushion, and being shut in from the world and back into the past by its circling woods – all this highly increased its impressiveness. The house is not large, as great houses go, and it sits, as I have said, upon the grass, without even a flagging or a footpath to conduct you from the point where the avenue stops to the beautiful sculptured doorway which admits you into the small, quaint, inner court. From this court you are at liberty to pass through the crookedest series of oaken halls and chambers, adorned with treasures of old wainscotting, and elaborate doors and chimney-pieces. Outside, you may walk all round the house on a grassy bank, which is raised above the level on which it stands, and find it from every point of view a more charming composition. I should not omit to mention that Compton Wyniates is supposed to have been in Scott's eye when he described the dwelling of the old royalist knight in *Woodstock*. In this case he simply transferred the house to the other side of the county. He has indeed given several of the features of the place, but he has not given what one may call its colour. I must add that if Sir Walter could not give the colour of Compton Wyniates, it is useless for any other writer to attempt it. It is a matter for the brush and not for the pen.

And what shall I say of the colour of Wroxton Abbey, which we visited last in order, and which in the thickening twilight, as we approached its great ivy-muffled face, made an ineffaceable impression on my fancy? Wroxton Abbey, as it stands, is a house of about the same period as Compton Wyniates – the latter years, I suppose, of the sixteenth century. But it is quite another affair. The place is inhabited, "kept up", and full of the most interesting and most splendid detail. Its happy occupants, however, were fortunately not actually staying there (happy occupants, in England, are almost always absent), and the house was exhibited with a civility worthy of its merit. Everything that in the material line can render life noble and charming has been gathered into it with a profusion which makes the whole place a monument to past opportunity. As I wandered from one rich room to another, looking at these things, that ineffaceable impression upon my fancy which I just mentioned was delightfully deepened. But who can tell the pleasures of fancy when fancy takes her ease in an old English countryhouse, while the twilight darkens the corners of expressive rooms, and the appreciative intruder, pausing at the window, turns his glance from the observing portrait of a handsome ancestral face and sees the great soft billows of the lawn melt away into the park?

XIII.

ABBEYS AND CASTLES.

1877.

It is a frequent reflection with the stranger in England that the beauty and interest of the country are private property, and that to get access to them a key is always needed. The key may be large or it may be small, but it must be something that will turn a lock. Of the things that contribute to the happiness of an American observer in the country of parks and castles, I can think of very few that do not come under this definition of private property. When I have mentioned the hedgerows and the churches I have almost exhausted the list. You can enjoy a hedgerow from the public road, and I suppose that even if you are a Dissenter you may enjoy a Norman abbey from the street. If, therefore, one talks of anything beautiful in England, the presumption will be that it is private; and indeed such is my admiration of this delightful country that I feel inclined to say that if one talk of anything private the presumption will be that it is beautiful. This is something of a dilemma. If the observer permit himself to commemorate charming impressions, he is in danger of giving to the world the fruits of friendship, and hospitality. If, on the other hand, he withhold his impression, he lets something admirable slip away without having marked its passage, without having done it proper honour. He ends by mingling discretion with enthusiasm, and he says to himself that it is not treating a country ill to talk of its treasures when the mention of each has tacit reference to an act of private courtesy.

The impressions I have in mind in writing these lines were gathered in a part of England of which I had not before had even a traveller's glimpse; but as to which, after a day or two, I found myself quite ready to agree with a friend who lived there, and who knew and loved it well, when he said very frankly, "I do believe it is the loveliest corner of the world!" This was not a dictum to quarrel about, and while I was in the neighbourhood I was quite of his opinion. I felt that it would not take a great deal to make me care for it very much as he cared for it; I had a glimpse of the peculiar tenderness with which such a country may be loved. It is a capital example of the great characteristic of English scenery – of what I should call density of feature. There are no waste details; everything in the landscape is something particular – has a history, has played a part, has a value to the imagination. It is a region of hills and blue undulations, and, though none of the hills are high, all of them are interesting – interesting as such things are interesting in an old, small country, by a kind of exquisite modulation, something suggesting that outline and colouring have been retouched and refined by the hand of time. Independently of its castles and abbeys, the definite relics of the ages, such a landscape seems historic. It has human relations, and it is intimately conscious of them. That little speech about the loveliness of his county, or of his own part of his county, was made to me by my companion as we walked up the grassy slope of a hill, or "edge", as it is called there, from the crest of which we seemed in an instant to look away over most of the remainder of England. Certainly I should have grown affectionate with regard to such a view as that. The "edge" plunged down suddenly, as if the corresponding slope on the other side had been excavated, and one might follow the long ridge for the space of an afternoon's walk with this vast, charming prospect before one's eyes. Looking across an English county into the next but one is a very pretty entertainment, the county seeming by no means so small as might be supposed. How can a county seem small in which, from such a vantage-point as the one I speak of, you see, as a darker patch across the lighter green, the great estate of one of their lordships? Beyond these are blue undulations of varying tone, and then another bosky-looking spot, which constitutes, as you are told, the residential umbrage of another peer. And to right and left of these, in wooded expanses, lie other domains of equal consequence. It was therefore not the smallness but the vastness of the country that struck me, and I was not at all in the mood of a certain American who once, in my hearing burst out laughing at an English answer to my inquiry as to whether my interlocutor often saw Mr. B—. "Oh no," the answer had been, "we never see him: he lives away off in the West." It was the western part of his county our friend meant, and my American humorist found matter for infinite jest in his meaning. "I should as soon think of saying my western hand and my eastern," he declared.

I do not think, even, that my disposition to form a sentimental attachment for this delightful region – for its hillside prospect of old red farmhouses lighting up the dark-green bottoms, of gables and chimneytops of great houses peeping above miles of woodland, and, in the vague places of the horizon, of far away towns and sites that one had always heard of – was conditioned upon having "property" in the neighbourhood, so that the little girls in the town should suddenly drop curtsies to me in the street; though that too would certainly have been pleasant. At the same time, having a little property would without doubt have made the sentiment stronger. People who wander about the world without money in their pockets indulge in dreams – dreams of the things they would buy if their pockets were complete. These dreams are very apt to have relation to a good estate in any neighbourhood in which the wanderer may happen to find himself. For myself, I have never been in a country so unattractive that it did not seem a peculiar felicity to be able to purchase the most considerable house it contained. In New England and other portions of the United States I have coveted the large mansion with Doric columns and a pediment of white-painted timber; in Italy I have made imaginary proposals for the yellow-walled villa with statues on the roof. In England I have rarely gone so far as to fancy myself in treaty for the best house, but, failing this, I have rarely failed to feel that ideal comfort for the time would be to call one's self owner of what is denominated here a "good" place. Is it that English country life seems to possess such irresistible charms? I have not always thought so; I have sometimes suspected that it is dull; I have remembered that there is a whole literature devoted to exposing it (that of the English novel "of manners"); and that its recorded occupations and conversations occasionally strike one as lacking a certain indispensable salt. But, for all that, when, in the region to which I allude, my companion spoke of this and that place being likely sooner or later to come to the hammer, it seemed as if nothing could be more delightful than to see the hammer hanging upon one's own liberality. And this in spite of the fact that the owners of the places in question would part with them because they could no longer afford to keep them up. I found it interesting to learn, in so far as was possible, what sort of income was implied by the possession of country-seats such as are not in America a concomitant of even the largest fortunes; and if in these revelations I sometimes heard of a very long rent-roll, on the other hand I was frequently surprised at the shortness of purse attributed to people living in the depths of an oak-studded park. Then, certainly, English country-life seemed to me the most advantageous thing in the world; on conditions such as these one would gladly be dull; surrounded by luxury of so moderate a cost one would joyfully stagnate.

There was one place in particular of which I said to myself that if I had the money to buy it, I would "move in" on the morrow. I saw this place, unfortunately, to small advantage; I saw it in the rain. But I am rather glad that fine weather did not meddle with the affair, for I think that in this case the irritation of envy might have made me ill. It was a long, wet Sunday, and the waters were deep. I had been in the house all day, for the weather can best be described by my saying that it had been deemed to exonerate me from churchgoing. But in the afternoon, the prospective interval between lunch and tea assuming formidable proportions, my host took me out to walk, and in the course of our walk he led me into a park which he described as "the paradise of a small English country-gentleman". It was indeed a modern Eden, and the trees might have been trees of knowledge. They were of high antiquity and magnificent girth and stature; they were strewn over the grassy levels in extraordinary profusion, and scattered upon and down the slopes in a fashion than which I have seen nothing more charming since I last looked at the chestnuts on the Lake of Como. It appears that the place was not very large, but I was unable to perceive its limits. Shortly before we turned into the park the rain had renewed itself, so that we were awkwardly wet and muddy; but, being near the house, my companion proposed to leave his card in a neighbourly way. The house was most agreeable; it stood on a kind of terrace, in the middle of a lawn and garden, and the terrace overlooked one of the most copious rivers in England, and across to those blue undulations of which I have already spoken. On the terrace also was a piece of ornamental water, and there was a small iron paling to divide the lawn from the park. All this I beheld in the rain. My companion gave his card to the butler, with the remark that we were too much bespattered to come in, and we turned away to complete our circuit. As we turned away I became acutely conscious of what I should have been tempted to call the cruelty of this proceeding. My imagination gauged the whole position. It was a Sunday afternoon, and it was raining. The house was charming, the terrace delightful, the oaks magnificent, the view most interesting. But the whole thing was – not to repeat the invidious epithet of which just now I made too gross a use – the whole thing was quiet. In the house was a drawing-room, and in the drawing-room, was – by which I meant *must be* – a lady, a charming English lady. It seemed to me that there was nothing fatuous in believing that on this rainy Sunday afternoon it would not please her to be told that two gentlemen had walked across the country to her door only to go through the ceremony of leaving a card. Therefore, when, before we had gone many yards, I heard the butler hurrying after us, I felt how just my sentiment of the situation had been. Of course we went back, and I carried my muddy boots into the drawing-room – just the drawing-room I had imagined – where I found – I will not say just the lady I had imagined, but a lady even more charming. Indeed, there were two ladies, one of whom was staying in the house. In whatever company you find yourself in England, you may always be sure that some one present is "staying". I seldom hear this participle nowadays without remembering an observation made to me in France by a lady who had seen much of English manners. "Ah, that dreadful word *staying!* I think we are so happy in France not to be able to translate it – not to have any word that answers to it." The large windows of the drawing-room I speak of looked away over the river to the blurred and blotted hills, where the rain was drizzling and drifting. It was very quiet, as I say; there was an air of large leisure. If one wanted to do something here, there was evidently plenty of time – and indeed of every other appliance – to do it. The two ladies talked about "town": that is what people talk about in the country. If I were disposed I might represent them as talking about it with a certain air of yearning. At all events, I asked myself how it was possible that one should live in this charming place and trouble one's head about what was going on in London in July. Then we had excellent tea.

I returned to the habitation of my companion – for I too was guilty of "staying" – through an old Norman portal, massively arched and quaintly sculptured, across whose hollow threshold the eye of fancy might see the ghosts of monks and the shadows of abbots pass noiselessly to and fro. This aperture admits you to a beautiful ambulatory of the thirteenth century – a long stone gallery or cloister, repeated in two stories, with the interstices of its traceries now glazed, but with its long low, narrow, charming vista still perfect and picturesque – with its flags worn away by monkish sandals, and with huge round-arched doorways opening from its inner side into great rooms roofed like cathedrals. These rooms are furnished with narrow windows, of almost defensive aspect, set in embrasures three feet deep, and ornamented with little grotesque mediæval faces. To see one of the small monkish masks grinning at you while you dress and undress, or while you look up in the intervals of inspiration from your letter writing, is a mere detail in the entertainment of living in a *ci-devant* priory. This entertainment is inexhaustible; for every step you take in such a house confronts you in one way or another with the remote past. You feast upon the pictorial, you inhale the historic. Adjoining the house is a beautiful ruin, part

of the walls and windows and bases of the piers of the magnificent church administered by the predecessor of your host,
the abbot. These relics are very desultory, but they are still
abundant, and they testify to the great scale and the stately
beauty of the abbey. You may lie upon the grass at the base of
an ivied fragment, measure the girth of the great stumps of the
central columns, half smothered in soft creepers, and think
how strange it is that in this quiet hollow, in the midst of
lonely hills, so exquisite and elaborate a work of art should
have arisen. It is but an hour's walk to another great ruin,
which has held together more completely. There the central
tower stands erect to half its altitude, and the round arches
and massive pillars of the nave make a perfect vista on the
unencumbered turf. You get an impression that when catholic
England was in her prime, great abbeys were as thick as milestones. By native amateurs, even now, the region is called
"wild", though to American eyes it seems almost suburban in
its smoothness and finish. There is a noiseless little railway
running through the valley, and there is an ancient little town
at the abbey-gates – a town, indeed, with no great din of vehicles, but with goodly brick houses, with a dozen "publics",
with tidy, whitewashed cottages, and with little girls, as I have
said, bobbing curtsies in the street. But even now, if one had
wound one's way into the valley by the railroad, it would be
rather a surprise to find a small ornamental cathedral in a spot
on the whole so natural and pastoral. How impressive then
must the beautiful church have been in the days of its prosperity, when the pilgrim came down to it from the grassy
hillside and its bells made the stillness sensible! The abbey was
in those days a great affair; as my companion said, it sprawled
all over the place. As you walk away from it you think you
have got to the end of its geography, but you encounter it still
in the shape of a rugged outhouse enriched with an early-

English arch, or an ancient well, hidden in a kind of sculptured cavern. It is noticeable that even if you are a traveller from a land where there are no early-English – and indeed few late-English – arches, and where the well-covers are, at their hoariest, of fresh-looking shingles, you grow used with little delay to all this antiquity. Anything very old seems extremely natural; there is nothing we accept so implicitly as transmitted associations. It is not too much to say that after spending twenty-four hours in a house that is six hundred years old, you seem yourself to have lived in it for six hundred years. You seem yourself to have hollowed the flags with your tread, and to have polished the oak with your touch. You walk along the little stone gallery where the monks used to pace, looking out of the gothic window-places at their beautiful church, and you pause at the big round, rugged doorway that admits you to what is now the drawing-room. The massive step by which you ascend to the threshold is a trifle crooked, as it should be; the lintels are cracked and worn by the myriad-fingered years. This strikes your casual glance. You look up and down the miniature cloister before you pass in; it seems wonderfully old and queer. Then you turn into the drawing-room, where you find modern conversation and late publications and the prospect of dinner. The new life and the old have melted together; there is no dividing-line. In the drawing-room wall is a queer funnel-shaped hole, with the broad end inward, like a small casemate. You ask what it is, but people have forgotten. It is something of the monks; it is a mere detail. After dinner you are told that there is of course a ghost – a gray friar who is seen in the dusky hours at the end of passages. Sometimes the servants see him; they afterwards go surreptitiously to sleep in the village. Then, when you take your chamber-candle and go wandering bedward by a short cut through empty rooms, you are conscious of a peculiar sentiment toward the

ABBEYS AND CASTLES 241

gray friar which you hardly know whether to interpret as a
hope or a reluctance.

A friend of mine, an American, who knew this country, had
told me not to fail, while I was in the neighbourhood, to go to
S— and two or three other places. "Edward IV and Elizabeth,"
he said, "are still hanging about there." So admonished, I
made a point of going at least to S—, and I saw quite what my
friend meant. Edward IV and Elizabeth, indeed, are still to be
met almost any where in the county; as regards domestic
architecture, few parts of England are still more vividly old
English. I have rarely had, for a couple of hours, the sensation
of dropping back personally into the past in a higher degree
than while I lay on the grass beside the well in the little sunny
court of this small castle, and lazily appreciated the still definite details of mediæval life. The place is a capital example of
what the French call a small *gentilhommière* of the thirteenth
century. It has a good deep moat, now filled with wild verdure, and a curious gatehouse of a much later period – the
period when the defensive attitude had been well-nigh aban-
doned. This gate-house, which is not in the least in the style of
the habitation, but gabled and heavily timbered, with quaint
cross-beams protruding from surfaces of coarse white plaster,
is a very effective anomaly in regard to the little gray fortress
on the other side of the court. I call this a fortress, but it is a
fortress which might easily have been taken, and it must have
assumed its present shape at a time when people had ceased to
peer through narrow slits at possible besiegers. There are slits
in the outer walls for such peering, but they are noticeably
broad and not particularly oblique, and might easily have been
applied to the uses of a peaceful parley. This is part of the
charm of the place; human life there must have lost an earlier
grimness; it was lived in by people who were begining to
believe in good intentions. They must have lived very much

together; that is one of the most obvious reflections in the
court of a mediæval dwelling. The court was not always grassy
and empty, as it is now, with only a couple of gentlemen in
search of impressions lying, at their length, one of whom has
taken a wine-flask out of his pocket and has coloured the clear
water drawn for them out of the well in a couple of tumblers
by a decent, rosy, smiling, talking old woman, who has come
bustling out of the gatehouse, and who has a large, dropsical,
innocent husband standing about on crutches in the sun, and
making no sign when you ask after his health. This poor man
has reached that ultimate depth of human simplicity at which
even a chance to talk about one's ailments is not appreciated.
But the civil old woman talks for every one, even for an artist
who has come out of one of the rooms, where I see him afterward reproducing its mouldering repose. The rooms are all
unoccupied and in a state of extreme decay, though the castle
is, as yet, far from being a ruin. From one of the windows I see
a young lady sitting under a tree, across a meadow, with her
knees up, dipping something into her mouth. It is a camel's
hair paint-brush; the young lady is sketching. These are the
only besiegers to which the place is exposed now, and they can
do no great harm, as I doubt whether the young lady's aim is
very good. We wandered about the empty interior, thinking it
a pity such things should fall to pieces. There is a beautiful
great hall – great, that is, for a small castle (it would be
extremely handsome in a modern house) – with tall, ecclesias-
tical-looking windows, and a long staircase at one end,
climbing against the wall into a spacious bedroom. You may
still apprehend very well the main lines of that simpler life;
and it must be said that, simpler though it was, it was apparently by no means destitute of many of our own conveniences.
The chamber at the top of the staircase ascending from the
hall is charming still, with its irregular shape, its low-browed

ceiling, its cupboards in the walls, and its deep bay window formed of a series of small lattices. You can fancy people stepping out from it upon the platform of the staircase, whose rugged wooden logs, by way of steps, and solid, deeply-guttered hand-rail, still remain. They looked down into the hall, where, I take it, there was always a congregation of retainers, much lounging and waiting and passing to and fro, with a door open into the court. The court, as I said just now, was not the grassy, æsthetic spot which you may find it at present of a summer's day; there were beasts tethered in it, and hustling men-at-arms, and the earth was trampled into puddles. But my lord or my lady, looking down from the chamber-door, commanded the position and, no doubt, issued their orders accordingly. The sight of the groups on the floor beneath, the calling up and down, the oaken tables spread, and the brazier in the middle – all this seemed present again; and it was not difficult to pursue the historic vision through the rest of the building – through the portion which connected the great hall with the tower (here the confederate of the sketching young lady without had set up the peaceful three-legged engine of his craft) through the dusky, roughly circular rooms of the tower itself, and up the corkscrew staircase of the same to that most charming part of every old castle, where visions must leap away off the battlements to elude you – the bright, dizzy platform at the tower-top, the place where the castle-standard hung and the vigilant inmates surveyed the approaches. Here, always, you really overtake the impression of the place – here, in the sunny stillness, it seems to pause, panting a little, and give itself up.

It was not only at Stokesay – I have written the name at last, and I will not efface it – that I lingered a while on the summit of the keep to enjoy the complete impression so overtaken. I spent such another half hour at Ludlow, which is a much grander and more famous monument. Ludlow, however, is a ruin – the most impressive and magnificent of ruins. The charming old town and the admirable castle form a capital object of pilgrimage. Ludlow is an excellent example of a small English provincial town that has not been soiled and disfigured by industry; it exhibits no tall chimneys and smoke-streamers, with their attendant purlieus and slums. The little city is perched upon a hill near which the goodly Severn wanders, and it has a remarkable air of civic dignity. Its streets are wide and clean, empty and a little grass-grown, and bordered with spacious, mildly-ornamental brick houses, which look as if there had been more going on in them in the first decade of the century than there is in the present, but which can still, nevertheless, hold up their heads and keep their window-panes clear, their knockers brilliant and their door steps whitened. The place seems to say that a hundred years, and less, ago it was the centre of a large provincial society, and that this society was very "good" of its kind. It must have transported itself to Ludlow for the season in rumbling coaches and heavy curricles – and there entertained itself in decent emulation of that metropolis which a choice of railway lines had not as yet placed within its immediate reach. It had balls at the assembly rooms; it had Mrs. Siddons to play; it had Catalani to sing. Miss Burney's and Miss Austen's heroines might perfectly well have had their first love-affair there; a journey to Ludlow would certainly have been a great event to Fanny Price or Emma Woodhouse, or even to those more exalted young ladies, Evelina and Cecilia. It is a place on which a provincial "gentry" has left a sensible stamp. I have seldom seen so good a collection of houses of the period between the elder picturesqueness and the modern baldness. Such places, such houses, such relics and intimations, always carry me back to the near antiquity of that pre-Victorian

England which it is still easy for a stranger to picture with a certain vividness, thanks to the partial survival of many of its characteristics. It is still easier for a stranger who has stayed a while in England to form an idea of the tone, the habits, the aspect of English social life before its classic insularity had begun to wane, as all observers agree that it did, about thirty years ago. It is true that the mental operation in this matter reduces itself to fancying some of the things which form what Mr. Matthew Arnold would call the peculiar "notes" of England infinitely exaggerated – the rigidly aristocratic constitution of society, for instance; the unæsthetic temper of the people; the private character of most kinds of comfort and entertainment. Let an old gentleman of conservative tastes, who can remember the century's youth, talk to you at a club *temporis acti* – tell you wherein it is that from his own point of view London, as a residence for a gentleman, has done nothing but fall off for the last forty years. You will listen, of course, with an air of decent sympathy, but privately you will say to yourself how difficult a place of sojourn London must have been in those days for a stranger – how little cosmopolitan, how bound in a thousand ways, with narrowness of custom. What is true of the metropolis at that time is of course doubly true of the provinces; and a genteel little city like the one I am speaking of must have been a kind of focus of insular propriety. Even then, however, the irritated alien would have had the magnificent ruins of the castle to dream himself back into good humour in. They would effectually have transported him beyond all waning or waxing Philistinisms.

XIV.

ENGLISH VIGNETTES.

1879.

I.

Toward the last of April, in Monmouthshire, the primroses were as big as your fist. I say "in Monmouthshire", because I believe that a certain grassy mountain which I gave myself the pleasure of climbing, and to which I took my way across the charming country, through lanes where the hedges were perched upon blooming banks, lay within the borders of this ancient province. It was the festive Eastertide, and a pretext for leaving London had not been wanting. Of course it rained, – it rained a good deal, – for man and the weather are usually at cross-purposes. But there were intervals of light and warmth, and in England a couple of hours of fine weather, islanded in moisture, assert their independence and leave an uncompromised memory. These bright episodes were even of longer duration; that whole morning, for instance, on which, with a companion, I scrambled up the little Skirrid. One had a feeling that one was very far from London; as, in fact, one was, after six or seven hours in a smooth, swift English train. In England this is a great remoteness; it seemed to justify the half-reluctant confession which I heard constantly made, that the country was extremely "wild". There is wildness and wildness, I thought; and though I had not been a great explorer, I compared this rough district with several neighbourhoods in another part of the world that passed for tame. I went even so far as to wish that some of its ruder features might be transplanted to that relatively unregulated landscape and commingled with its suburban savagery. I went over the elements of this English prospect and of human life in the midst of it, and wondered whether, if I were to enumerate them and leave them to be added up by the dwellers beyond the sea, the total would be set down as a wilderness. We were close to the Welsh border, and a dozen little mountains in the distance were peeping over each other's shoulders. But nature was open to the charge of no worse disorder than this. The Skirrid (I like to repeat the name) wore, it is true, at a distance, the aspect of a magnified extinguisher; but when, after a bright, breezy walk through lane and meadow, we had scrambled over the last of the thickly-flowering hedges which lay around its shoulders like loosened strings of coral and began to ascend the grassy cone (very much in the attitude of Nebuchadnezzar), it proved as smooth-faced as a garden-mound. Hard by, on the flanks of other hills, were troops of browsing sheep, and the only thing in which there was any harshness of suggestion was the strong, damp wind. But even this had a good deal of softness in it, and ministered to my sense of the agreeable in scenery by the way it blew about the pearly morning mists that were airing themselves upon neighbouring ridges, and kept shaking the vaporous veil that fluttered down in the valley over the picturesque little town of Abergavenny. A breezy, grassy English hill-top, looking down on a country full of suggestive names and ancient memories, belongs (especially if you are exhilarated by a beautiful walk, and you have a flask in your pocket) decidedly to the category of smooth scenery. And so with all the rest of it.

On Sunday I stayed away from church, because I learned that the sacred edifice had a mediæval chill, and that if I should sit there for a couple of hours I might inherit a lumbago three hundred years old. The fact was formidable, but the idea was, in a certain way, attractive; there was nothing crude in a rheumatism which descended from the Norman times. Practical considerations, however, determined me not to expose myself to this venerable pain; so in the still hours, when the roads and lanes were empty, I simply walked to the churchyard and sat upon one of the sun-warmed gravestones. I say the roads were empty, but they were peopled with the big primroses I just now spoke of – primroses of the size of ripe apples, and yet, in spite of their rank-growth, of as pale and tender a yellow as if their gold had been diluted with silver. It was indeed a mixture of gold and silver, for there was a wealth of the white wood-anemone as well, and these delicate flowers, each of so perfect a coinage, were tumbled along the green wayside as if a prince had been scattering largesse. The outside of an old English country-church in service-time is a very pleasant place; and this is as near as I often care to approach to the celebration of the Anglican mysteries. A just sufficient sense of their august character may be gathered from that vague sound of village-music which makes its way out into the stillness, and from the perusal of those portions of the Prayer-Book which are inscribed upon mouldering slabs and dislocated headstones. The church I speak of was a beautiful specimen of its kind – intensely aged, variously patched, but still solid and useful, and with no touch of restoration. It was very big and massive, and, hidden away in the fields, it had a kind of lonely grandeur; there was nothing in particular near it but its out-of-the-world little parsonage. It was only one of ten thousand; I had seen a hundred such before. But I watched the watery sunshine upon the rugosities of its ancient masonry; I stood a while in the shade of two or three spreading yews which stretched their black arms over graves decorated for Easter, according to the custom of that country, with garlands of primrose and dog-violet; and I reflected that in a wild region it was a blessing to have so quiet a place of refuge as that.

Later, I chanced upon a couple of other asylums which were more spacious and no less tranquil. Both of them were old country-houses, and each in its way was charming. One was a half-modernised feudal dwelling, lying in a wooded hollow – a large concavity filled with a delightful old park. The house had a long gray façade and half a dozen towers, and the usual supply of ivy and of clustered chimneys relieved against a background of rook-haunted elms. But the windows were all closed and the avenue was untrodden; the house was the property of a lady who could not afford to live in it in becoming state, and who had let it, furnished, to a rich young man "for the shooting". The rich young man occupied it but for three weeks in the year, and for the rest of the time left it a prey to the hungry gaze of the passing stranger, the would-be redresser of æsthetic wrongs. It seemed a great æsthetic wrong that so charming a place should not be a conscious, sentient home. But in England all this is very common. It takes a great many plain people to keep a gentleman going; it takes a great deal of wasted sweetness to make up a property. It is true that, in the other case I speak of, the sweetness, which here was even greater, was less sensibly squandered. If there was no one else in the house, at least there were ghosts. It had a dark red front and grim-looking gables; it was perched upon a sort of terrace, quite high in the air, which was reached by steep, crooked, mossy steps. Beneath these steps was an ancient bit of garden, and from the hither side of the garden stretched a great expanse of turf. Out of the midst of the turf sprang a magnificent avenue of Scotch firs – a perfect imitation of the Italian stone-pine. It looked like the Villa Borghese transplanted to the Welsh hills. The huge, smooth stems, in their double row, were crowned with dark parasols. In the Scotch fir or the Italian pine there is always an element of grotesqueness; the open umbrella in a rainy country is not a poetical analogy, and the case is not better if you compare the tree to a colossal mushroom. But, without analogies, there was something very striking in the effect of this enormous, rigid vista, and in the grassy carpet of the avenue, with the dusky, lonely, high-featured house looking down upon it. There was something solemn and tragical; the place was made to the hand of a romancer, and he might have found his characters within; the leaden lattices were open.

II.

The Isle of Wight is disappointing at first. I wondered why it should be, and then I found the reason in the influence of the detestable little railway. There can be no doubt that a railway in the Isle of Wight is a gross impertinence; it is in evident contravention to the natural style of the place. The place is minutely, delicately picturesque, or it is nothing at all. It is purely ornamental; it exists for the entertainment of tourists. It is separated by nature from the dense railway-system of the less diminutive island, and it is the corner of the world where a good carriage-road is most in keeping. Never was there a better place for sacrificing to prettiness; never was there a better chance for not making a railway. But now there are twenty trains a day, and the prettiness is twenty times less. The island is so small that the hideous embankments and tunnels are obtrusive; the sight of them is as painful as it would be to see a pedlar's pack on the shoulders of a pretty woman. This is your first impression as you travel (naturally by the objectionable conveyance) from Ryde to Ventnor; and the fact that the train rumbles along very smoothly, and stops at half a dozen little stations, where the groups on the platform enable you to perceive that the population consists almost exclusively of gentlemen in costumes suggestive of unlimited leisure for attention to cravats and trousers (an immensely large class in England), of old ladies of the species denominated in France *rentières*, of young ladies of the highly-educated and sketching variety, this circumstance fails to reconcile you to the chartered cicatrix which forms your course. At Ventnor, however, face to face with the sea, and with the blooming shoulder of the Undercliff close behind you, you lose sight to a certain extent of the superfluities of civilisation. Not, indeed, that Ventnor has not been diligently civilised. It is a well-regulated little watering-place, and it has been subjected to a due measure of cockneyfication. But the glittering ocean remains, shimmering at moments with blue and silver, and the large gorse-covered downs rise superbly above it. Ventnor hangs upon the side of a steep hill, and here and there it climbs and scrambles, it is propped and terraced, like one of the bright-faced little towns that look down upon the Mediterranean. To add to the Italian effect, the houses are all denominated villas, though it must be added that nothing is less like an Italian villa than an English one. Those which ornament the successive ledges at Ventnor are for the most part small semi-detached boxes, predestined, even before they had fairly come into the world, to the entertainment of lodgers. They stand in serried rows all over the place, with the finest names in the British *Peerage* painted upon their gate-posts. Their severe similarity of aspect, however, is such that even the difference between Plantagenet and Percival, between Montgomery and Montmorency, is hardly sufficient to enlighten the puzzled visitor. An English watering-place is much more comfortable than an American; in a Plantagenet villa the art of receiving "summer guests" has usually been brought to a higher perfection than in an American rural hotel. But what strikes an American, with regard to even so charmingly-nestled a little town as Ventnor, is that it is far less natural, less pastoral and bosky, than his own fond image of a summer-retreat. There is too much brick and mortar; there are too many smoking chimneys and shops and public-houses; there are no woods nor brooks, nor lonely headlands; there is none of the virginal stillness of Nature. Instead of these things, there is an esplanade, mostly paved with asphalt, bordered with benches and little shops, and provided with a German band. To be just to Ventnor, however, I must hasten to add that once you get away from the asphalt there is a great deal of vegetation. The little village of Bonchurch, which closely adjoins it, is buried in the most elaborate verdure, muffled in the smoothest lawns and the densest shrubbery. Bonchurch is simply delicious, and indeed in a manner quite absurd. It is like a model village in imitative substances, kept in a glass case; the turf might be of green velvet and the foliage of cut paper. The villagers are all happy gentlefolk, the cottages have plate-glass windows, and the rose-trees on their walls are tended by an under-gardener. Passing from Ventnor through the elegant umbrage of Bonchurch, and keeping along the coast toward Shanklin, you come to the prettiest part of the Undercliff, or, in other words, to the prettiest place in the world. The immense grassy cliffs which form the coast of the island make what the French would call a "false descent" to the sea. At a certain point the descent is broken, and a wide natural terrace, all overtangled with wild shrubs and flowers, hangs there in mid-air, half-way above the ocean. It is impossible to imagine anything more charming than this long, blooming platform, protected from the north by huge green bluffs and plunging on the other side into the murmuring tides. This delightful arrangement constitutes for a distance of some fifteen miles the south shore of the Isle of Wight; but the best of it, as I have said, is to be found in the four or five miles that separate Ventnor from Shanklin. Of a lovely afternoon in April these four or five miles are an enchanting walk.

Of course you must first catch your lovely afternoon. I caught one; in fact, I caught two. On the second I climbed up the downs, and perceived that it was possible to put their gorse-covered stretches to still other than pedestrian uses – to devote them to sedentary pleasures. A long lounge in the lee of a stone wall, the lingering, fading afternoon light, the reddening sky, the band of blue sea above the level-topped bunches of gorse – these things, enjoyed as an undertone to the conversation of an amiable compatriot, seemed indeed a very sufficient substitute for that primitive stillness of the absence of which I ventured just now to complain.

III.

It was probably a mistake to stop at Portsmouth. I had done so, however, in obedience to a familiar theory that seaport-towns abound in local colour, in curious types, in the quaint and the strange. But these charms, it must be confessed, were signally wanting to Portsmouth, along whose sordid streets I strolled for an hour, vainly glancing about me for an over-hanging façade or a group of Maltese sailors. I was distressed to perceive that a famous seaport could be at once untidy and prosaic. Portsmouth is dirty, but it is also dull. It may be roughly divided into the dock-yard and the public-houses. The dock-yard, into which I was unable to penetrate, is a colossal enclosure, signalised externally by a grim brick wall, as featureless as an empty blackboard. The dockyard eats up the town, as it were, and there is nothing left over but the gin-shops, which the town drinks up. There is not even a crooked old quay of any consequence, with brightly patched houses looking out upon a forest of masts. To begin with, there are no masts; and then there are no polyglot sign-boards, no over-hanging upper stories, no outlandish parrots and macaws perched in open lattices. I had another hour or so before my train departed, and it would have gone hard with me if I had not bethought myself of hiring a boat and being pulled about in the harbour. Here a certain amount of entertainment was to be found. There were great iron-clads, and white troopships that looked vague and spectral, like the floating home of the Flying Dutchman, and small, devilish vessels whose mission was to project the infernal torpedo. I coasted about these metallic islets; and then, to eke out my entertainment, I boarded the *Victory*. The *Victory* is an ancient frigate of enor-mous size, which in the days of her glory carried I know not how many hundred guns, but whose only function now is to stand year after year in Portsmouth waters and exhibit herself to the festive cockney. Bank-holiday is now her great date; once upon a time it was Trafalgar. The *Victory*, in short, was Nelson's ship; it was on her huge deck that he was struck and in her deep bowels he breathed his last. The venerable vessel is provided with a company of ushers, like the Tower of London or Westminster Abbey, and it is hardly less solid and spacious than either of those edifices. A good man in uniform did me the honours of the ship with a terrible displacement of *h*'s, and there seemed something strange in the way it had lapsed from its heroic part. It had carried two hundred guns and a mighty warrior, and boomed against the enemies of England; it had been the scene of one of the most thrilling and touching events in English history. Now, it was hardly more than a mere source of income to the Portsmouth watermen – an objective point for Whitsuntide excursionists – a thing that a foreign observer must allude to very casually, for fear of seeming vulgar, or even serious.

IV.

But I recouped myself, as they say in England, by stopping afterwards at Chichester. In this dense and various old England two places may be very near together and yet strike a very different note. I knew in a general way that there was a cathedral at Chichester; indeed, I had seen its beautiful spire from the window of the train. I had always regarded an afternoon in a little cathedral-town as a high order of entertainment, and a morning at Portsmouth had left me in the mood for not missing such an exhibition. The spire of Chichester at a little distance geatly resembles that of Salisbury. It is on a smaller scale, but it tapers upward with a delicate slimness which, like that of its famous rival, makes a picture of the level landscape in which it stands. Unlike the spire of Salisbury, however, it has not at present the charm of antiquity. A few years ago the old steeple collapsed and tumbled into the church, and the present structure is but a modern facsimile. The cathedral is not of the highest interest; it is rather plain and bare, and, except a curious old detached bell-tower which stands beside it, has no particular element of unexpectedness. But an English cathedral of restricted grandeur may yet be a very charming affair; and I spent an hour or so lounging around this highly respectable edifice, without the spell of contemplation being broken by satiety. I approached it, from the station, by the usual quiet red-brick street of the usual cathedral town – a street of small, excellent shops, before which, here and there, one of the vehicles of the neighbouring gentry was drawn up beside the curbstone, while the grocer or the bookseller, who had hurried out obsequiously, was waiting upon the comfortable occupant. I went into a bookseller's to buy a Chichester guide, which I perceived in the window; I found the shopkeeper talking to a young curate in a soft hat. The guide seemed very desirable, though it appeared to have been but scantily desired; it had been published in the year 1841, and a very large remnant of the edition, with a muslin back and a little white label and paper-covered boards, was piled up on the counter. It was dedicated, with terrible humility, to the Duke of Richmond, and ornamented with primitive woodcuts and steel plates; the ink had turned brown and the page musty; and the style itself – that of a provincial antiquary of upwards of forty years ago penetrated with the grandeur of the aristocracy – had grown rather sallow and stale. Nothing could have been more mellifluous and urbane than the young curate: he was arranging to have the *Times* newspaper sent him every morning for perusal. "So it will be a penny if it is fetched away at noon?" he said, smiling very sweetly and with the most gentlemanly voice possible; "and it will be three halfpence if it is fetched away at four o'clock?" At the top of the street, into which, with my guide-book, I relapsed, was an old market-cross, of the fifteenth century – a florid, romantic little structure. It consists of a stone pavilion, with open sides and a number of pinnacles and crockets and buttresses, besides a goodly medallion of the high-nosed visage of Charles I, which was placed above one of the arches, at the Restoration, in compensation for the violent havoc wrought upon the little town by the Parliamentary soldiers, who had wrested the place from the Royalists, and who amused themselves, in their grim fashion, with infinite hacking and hewing in the cathedral. Here, to the left, the cathedral discloses itself, lifting its smart gray steeple out of a pleasant garden. Opposite to the garden was the Dolphin or the Dragon – in fine, the most eligible inn. I must confess that for a time it divided my attention with the cathedral, in virtue of an ancient, musty parlour on the second floor, with hunting-pictures hung above haircloth sofas; of a red-faced waiter, in evening dress; of a big round of cold beef and a tankard of ale. The prettiest thing at Chichester is a charming little three-sided cloister, attached to the cathedral, where, as is usual in such places, you may sit upon a gravestone amid the deep grass in the middle, and measure the great central mass of the church – the large gray sides, the high foundations of the spire, the parting of the nave and transept. From this point the greatness of a cathedral seems more complex and impressive. You watch the big shadows slowly change their relations; you listen to the cawing of rooks and the twittering of swallows; you hear a slow footstep echoing in the cloisters.

V.

If Oxford were not the finest thing in England, Cambridge would certainly be. Cambridge was so, for that matter, to my imagination, for thirty-six hours. To the barbaric mind, ambitious of culture, Oxford is the usual image of the happy reconciliation between research and acceptance. It typifies, to an American, the union of science and sense – of aspiration and ease. A German university gives a greater impression of science, and an English country-house or an Italian villa a greater impression of idle enjoyment; but in these cases, on one side, knowledge is too rugged, and on the other, satisfaction is too trivial. Oxford lends sweetness to labour and dignity to leisure. When I say Oxford, I mean Cambridge, for a barbarian is not in the least obliged to know the difference, and it suddenly strikes me as being both very pedantic and very good-natured in him to pretend to know it. What insti-

tution is more majestic than Trinity College? what can be more
touching to an American than the hospitality of such an institution? The first quadrangle is of immense extent, and the
buildings that surround it, with their long, rich fronts of time-
deepened gray, are the stateliest in the world. In the centre of
the court are two or three acres of close-shaven lawn, in the
midst of which rises a splendid gothic fountain, where the
serving-men fill up their buckets. There are towers and battlements and statues, and besides these things there are cloisters
and gardens and bridges. There are charming rooms in a kind
of stately gate-tower, and the rooms, occupying the thickness
of the building, have windows looking out on one side over
the magnificent quadrangle, with half a mile or so of
Decorated architecture, and on the other into deep-bosomed
trees. And in the rooms is the best company conceivable – dis-
tintguished men who are remarkably good fellows. I spent a
beautiful Sunday morning walking about Cambridge, with one
of these gentlemen, and attempting as the French say, to
débrouiller its charms. These are a very complicated affair, and
I do not pretend, in memory, to keep the colleges apart. There
are, however, half a dozen points that make ineffaceable pictures. Six or eight of the colleges stand in a row, turning their
backs to the river; and hereupon ensues the loveliest confusion
of gothic windows and ancient trees, of grassy banks and
mossy balustrades, of sun-chequered avenues and groves, of
lawns and gardens and terraces, of single-arched bridges span-
ning the little stream, which is small and shallow, and looks as
if it had been "turned on" for ornamental purposes. The
scantily-flowing Cam appears to exist simply as an occasion
for these enchanting little bridges – the beautiful covered
gallery of John's or the slightly-collapsing arch of Clare. In the
way of college-courts and quiet scholastic porticoes, of gray-
walled gardens and ivied nooks of study, in all the pictorial

accidents of a great English university, Cambridge is delightfully and inexhaustibly rich. I looked at these one by one, and
said to myself always that the last was the best. If I were called
upon, however, to mention the prettiest corner of the world,
I should heave a tender sigh and point the way to the garden
of Trinity Hall. My companion, who was very competent to
judge (but who spoke, indeed, with the partiality of a son of
the house), declared, as he ushered me into it, that it was, to
his mind, the most beautiful *small* garden in Europe. I freely
accepted, and I promptly repeat, an affirmation so ingeniously
conditioned. The little garden at Trinity Hall is narrow and
crooked; it leans upon the river, from which a low parapet, all
muffled in ivy, divides it; it has an ancient wall, adorned with
a thousand matted creepers on one side, and on the other a
group of extraordinary horse-chestnuts. These trees are of
prodigious size; they occupy half the garden, and they are
remarkable for the fact that their giant limbs strike down into
the earth, take root again, and emulate, as they rise, the
majesty of the parent tree. The manner in which this magnificent group of horse-chestnuts sprawls about over the grass,
out into the middle of the lawn, is one of the most picturesque
features of the garden of Trinity Hall. Of course the single
object at Cambridge that makes the most abiding impression
is the famous chapel of King's College – the most beautiful
chapel in England. The effect it attempts to produce within
belongs to the order of sublimity. The attempt succeeds, and
the success is attained by means so light and elegant that at
first it almost defeats itself. The sublime usually has more of a
frown and straddle, and it is not until after you have looked
about you for ten minutes that you perceive that the chapel is
saved from being the prettiest church in England by the accident of its being one of the noblest. It is a cathedral without
aisles or columns or transepts, but (as a compensation) with

such a beautiful slimness of clustered tracery soaring along the walls, and spreading, bending and commingling in the roof, that its simplicity seems only a richness the more. I stood there for a quarter of an hour on a Sunday morning; there was no service, but in the choir behind the great screen which divides the chapel in half, the young choristers were rehearsing for the afternoon. The beautiful boy-voices rose together and touched the splendid vault; they hung there, expanding and resounding, and then, like a rocket that spends itself, they faded and melted toward the end of the building. The sound was angelic.

VI.

Cambridgeshire is one of the so-called ugly counties; which means that it is observably flat. It is for this reason that Newmarket is, in its own peculiar fashion, so thriving a locality. The country is like a board of green cloth, the turf presents itself as a friendly provision of nature. Nature offers her gentle bosom as a gaming-table; card-tables, billiard-tables are but a humble imitation of Newmarket Heath. It was odd to think that amid this gentle, pastoral scenery, there is more betting than anywhere else in the world. The large, neat English meadows roll away to a humid-looking sky, the young partridges jump about in the hedges, and nature does not look in the least as if she were offering you odds. The gentlemen do, though – the gentlemen whom you meet on the roads and in the railway carriage; they have that indefinable look – it pervades a man from the cut of his whisker to the shape of his boot-toe – which denotes a familiarity with the turf. It is brought home to you that to an immense number of people in England the events in the *Racing Calendar* constitute the most important portion of contemporary history. The very air about Newmarket appears to contain a vague echo of stable-talk, and you perceive that this is the landscape depicted in those large coloured prints of the "sporting" genus which you have admired in inn-parlours.

The destruction of partridges is, if an equally classical, a less licentious pursuit, for which, I believe, Cambridgeshire offers peculiar facilities. Among these is a certain shooting-box, which is a triumph of accidental picturesqueness (the highest order) and a temple of delicate hospitality. The shooting belongs to the autumn, not to this vernal period; but as I have spoken of echoes, I suppose that if I had listened attentively I might have heard the ghostly crack of some of the famous shots that have been discharged there. The air, I believe, had vibrated to several august rifles, but all that I happened to hear by listening was some excellent talk.

In England, I said just now, a couple of places may be very near together, and yet have what the philosophers call a con-notation strangely different. Only a few miles beyond Newmarket lies Bury St. Edmunds, a town whose tranquil antiquity makes horse-racing, and even partridge-shooting, appear a restless and fidgety mode of passing the time. I con-fess that I went to Bury St. Edmunds simply on the strength of its name, which I had often encountered, and which had always seemed to me to have a high value for the tourist. I knew that St. Edmund had been an Anglo-Saxon worthy, but my conviction that the little town that bore his name would afford entertainment between trains had nothing definite to rest upon. The event, however, rewarded my faith – rewarded it with the sight of a magnificent old gatehouse of the thir-teenth century, the most substantial of many relics of the great abbey which once flourished there. There are many others; they are scattered about the old precinct of the abbey, a large portion of which has been converted into a rambling botanic garden, the resort at Whitsuntide of a thousand very modern merrymakers. The monument I speak of has the proportions of a triumphal arch; it is at once a gateway and a fortress; it is covered with beautiful ornament, and is altogether the lion of Bury.

XV.

AN ENGLISH NEW YEAR.

1879.

It will hardly be pretended this year that the English Christmas has been a merry one, or that the New Year has the promise of being particularly happy. The winter is proving very cold and vicious – as if nature herself were loath to be left out of the general conspiracy against the comfort and self-complacency of man. The country at large has a sense of embarrassment and depression, which is brought home more or less to every class in the closely-graduated social hierarchy, and the light of Christmas firesides has by no means dispelled the gloom. Not that I mean to overstate the gloom. It is difficult to imagine any combination of adverse circumstances powerful enough to infringe very sensibly upon the appearance of activity and prosperity, social stability and luxury, which English life must always present to a stranger. Nevertheless, the times are distinctly hard – there is plenty of evidence of it – and the spirits of the public are not high. The depression of business is extreme and universal; I am ignorant whether it has reached so calamitous a point as that almost hopeless prostration of every industry which you have lately witnessed in America, and I believe things are by no means so bad as they have been on two or three occasions within the present century. The possibility of distress among the lower classes has been minimised by the gigantic poor-relief system, which is so characteristic a feature of English civilisation, and which on particular occasions is supplemented (as is the case at present) by private charity proportionately huge. I notice, too, that in some parts of the country discriminating groups of work-people have selected these dismal days as a happy time for striking. When the labouring classes are able to indulge in the luxury of a strike I suppose the situation may be said to have its cheerful side. There is, however, great distress in the North, and there is a general feeling of impecuniosity throughout the country. The *Daily News* has sent a correspondent to the great industrial regions, and almost every morning for the last three weeks a very cleverly-executed picture of the misery of certain parts of Yorkshire and Lancashire has been served up with the matutinal tea and toast. The work is a good one and, I take it, eminently worth doing, as it appears to have had a visible effect upon the purse-strings of the well-to-do. There is nothing more striking in England than the success with which an "appeal" is always made. Whatever the season or whatever the cause, there always appears to be enough money and enough benevolence in the country to respond to it in sufficient measure – a remarkable fact when one remembers that there is never a moment of the year when the custom of "appealing" intermits. Equally striking, perhaps, is the perfection to which the science of distributing charity has been raised – the way it has been analysed and explored and made one of the exact sciences. One perceives that it has occupied for a long time a foremost place among administrative questions, and has received all the light that experience and practice can throw upon it. The journal I quoted just now may perhaps, without reproach, be credited with a political *arrière-pensée*. It would obviously like its readers to supply in this matter of the stagnation of trade the missing link between effect and cause – or the link which, if not absolutely missing, is at any rate difficult to lay one's hand upon. The majority in Parliament were not apparently of the opinion that the disorganisation of business is the fault of Lord Beaconsfield; but there is no doubt that it is a misfortune for the Conservative party that this bad state of things coincides very much with its tenure of office. When an Administration may be invidiously described as "restless", "reckless", and "adventurous", and when at the same time business is very bad and distress increasing, it requires no great ingenuity to represent the former fact as responsible for the latter.

I have spoken of the rigour of the time in the lower walks of English life; and it is not out of place to say that among those happier people who stand above the reach of material incommodity, the Christmas season has been overshadowed sentimentally – or at least conventionally – by the death of Princess Alice. If I had written to you at the moment this event occurred I should have been tempted to make some general reflections upon it, and it is even now perhaps not too late to say that there was, to an observer, something very interesting and characteristic in the manner in which the news was received. Broadly speaking, it produced much more commotion than I should have expected; the papers overflowed with articles on the subject, the virtues of the deceased lady and the grief of the Queen were elaborately commemorated; many shops, on the day of the Princess's funeral, were partially closed, and the whole nation, it may be said – or the whole of what professes, in any degree whatever, to be "society" – went into mourning. There was enough in all this to make a stranger consider and interrogate; and the result of his reflections would, I think, have been that, after all abatements are made, the monarchy has still a great hold upon the affections of the people. The people takes great comfort in its royal family. The love of social greatness is extraordinarily strong in

England, and the royal family appeals very conveniently to this sentiment. People in the immense obscurity of that middle class which constitutes the bulk of the English world like to feel that they are related in some degree to something that is socially great. They cannot pretend that they are related to dukes and earls and people of that sort; but they are able to cultivate a certain sense of being related to the royal family. They may talk of "our" princes and princesses – and the most exalted members of the peerage may do no more than that; they may possess photographs of the Queen's children, and read of their daily comings and goings with an agreeable sense of property, and without incurring that reproach of snobbishness which sometimes attaches to too eager an interest in the doings of the great nobility. There is no reason to suppose that the Queen takes the humorous view of this situation; her Majesty is indeed credited with a comfortable, motherly confidence in the salutary effect of the court-circle upon the mind of the middle class; and there is a kind of general feeling that, socially speaking, the Queen and the middle class understand each other. There was something natural, therefore, in the great impression made by the death of a princess who was personally known but to an incalculably small proportion of the people who mourned for her, and on whose behalf propriety would have resented the idea that she could personally be missed. It is nevertheless true that Lord Beaconsfield is felt rather to have overdone his part in announcing the event to the House of Lords in language in which he might have proclaimed some great national catastrophe. I was told by a person who was present that the House felt itself to be at the mercy of his bad taste – that men looked at each other with a blush and a kind of shudder, and asked each other what was coming next. He remarked, among other things, that the manner in which the Princess Alice had contracted her fatal illness (her tender imprudence in kissing her sick children) was an act worthy to be commemorated in art – "in painting, in sculpture, and in gems." I have heard these last two words wittily quoted in illustration of his Semitic origin. An ordinarily florid speaker would have contented himself with saying "in painting and in sculpture." The addition "in gems" betrays the genius of the race which supplies the world with pawnbrokers.

I left town a short time before Christmas and went to spend the festive season in the North, in a part of the country with which I was unacquainted. It was quite possible to absent one's self from London without a sense of sacrifice, for the charms of the metropolis during the last several weeks have been obscured by peculiarly atrocious weather. It is, of course, a very old story that London is foggy, and this simple statement is not of necessity alarming. But there are fogs and fogs, and these murky visitations, during the present winter, have been of the least tolerable sort. The fog that draws down and absorbs the smoke of the housetops, causes it to hang about the streets in impenetrable density, forces it into one's eyes and down one's throat, so that one is half-blinded and quite sickened – this atmospheric abomination has been much more frequent than usual. Just before Christmas, too, there was a heavy snow-storm, and even a tolerably light fall of snow has London quite at its mercy. The emblem of purity is almost immediately converted into a sticky, lead-coloured mush, the cabs skulk out of sight or take up their stations before the lurid windows of a public-house, which glares through the sleety darkness at the desperate wayfarer with an air of vulgar bravado. This state of things in the London streets made a rather sorry Christmas, though I believe the Christmas hearth is supposed to burn the more brightly in proportion as the outer world is less attractive. The wonderful London shops were, of course, duly transfigured, but they seemed to me, for the most part, to have an aspect of vain expectation, and I hear that their proprietors give a melancholy account of the profits of the season. It was only at a certain charming little French establishment in Bond Street that I observed any great activity – a little chocolate-shop where light-fingered young women from Paris dispense the most wonderful bonbonnières.

To keep one's self in good humour with English civilisation, however, one must do what I alluded to just now – one must go into the country; one must limit one's horizon, for the time, to the spacious walls of one of those admirable homes which at this season overflow with hospitality and good cheer. By this means the result is triumphantly attained – these are conditions that you cordially appreciate. Of all the great things that the English have invented and made a part of the glory of the national character, the most perfect, the most characteristic, the one they have mastered most completely in all its details, so that it has become a compendious illustration of their social genius and their manners, is the well-appointed, well-administered, well-filled country-house. The grateful stranger makes these reflections – and others besides – as he wanders about in the beautiful library of such a dwelling of an inclement winter afternoon just at the hour when six o'clock tea is impending. Such a place and such a time abound in agreeable episodes; but I suspect that the episode from which, a fortnight ago, I received the most ineffaceable impression was but indirectly connected with the charms of a luxurious fireside. The country I speak of was a populous manufacturing region, full of tall chimneys and of an air that is gray and gritty. A lady had made a present of a Christmas-tree to the children of a workhouse, and she invited me to go with her and assist at the distribution of the toys. There was a drive through the early dusk of a very cold Christmas eve, followed by the drawing-up of a lamp-lit brougham in the snowy quadrangle of a grim-looking charitable institution. I had never been in an English workhouse before, and this one transported me, with the aid of memory, to the early pages of *Oliver Twist*. We passed through certain cold, bleak passages, to which an odour of suet-pudding, the aroma of Christmas cheer, failed to impart an air of hospitality; and then, after waiting a while in a little parlour appertaining to the superintendent, where the remainder of a dinner of by no means eleemosynary sim- plicity and the attitude of a gentleman asleep with a flushed face on the sofa seemed to effect a tacit exchange of refer- ences, we were ushered into a large frigid refectory, chiefly illumined by the twinkling tapers of the Christmas-tree. Here entered to us some hundred and fifty little children of charity, who had been making a copious dinner, and who brought with them an atmosphere of hunger memorably satisfied – together with other traces of the occasion upon their pinafores and their small red faces. I have said that the place reminded me of *Oliver Twist*, and I glanced through this little herd for an infant figure that should look as if it were cut out for romantic adventures. But they were all very prosaic little mor- tals. They were made of very common clay indeed, and a certain number of them were idiotic. They filed up and received their little offerings, and then they compressed them- selves into a tight infantine bunch, and lifting up their small hoarse voices, directed a melancholy hymn toward their bene- factress. The scene was a picture I shall not forget, with its curious mixture of poetry and sordid prose – the dying wintry light in the big, bare, stale room; the beautiful Lady Bountiful, standing in the twinkling glory of the Christmas-tree; the little multitude of staring and wondering, yet perfectly expression- less, faces.

XVI.

AN ENGLISH WINTER
WATERING-PLACE.

1879.

I have just been spending a couple of days at a well-known resort upon the Kentish coast, and though such an exploit is by no means unprecedented, yet, as to the truly observing mind no opportunity is altogether void and no impressions are wholly valueless, I have it on my conscience to make a note of my excursion. Superficially speaking, it was certainly wanting in originality; but I am afraid that it afforded me as much entertainment as if the idea of paying a visit to Hastings had been an invention of my own. This is so far from being the case that the most striking feature of the town in question is the immense provision made there for the entertainment of visitors. Hastings and St. Leonard's, standing side by side, present a united sea-front of more miles in length than I shall venture to compute. It is sufficient that in going from one end of the place to the other I had a greater sense of having taken a long, straight walk, than I had done since I last measured the remarkable length of Broadway. This is not a strikingly picturesque image, and it must be confessed that the beauty of Hastings does not reside in a soft irregularity or a rural exuberance. Like all the larger English watering-places it is simply a little London *super mare*. The pictorial is always to be found in England if one will take the trouble of looking for it; but it

must be conceded that at Hastings this element is less obtrusive than it might be. I had heard it described as a "dull
Brighton", and this description had been intended to dispose
of the place. In fact, however – such is the perversity of the
inquiring mind – it had rather quickened than quenched my
interest. It occurred to me that it might be entertaining to
follow out the variations and modifications of Brighton. Four
or five miles of lodging-houses and hotels staring at the sea
across a "parade" adorned with iron benches, with hand-
organs and German bands, with nursemaids and British
babies, with ladies and gentleman of leisure – looking rather
embarrassed with it, and trying, rather unsuccessfully, to get
rid of it – this is the great feature which Brighton and Hastings
have in common. At Brighton there is a certain variety and
gaiety of colour – something suggesting crookedness and
yellow paint – which gives the place a kind of cheerful, easy,
more or less vulgar, foreign air. But Hastings is very gray and
sober and English, and, indeed, it is because it seemed to me
so English that I gave my best attention to it. If one is
attempting to gather impressions of a people and to learn to
know them, everything is interesting that is characteristic,
quite apart from its being beautiful. English manners are made
up of such a multitude of small details that the portrait a
stranger has privately sketched in is always liable to receive
new touches. And this, indeed, is the explanation of his noting
a great many small points, on the spot, with a degree of relish
and appreciation which must often, to persons who are not in
his position, appear exaggerated. He has formed a mental picture of the civilisation of the people he lives among, and
whom, when he has a great deal of courage, he makes bold to
say he is "studying"; he has drawn-up a kind of tabular view
of their manners and customs, their idiosyncrasies, their social
institutions, their general features and properties; and when

once he has suspended this rough cartoon in the chambers of his imagination, he finds a great deal of occupation in touching it up and filling it in. Wherever he goes, whatever he sees, he adds a few strokes. That is how I spent my time at Hastings.

I found it, for instance, a question more interesting than it might superficially appear, to choose between the inns – between the Royal Hotel upon the Parade and an ancient hostel – a survival of the posting-days – in a side-street. A friend had described the latter establishment to me as "mellow", and this epithet complicated the problem. The term mellow, as applied to an inn, is the comparative degree of a state of things of which (say) "musty" would be the superlative. If you can seize this tendency in its comparative stage you may do very well indeed; the trouble is that, like all tendencies, it contains, even in its earlier phases, the germs of excess. I thought it very possible that the Swan would be over-ripe; but I thought it equally probable that the Royal would be crude. I could claim a certain acquaintance with "royal" hotels – I knew just how they were constituted. I foresaw the superior young woman sitting at a ledger, in a kind of glass cage, at the bottom of the stairs, and expressing by refined intonations her contempt for a gentleman who should decline to "require" a sitting-room. The functionary whom in America we know and dread as an hotel-clerk belongs in England to the sex which, when need be, has an even more perfect command of the supercilious. Large hotels here are almost always owned and carried on by companies, and the company is represented by a well-shaped female figure belonging to the class whose members are more particularly known as "persons". The chambermaid is a young woman, and the female tourist is a lady; but the occupant of the glass cage, who hands you your key and assigns you your apartment, is designated in the manner I have mentioned. The "person" has various methods of revenging herself for her shadowy position in the social scale, and I think it was from a vague recollection of having on former occasions felt the weight of her embittered spirit that I determined to seek the hospitality of the humbler inn, where it was probable that one who was himself humble would enjoy a certain consideration. In the event, I was rather oppressed by the feather-bed quality of the welcome extended to me at the Swan. Once established there, in a sitting-room (after all), the whole affair was as characteristically English as I could desire.

I have sometimes had occasion to repine at the meagreness and mustiness of the old-fashioned English inn, and to feel that in poetry and in fiction these defects had been culpably glossed over. But I said to myself the other evening that there is a kind of venerable decency even in some of its dingiest idiosyncrasies, and that in an age of vulgarisation one should do justice to an institution which is still more or less of a stronghold of the ancient amenities. It is a satisfaction in moving about the world to be treated as a gentleman, and this gratification appears to be more than, in the light of modern science, a Company can profitably undertake to bestow. I have an old friend, a person of admirably conservative instincts, from whom, a short time since, I borrowed a hint of this kind. This lady had been staying at a small inn in the country, with her daughter; the daughter, whom we shall call Mrs. B., had left the house a few days before the mother. "Did you like the place?" I asked of my friend; "was it comfortable?" "No, it was not comfortable; but I liked it. It was shabby, and I was much overcharged; but it pleased me." "What was the mysterious charm?" "Well, when I was coming away, the landlady – she had cheated me horribly – came to my carriage, and dropped a curtsey, and said: 'My duty to Mrs. B., ma'am.' Que voulez-vous? That pleased me." There was an old waiter at

Hastings who would have been capable of that – an old waiter who had been in the house for forty years, and who was not so much an individual waiter as the very spirit and genius, the incarnation and tradition of waiterhood. He was faded and weary and rheumatic, but he had a sort of mixture of the paternal and the deferential, the philosophic and the punctilious, which seemed but grossly requited by a present of a small coin. I am not fond of jugged hare for dinner, either as a light *entrée* or as a *pièce de résistance*; but this accomplished attendant had the art of presenting you such a dish in a manner that persuaded you, for the time, that it was worthy of your serious consideration. The hare, by the way, before being subjected to the mysterious operation of jugging, might have been seen dangling from a hook in the bar of the inn, together with a choice collection of other viands. You might peruse the bill of fare in an elementary form as you passed in and out of the house, and make up your *menu* for the day by poking with your stick at a juicy-looking steak or a promising fowl. The landlord and his spouse were always on the threshold of the bar, polishing a brass candlestick and paying you their respects; the place was pervaded by an aroma of rum-and-water and of commercial travellers' jokes.

This description, however, is lacking in the element of gentility, and I will not pursue it farther, for I should give a very false impression of Hastings if I were to omit so characteristic a feature. It was, I think, the element of gentility that most impressed me. I know that the word I have just ventured to use is under the ban of contemporary taste; so I may as well say outright that I regard it as indispensable in almost any attempt at portraiture of English manners. It is vain for an observer of such things to pretend to get on without it. One may talk of foreign life indefinitely – of the manners and customs of France, Germany, and Italy – and never feel the need of this suggestive, yet mysteriously discredited, epithet. One may survey the remarkable face of American civilisation without finding occasion to strike this particular note. But in England no circumlocution will serve – the note must be definitely struck. To attempt to speak of an English watering-place in winter and yet pass it over in silence, would be to forfeit all claims to analytic talent. For a stranger, at any rate, the term is invaluable – it is more convenient than I should find easy to say. It is instantly evoked in my mind by long rows of smuttily-plastered houses, with a card inscribed "Apartments" suspended in the window of the ground-floor sitting-room – that portion of the dwelling which is known in lodging-house parlance as "the parlours". Everything, indeed, suggests it – the bath-chairs, drawn up for hire in a melancholy row; the innumerable and excellent shops, adorned with the latest photographs of the royal family and of Mrs. Langtry; the little reading-room and circulating library on the Parade, where the daily papers, neatly arranged, may be perused for a trifling fee, and the novels of the season are stacked away like the honeycombs in an apiary; the long pier, stretching out into the sea, to which you are admitted by the payment of a penny at a wicket, and where you may enjoy the music of an indefatigable band, the enticements of several little stalls for the sale of fancy-work, and the personal presence of good local society. It is only the winking, twinkling, easily-rippling sea that is not genteel. But, really, I was disposed to say at Hastings that if the sea were not genteel, so much the worse for Neptune; for it was the favourable aspect of the great British proprieties and solemnities that struck me. Hastings and St. Leonards, with their long, warm seafront, and their multitude of small, cheap comforts and conveniences, offer a kind of résumé of middle-class English civilisation and of advantages of which it would ill become an American to make light. I don't suppose that life at Hastings is the most exciting or the most gratifying in the world, but it must certainly have its advantages. If I were a quiet old lady of modest income and nice habits – or even a quiet old gentleman of the same pattern – I should certainly go to Hastings. There, amid the little shops and the little libraries, the bathchairs and the German bands, the Parade and the long Pier, with a mild climate, a moderate scale of prices, and the consciousness of a high civilisation, I should enjoy a seclusion which would have nothing primitive or crude.

XVII.

SARATOGA.

1870.

The sentimental tourist makes images in advance; they grow up in his mind by a logic of their own. He finds himself thinking of an unknown, unseen place, as having such and such a shape and figure rather than such another. It assumes in his mind a certain complexion, a certain colour which frequently turns out to be singularly at variance with reality. For some reason or other, I had supposed Saratoga to be buried in a sort of elegant wilderness. I imagined a region of shady forest drives, with a bright, broad-terraced hotel gleaming here and there against a background of mysterious groves and glades. I had made a cruelly small allowance for the stern vulgarities of life – for the shops and sidewalks and loafers, the complex machinery of a city of pleasure. The fault was so wholly my own that it is quite without bitterness that I proceed to affirm that the Saratoga of experience is sadly different from this. I confess, however, that it has always seemed to me that one's visions, on the whole, gain more than they lose by being transmuted into fact. There is an essential indignity in indefiniteness; you cannot allow for accidents and details until you have seen them. They give more to the imagination than they receive from it. I frankly admit, therefore, that the Saratoga of reality is a much more satisfactory place than the all-too-primitive Elysium I had constructed. It is indeed, as I say, immensely different. There is a vast number of brick – nay, of asphalt-sidewalks, a great many shops, and a magnificent array of loafers. But what indeed are you to do at Saratoga – the morning draught having been achieved – unless you loaf? "Que faire en un gîte à moins que l'on ne songe?" Loafers being assumed, of course shops and sidewalks follow. The main avenue of Saratoga does not scruple to call itself Broadway. The untravelled reader may form a very accurate idea of it by recalling as distinctly as possible, not indeed the splendours of that famous thoroughfare, but the secondary charms of the Sixth Avenue. The place has what the French would call the "accent" of the Sixth Avenue. Its two main features are the two monster hotels which stand facing each other along a goodly portion of its course. One, I believe, is considered much better than the other, – less of a monster and more of a refuge, – but in appearance there is little choice between them. Both are immense brick structures, directly on the crowded, noisy street, with vast covered piazzas running along the façade, supported by great iron posts. The piazza of the Union Hotel, I have been repeatedly informed, is the largest "in the world". There are a number of objects in Saratoga, by the way, which in their respective kinds are the finest in the world. One of these is Mr. John Morrissey's casino. I bowed my head submissively to this statement, but privately I thought of the blue Mediterranean, and the little white promontory of Monaco, and the silver-gray verdure of olives, and the view across the outer sea toward the bosky cliffs of Italy. The Congress waters, too, it is well known, are excellent in the superlative degree; this I am perfectly willing to maintain.

The piazzas of these great hotels may very well be the biggest of all piazzas. They have not architectural beauty; but they doubtless serve their purpose – that of affording sitting-space in the open air to an immense number of persons. They are, of course, quite the best places to observe the Saratoga world. In the evening, when the "boarders" have all come forth and seated themselves in groups, or have begun to stroll in (not always, I regret to say, to the sad detriment of the dramatic interest, bisexual) couples, the big heterogeneous scene affords a great deal of entertainment. Seeing it for the first time, the observer is likely to assure himself that he has neglected an important item in the sum of American manners. The rough brick wall of the house, illumined by a line of flaring gas-lights, forms a natural background to the crude, impermanent, discordant tone of the assembly. In the larger of the two hotels, a series of long windows open into an immense parlour – the largest, I suppose, in the world, and the most scantily furnished in proportion to its size. A few dozen rocking chairs, an equal number of small tables, tripods to the eternal ice-pitcher, serve chiefly to emphasise the vacuous grandeur of the spot. On the piazza, in the outer multitude, ladies largely prevail, both by numbers and (you are not slow to perceive) by distinction of appearance. The good old times of Saratoga, I believe, as of the world in general, are rapidly passing away. The time was when it was the chosen resort of none but "nice people". At the present day, I hear it constantly affirmed, "the company is dreadfully mixed." What society may have been at Saratoga when its elements were thus simple and severe, I can only vaguely and mournfully conjecture. I confine myself to the dense, democratic, vulgar Saratoga of the current year. You are struck, to begin with, at the hotels, by the numerical superiority of the women; then, I think, by their personal superiority. It is incontestably the case that in appearance, in manner, in grace and completeness of aspect, American women surpass their husbands and brothers; the relation being reversed among some of the nations of Europe. Attached to the main entrance of the Union Hotel, and adjoining the ascent from the street to the piazza, is a "stoop" of mighty area, which, at most hours of the day and evening is a favoured lounging-place of men. I should add, after the remark I have just made, that even in the appearance of the usual American male there seems to me to be a certain plastic intention. It is true that the lean, sallow, angular Yankee of tradition is dignified mainly by a look of decision, a hint of unimpassioned volition, the air of "smartness". This in some degree redeems him, but it fails to make him handsome. But in the average American of the present time, the typical leanness and sallowness are less than in his fathers, and the individual acuteness is at once equally marked and more frequently united with merit of form. Casting your eye over a group of your fellow-citizens in the portico of the Union Hotel, you will be inclined to admit that, taking the good with the bad, they are worthy sons of the great Republic. I have found, at any rate, a great deal of entertainment in watching them. They suggest to my fancy the swarming vastness – the multifarious possibilities and activities – of our young civilisation. They come from the uttermost ends of the Union – from San Francisco, from New Orleans, from Alaska. As they sit with their white hats tilted forward, and their chairs tilted back, and their feet tilted up, and their cigars and toothpicks forming various angles with these various lines, I seem to see in their faces a tacit reference to the affairs of a continent. They are obviously persons of experience – of a somewhat narrow and monotonous experience certainly; an experience of which the diamonds and laces which their wives are exhibiting hard by are, perhaps, the most substantial and beautiful result; but, at any rate, they have lived, in every fibre of the will. For the time, they are lounging with the negro waiters, and the boot-blacks, and the news-vendors; but it was not in lounging that they gained their hard wrinkles and the level impartial regard which they direct from beneath their hat-rims. They are not the mellow fruit of a society which has walked hand-in-hand with tradition and culture; they are hard nuts, which have grown and ripened as they could. When they talk among themselves, I seem to hear the cracking of the shells.

If the men are remarkable, the ladies are wonderful. Saratoga is famous, I believe, as the place of all places in America where women adorn themselves most, or as the place, at least, where the greatest amount of dressing may be seen by the greatest number of people. Your first impression is therefore of the – what shall I call it? – of the abundance of petticoats. Every woman you meet, young or old, is attired with a certain amount of richness, and with whatever good taste may be compatible with such a mode of life. You behold an interesting, indeed a quite momentous spectacle; the democratisation of elegance. If I am to believe what I hear – in fact, I may say what I overhear – many of these sumptuous persons have enjoyed neither the advantages of a careful education nor the privileges of an introduction to society. She walks more or less of a queen, however, each uninitiated nobody. She often has, in dress, an admirable instinct of elegance and even of what the French call "chic". This instinct occasionally amounts to a sort of passion; the result then is wonderful. You look at the coarse brick walls, the rusty iron posts of the piazza, at the shuffling negro waiters, the great tawdry steamboat-cabin of a drawing-room – you see the tilted ill-dressed loungers on the steps – and you finally regret that a figure so exquisite should have so vulgar a setting. Your resentment, however, is speedily tempered by reflection. You feel the impertinence of your old reminiscences of English and French novels, and of the dreary social order in which privacy was the presiding genius and women arrayed themselves for the appreciation of the few. The crowd, the tavern-loungers, the surrounding ugliness and tumult and license, constitute the social medium of the young lady you are so inconsistent as to admire; she is dressed for publicity. The thought fills you with a kind of awe. The social order of tradition is far away indeed, and as for the transatlantic novels, you begin to doubt whether she is so amiably curious as to read even the silliest of them. To be dressed up to the eyes is obviously to give pledges to idleness. I have been forcibly struck with the apparent absence of any warmth and richness of detail in the lives of these wonderful ladies of the piazzas. We are freely accused of being an eminently wasteful people; and I know of few things which so largely warrant the accusation as the fact that these conspicuous *élégantes* adorn themselves, socially speaking, to so little purpose. To dress for every one is, practically, to dress for no one. There are few prettier sights than a charmingly-dressed woman, gracefully established in some shady spot, with a piece of needlework or embroidery, or a book. Nothing very serious is accomplished, probably, but an æsthetic principle is recognised. The embroidery and the book are a tribute to culture, and I suppose they really figure somewhere out of the opening scenes of French comedies. But here at Saratoga, at any hour of morning or evening, you may see a hundred rustling beauties whose rustle is their sole occupation. One lady in particular there is, with whom it appears to be an inexorable fate that she shall be nothing more than dressed. Her apparel is tremendously modern, and my remarks would be much illumined if I had the learning necessary for describing it. I can only say that every evening for a fortnight she has revealed herself as a fresh creation. But she especially, as I say, has struck me as a person dressed beyond her life and her opportunities. I resent on her behalf – or on behalf at least of her finery – the extreme severity of her circumstances. What is she, after all, but a "regular boarder"? She ought to sit on the terrace of a stately castle, with a great baronial park shutting out the undressed world, and bandy quiet small-talk with an ambassador or a duke. My imagination is shocked when I behold her seated in gorgeous relief against the dusty clapboards of the hotel, with her beautiful hands folded in her silken lap, her head drooping slightly beneath the weight of her chignon, her lips parted in a vague contemplative gaze at Mr. Helmbold's well-known advertisement on the opposite fence, her husband beside her reading the New York *Herald*.

I have indeed observed cases of a sort of splendid social isolation here, which are not without a certain amount of pathos – people who know no one, who have money and finery and possessions, only no friends. Such at least is my inference, from the lonely grandeur with which I see them invested. Women, of course, are the most helpless victims of this cruel situation, although it must be said that they befriend each other with a generosity for which we hardly give them credit. I have seen women, for instance, at various "hops", approach their lonely sisters and invite them to waltz, and I have seen the fair invited surrender themselves eagerly to this humiliating embrace. Gentlemen at Saratoga are at a much higher premium than at European watering-places. It is an old story that in this country we have no "leisure-class" – the class from which the Saratogas of Europe recruit a large number of their male frequenters. A few months ago, I paid a visit to an English "bath", commemorated in various works of fiction, where, among many visible points of difference from American resorts, the most striking was the multitude of young men who had the whole day on their hands. While their sweethearts and sisters are waltzing together, our own young men are rolling up greenbacks in counting-houses and stores. I was recently reminded in another way, one evening, of the

unlikeness of Saratoga to Cheltenham. Behind the biggest of
the big hotels is a large planted yard, which it is the fashion at
Saratoga to talk of as a "park", and which is perhaps believed
to be the biggest in the world. At one end of it stands a great
ballroom, approached by a range of wooden steps. It was late
in the evening; the room, in spite of the intense heat, was
blazing with light and the orchestra thundering a mighty
waltz. A group of loungers, including myself, were hanging
about to watch the ingress of the festally-minded. In the basement of the edifice, sunk beneath the ground, a noisy
auctioneer, in his shirt and trousers, black in the face with heat
and vociferation, was selling "pools" of the races to a dense
group of frowsy betting-men. At the foot of the steps was stationed a man in a linen coat and straw hat, without waistcoat
or necktie, to take the tickets of the ball-goers. As the latter
failed to arrive in sufficient numbers, a musician came forth to
the top of the steps and blew a loud summons on a horn. After
this they began to straggle along. On this occasion, certainly,
the company promised to be decidedly "mixed". The women,
as usual, were much bedizened, though without any constant
adhesion to the technicalities of full-dress. The men adhered
to it neither in the letter nor the spirit. The possessor of a pair
of satin-shod feet, twinkling beneath an uplifted volume of
gauze and lace and flowers, tripped up the steps with her
gloved hand on the sleeve of a railway "duster". Now and
then two ladies arrived alone; generally a group of them
approached under convoy of a single man. Children were
freely scattered among their elders, and frequently a small boy
would deliver his ticket and enter the glittering portal, beautifully unembarrassed. Of the children of Saratoga there would
be wondrous things to relate. I believe that, in spite of their
valuable aid, the festival of which I speak was rated rather a
"fizzle". I see it advertised that they are soon to have, for their

own peculiar benefit, a "Masquerade and Promenade Concert, beginning at 9 P.M." I observe that they usually open the "hops," and that it is only after their elders have borrowed confidence from the sight of their unfaltering paces that the latter dare to dance. You meet them far into the evening, roaming over the piazzas and corridors of the hotels – the little girls especially – lean, pale, formidable. Occasionally childhood confesses itself, even when maternity resists, and you see at eleven o'clock at night some poor little bedizened precocity collapsed in slumber in a lonely wayside chair. The part played by children in society here is only an additional instance of the wholesale equalisation of the various social atoms which is the distinctive feature of collective Saratoga. A man in a "duster" at a ball is as good as a man in regulation-garments; a young woman dancing with another young woman is as good as a young woman dancing with a young man; a child of ten is as good as a woman of thirty; a double negative in conversation is rather better than a single.

An important feature in many a watering-place is the facility for leaving it a little behind you and tasting of the unmitigated country. You may wander to some shady hillside and sentimentalise upon the vanity of a high civilisation. But at Saratoga civilisation holds you fast. The most important feature of the place, perhaps, is the impossibility of carrying out any such pastoral dream. The surrounding country is a charming wilderness, but the roads are so abominably bad that walking and driving are alike unprofitable. Of course, however, if you are bent upon a walk, you will take a walk. There is a striking contrast between the concentrated prodigality of life in the immediate neighbourhood of the hotels and the pastoral solitudes into which a walk of half an hour may lead you. You have left the American citizen and his wife, the orchestras, the pools, the precocious infants, the cocktails, the importations from Worth, but a mile or two behind, but already the forest is primeval and the landscape is without figures. Nothing could be less manipulated than the country about Saratoga. The heavy roads are little more than sandy wheel-tracks; by the tangled wayside the blackberries wither unpicked. The horizon undulates with an air of having it all its own way. There are no white villages gleaming in the distance, no spires of churches, no salient details. It is all green, lonely, and vacant. If you wish to enjoy a detail, you must stop beneath a cluster of pines and listen to the murmur of the softly-troubled air, or follow upward the scaly straightness of their trunks to where the afternoon light gives it a colour. Here and there on a slope by the roadside stands a rough unpainted farmhouse, looking as if its dreary blackness were the result of its standing dark and lonely amid so many months – and such a wide expanse – of winter snow. It has turned black by contrast. The principal feature of the grassy unfurnished yard is the great wood-pile, telling grimly of the long reversion of the summer. For the time, however, it looks down contentedly enough over a goodly appanage of grain-fields and orchards, and I can fancy that it may be amusing to be a boy there. But to be a man, it must be quite what the lean, brown, serious farmers physiognomically hint it to be. You have, however, at the present season, for your additional beguilement, on the eastern horizon, the vision of the long bold chain of the Green Mountains, clad in that single coat of simple, candid blue which is the favourite garment of our American hills. As a visitor, too, you have for an afternoon's excursion your choice between a couple of lakes. Saratoga Lake, the larger and more distant of the two, is the goal of the regular afternoon drive. Above the shore is a well-appointed tavern – "Moon's" it is called by the voice of fame – where you may sit upon a broad piazza and partake of fried potatoes and "drinks"; the latter, if you happen to have come from poor dislicensed Boston, a peculiarly gratifying privilege. You enjoy the felicity sighed for by that wanton Italian lady of the anecdote, when, one summer evening, to the sound of music, she wished that to eat an ice were a sin. The other lake is small, and its shores are unadorned by any edifice but a boat-house, where you may hire a skiff and pull yourself out into the minnow-tickled, wood-circled oval. Here, floating in its darkened half, while you watch on the opposite shore the tree-stems, white and sharp in the declining sunlight, and their foliage whitening and whispering in the breeze, and you feel that this little solitude is part of a greater and more portentous solitude, you may recall certain passages of Ruskin, in which he dwells upon the needfulness of some human association, however remote, to make natural scenery fully impressive. You may recall that magnificent page in which he relates having tried with such fatal effect, in a battle-haunted valley of the Jura, to fancy himself in a nameless solitude of our own continent. You feel around you, with irresistible force, the elo-quent silence of undedicated nature – the absence of serious associations, the nearness, indeed, of the vulgar and trivial associations of the least complete of all the cities of pleasure – you feel this, and you wonder what it is you so deeply and calmly enjoy. You make up your mind, possibly, that it is a great advantage to be able at once to enjoy Mr. Ruskin and to enjoy Mr. Ruskin's alarms. And hereupon you return to your hotel and read the New York papers on the plan of the French campaign and the Nathan murder.

XVIII.

NEWPORT.

1870.

The season at Newport has an obstinate life. September has
fairly begun, but as yet there is small visible diminution in the
steady stream – the splendid, stupid stream – of carriages
which rolls in the afternoon along the Avenue. There is, I
think, a far more intimate fondness between Newport and its
frequenters than that which in most American watering-places
consecrates the somewhat mechanical relation between the
visitors and the visited. This relation here is for the most part
slightly sentimental. I am very far from professing a cynical
contempt for the gaieties and vanities of Newport life: they
are, as a spectacle, extremely amusing; they are full of a certain warmth of social colour which charms alike the eye and
the fancy; they are worth observing, if only to conclude
against them; they possess at least the dignity of all extreme
and emphatic expressions of a social tendency; but they are
not so untouched with Philistinism that I do not seem to overhear at times the still, small voice of this tender sense of the
sweet, superior beauty of the natural things that surround
them, pleading gently in their favour to the fastidious critic. I
feel almost warranted in saying that here the background of
life has sunk less in relative value and suffered less from the
encroachments of pleasure-seeking man than the scenic dispo-
sitions of any other watering-place. For this, perhaps, we may

thank rather the modest, incorruptible integrity of the Newport landscape than any very intelligent forbearance on the part of the summer colony. The beauty of this landscape is so subtle, so essential, so humble, so much a thing of character and expression, so little a thing of feature and pretension, that it cunningly eludes the grasp of the destroyer or the reformer, and triumphs in impalpable purity even when it seems to make concessions. I have sometimes wondered, in rational moods, why it is that Newport is so much appreciated by the votaries of idleness and pleasure. Its resources are few in number. It is extremely circumscribed. It has few drives, few walks, little variety of scenery. Its charms and its interest are confined to a narrow circle. It has of course the unlimited ocean, but sea-faring idlers are not true Newporters, for any other sea would suit them as well. Last evening, it seemed to me, as I drove along the Avenue, that I guessed the answer to the riddle. The atmospheric tone, the careful selection of ingredients, your pleasant sense of a certain climatic ripeness – these are the real charm of Newport, and the secret of her supremacy. You are affected by the admirable art of the landscape, by seeing so much that is lovely and impressive achieved with such a fru-gality of means – with so little parade of the vast, the various, or the rare, with so narrow a range of colour and form. I could not help thinking, as I turned from the harmonies and purities which lay deepening on the breast of nature, with the various shades of twilight, to the heterogeneous procession in the Avenue, that, quite in their own line of effect, the usual per-formers in this exhibition might learn a few good lessons from the daily prospect of the great western expanse of rock and ocean in its relations with the declining sun. But this is asking too much. Many persons of course come to Newport simply because others come, and in this way the present brilliant colony has grown up. Let me not be suspected, when I speak

of Newport, of the untasteful heresy of meaning primarily
rocks and waves rather than ladies and gentlemen.

The ladies and gentlemen are in great force – the ladies, of
course, especially. It is true everywhere, I suppose, that women
are the animating element of "society"; but you feel this to be
especially true as you pass along Bellevue Avenue. I doubt
whether anywhere else so many women have a "good time"
with so small a sacrifice of the luxury of self-respect. I heard a
lady yesterday tell another, with a quiet ecstasy of tone, that
she had been having a "most perfect time". This is the very
poetry of pleasure. It is a part of our complacent tradition that
in those foreign lands where women are supposed to be
socially supreme, they maintain their empire by various clan-
destine and reprehensible arts. With us – we say it at Newport
without bravado – they are both conspicuous and unsophisti-
cated. You feel this most gratefully as you receive a confident
bow from a pretty girl in her basket-phaeton. She is very
young and very pretty, but she has a certain habitual assurance
which is only a grace the more. She combines, you reflect with
respectful tenderness, all that is possible in the way of modesty
with all that is delightful in the way of facility. Shyness is certainly very pretty – when it is not very ugly; but shyness may
often darken the bloom of genuine modesty, and a certain
frankness and confidence may often incline it toward the light.
Let us assume, then, that all the young ladies whom you may
meet here are of the highest modern type. In the course of
time they ripen into the delightful matrons who divide your
admiration. It is easy to see that Newport must be a most
agreeable sojourn for the male sex. The gentlemen, indeed,
look wonderfully prosperous and well-conditioned. They
gallop on shining horses or recline in a sort of coaxing
Herculean submission beside the lovely mistress of a curricle.
Young men – and young old men – I have occasion to observe,

are far more numerous than at Saratoga, and of vastly superior quality. There is, indeed, in all things a striking difference in tone and aspect between these two great centres of pleasure. After Saratoga, Newport seems really substantial and civilised. Æsthetically speaking, you may remain at Newport with a fairly good conscience; at Saratoga you linger under passionate protest. At Newport life is public, if you will; at Saratoga it is absolutely common. The difference, in a word, is the difference between a group of undiscriminating hotels and a series of organised homes. Saratoga perhaps deserves our greater homage, as being characteristically democratic and American; let us, then, make Saratoga the heaven of our aspiration, but let us yet a while content ourselves with Newport as the lowly earth of our residence.

The villas and "cottages", the beautiful idle women, the beautiful idle men, the brilliant pleasure-fraught days and evenings, impart, perhaps, to Newport life a faintly European expression, in so far as they suggest the somewhat alien presence of leisure – "fine old leisure", as George Eliot calls it. Nothing, it seems to me, however, can take place in America without straightway seeming very American; and, after a week at Newport, you begin to fancy that to live for amusement simply, beyond the noise of commerce or of care, is a distinctively national trait. Nowhere else in this country – nowhere, of course, within the range of our better civilisation – does business seem so remote, so vague, and unreal. It is the only place in America in which enjoyment is organised. If there be any poetry in the ignorance of trade and turmoil and the hard processes of fortune, Newport may claim her share of it. She knows – or at least appears to know – for the most part nothing but results. Individuals here, of course, have private cares and burdens to preserve the balance and the dignity of life; but collective society conspires to forget everything that

worries. It is a singular fact that a society that does nothing is
decidedly more pictorial, more interesting to the eye of contemplation, than a society which is hard at work. Newport, in
this way, is infinitely more fertile in combinations than
Saratoga. There you feel that idleness is occasional, empirical.
Most of the people you see are asking themselves, you
imagine, whether the game is worth the candle and work is
not better than such difficult play. But here, obviously, the
habit of pleasure is formed, and (within the limits of a severe
morality) many of the secrets of pleasure are known. Do what
we will, on certain lines Europe is in advance of us yet.
Newport lags altogether behind Trouville and Brighton in her
exhibition of the unmentionable. All this is markedly absent
from the picture, which is therefore signally destitute of the
enhancing tints produced by the mysteries and fascinations of
vice. But idleness *per se* is vicious, and of course you may
imagine what you please. For my own part, I prefer to imagine
nothing but the graceful and the pure; and with the help of
such imaginings you may construct a very pretty sentimental
undercurrent to the superficial movement of society. This I
lately found very difficult to do at Saratoga. Sentiment there is
pitifully shy and elusive. Here, the multiplied relations of men
and women, under the permanent pressure of luxury and idleness, give it a very fair chance. Sentiment, indeed, of masterly
force and interest, springs up in every soil, with a sovereign
disregard of occasion. People love and hate and aspire with
the greatest intensity when they have to make their time and
opportunity. I should hardly come to Newport for the materials of a tragedy. Even in their own kind, the social elements
are as yet too light and thin. But I can fancy finding here the
motive of a drama which should depend more on smiles than
tears. I can almost imagine, indeed, a transient observer of the
Newport spectacle dreaming momentarily of a great American

novel, in which the heroine might be infinitely realistic and yet neither a schoolmistress nor an outcast. I say intentionally the "transient" observer, because it is probable that here the suspicion only is friendly to dramatic point; the knowledge is hostile. The observer would discover, on a nearer view, I rather fear, that his possible heroines have too perfect a time.

This will remind the reader of what he must already have heard affirmed, that to speak of a place with abundance you must know it, but not too well. I suffer from knowing the natural elements of Newport too well to attempt to describe them. I have known them so long that I hardly know what I think of them. I have little more than a simple consciousness of enjoying them very much. Even this consciousness at times lies dumb and inert. I wonder at such times whether, to appeal fairly to the general human sense, the horizon has not too much of that mocking straightness which is such a misrepresentation of the real character of the sea – as if, forsooth, it were level. Life seems too short, space too narrow, to warrant you in giving in an unqualified adhesion to a *paysage* which is two-thirds ocean. For the most part, however, I am willing to take the landscape as it stands, and to think that, without the water to make it precious, the land would be much less lovable. It is, in fact, a land exquisitely modified by marine influences. Indeed, in spite of all the evil it has done me, I could almost speak well of the ocean when I remember the charming tricks it plays with the Newport promontories.

The place consists, as the reader will know, of an ancient and honourable town, a goodly harbour, and a long, broad neck of land, stretching southward into the sea and forming the chief habitation of the summer colony. Along the greater part of its eastward length, this projecting coast is bordered with cliffs of no great height, and dotted with seaward-gazing villas. At the head of the promontory the villas enjoy a magnificent reach of prospect. The pure Atlantic – the old world westward tides – expire directly at their feet. Behind the line of villas runs the Avenue, with more villas yet – of which there is nothing at all to say but that those built recently are a hundred times prettier than those built fifteen years ago, and give one some hope of a revival of the architectural art. Some years ago, when I first knew Newport, the town proper was considered remarkably quaint. If an antique shabbiness that amounts almost to squalor is a pertinent element, as I believe it is, of this celebrated quality, the little main street at least – Thames Street by name – still deserves the praise. Here, in their crooked and dwarfish wooden mansions, are the shops that minister to the daily needs of the expanded city; and here of a summer morning, jolting over the cobble stones of the narrow roadway, you may see a hundred superfine ladies seeking with languid eagerness what they may buy – to "buy something", I believe, being a diurnal necessity of the conscientious American woman. This busy region gradually melts away into the grass-grown stillness of the Point, in the eyes of many persons the pleasantest quarter of Newport. It has superficially the advantage of being as yet uninvaded by fashion. When I first knew it, however, its peculiar charm was even more undisturbed than at present. The Point may be called the old residential, as distinguished from the commercial, town. It is meagre, shallow and scanty – a mere pinch of antiquity – but, so far as it goes, it retains an exquisite tone. It leaves the shops and the little wharves, and wanders close to the harbour, where the breeze-borne rattle of shifted sails and spars alone intrudes upon its stillness, till its mouldy-timbered quiet subsides into the low, tame rocks and beaches which edge the bay. Several matter-of-course modern houses have recently been erected on the water-side, absorbing the sober, primitive tenements which used to maintain the picturesque character of the place. They improve it, of course, as a residence, but they injure it as an unexpected corner. Enough of early architecture still remains, however, to suggest a multitude of thoughts as to the severe simplicity of the generation which produced it. The plain gray nudity of these little warped and shingled boxes seems to make it a hopeless task on their part to present any positive appearance at all. But here, as elsewhere, the magical Newport atmosphere wins half the battle. It aims at no mystery – it simply makes them scintillate in their bareness. Their homely notches and splinters twinkle till the mere friendliness of the thing makes a surface. Their steep gray roofs, barnacled with lichens, remind you of old barges, overturned on the beach to dry.

One of the more recent monuments of fashion is the long drive which follows the shore. The Avenue, where the Neck abruptly terminates, has been made to extend itself to the west, and to wander for a couple of miles over a lovely region of beach and lowly down and sandy meadow and salt brown sheep-grass. This region was formerly the most beautiful part of Newport – the least frequented and the most untamed by fashion. I by no means regret the creation of the new road, however. A walker may very soon isolate himself, and the occupants of carriages are exposed to a benefit quite superior to their power of injury. The peculiar charm of this great westward expanse is very difficult to define. It is in an especial degree the charm of Newport in general – the combined lowness of tone, as painters call it, in all the elements of *terra firma*, and the extraordinary elevation of tone in the air. For miles and miles you see at your feet, in mingled shades of yellow and gray, a desolate waste of moss-clad rock and sand-starved grass. At your left is nothing but the shine and surge of the ocean, and over your head that wonderful sky of Newport, which has such an unexpected resemblance to the sky of Venice. In spite of the bare simplicity of this prospect, its beauty is far more a beauty of detail than that of the average American landscape. Descend into a hollow of the rocks, into one of the little warm climates, five feet square, which you may find there, beside the grateful ocean glare, and you will be struck quite as much by their fineness as by their roughness. From time to time, as you wander, you will meet a lonely, stunted tree, which is sure to be a charming piece of the individual grotesque. The region of which I speak is perhaps best seen in the late afternoon, from the high seat of a carriage on the Avenue. You seem to stand just outside the threshold of the west. At its opposite extremity sinks the sun, with such a splendour, perhaps, as I lately saw – a splendour of the deepest blue, more luminous and fiery than the usual redness of evening, and all streaked and barred with blown and drifted gold. The whole large interval, with its rocks and marshes and ponds, seems bedimmed with a kind of purple glaze. The near Atlantic fades and turns cold with that desolate look of the ocean when the day ceases to care for it. In the foreground, a short distance from the road, an old orchard uplifts its tangled stems and branches against the violet mists of the west. It seems strangely grotesque and enchanted. No ancient olive-grove of Italy or Provence was ever more hoarily romantic. This is what people commonly behold on the last homeward bend of the drive. For such of them as are happy enough to occupy one of the villas on the cliffs, the beauty of the day has even yet not expired. The present summer has been emphatically the summer of moonlights. Not the nights, however, but the long days, in these agreeable homes, are what especially appeal to my fancy. Here you find a solution of the insoluble problem – to combine an abundance of society with an abundance of solitude. In their charming broad-windowed drawing-rooms, on their great seaward piazzas, within sight of the serious Atlantic horizon, which is so familiar to the eye and so mysterious to the heart, caressed by the gentle breeze which makes all but simple, social, delightful *now* and *here* seem unreal and untasteful – the sweet fruit of the lotus grows more than ever succulent and magical. How sensible they ought to be, the denizens of these pleasant places, of their peculiar felicity and distinction! How it should purify their temper and refine their tastes! How delicate, how wise, how discriminating they should become! What excellent manners – what enlightened opinions – their situation should produce! How it should purge them of vulgarity! Happy *villeggianti* of Newport!

XIX.

QUEBEC.

1871.

I.

A traveller who combines a taste for old towns with a love of letters ought not, I suppose, to pass through "the most picturesque city in America" without making an attempt to commemorate his impressions. His first impression will certainly have been that not America, but Europe, should have the credit of Quebec. I came, some days since, by a dreary night-journey, to Point Levi, opposite the town, and as we rattled toward our goal in the faint raw dawn, and, already attentive to "effects", I began to consult the misty window-panes and descried through the moving glass little but crude, monotonous woods, suggestive of nothing that I had ever heard of in song or story, I felt that the land would have much to do to give itself a romantic air. And, in fact, the feat is achieved with almost magical suddenness. The old world rises in the midst of the new in the manner of a change of scene on the stage. The St. Lawrence shines at your left, large as a harbour-mouth, gray with smoke and masts, and edged on its hither verge by a bustling water-side *faubourg* which looks French or English, or anything not local that you please; and beyond it, over against you, on its rocky promontory, sits the ancient town, belted with its hoary wall and crowned with its granite citadel. Now that I have been here a while I find myself wondering how the city would strike one if the imagination had not been bribed beforehand. The place, after all, is of the soil on which it stands; yet it appeals to you so cunningly with its little stock of transatlantic wares that you overlook its flaws and lapses, and swallow it whole. Fancy lent a willing hand the morning I arrived, and zealously retouched the picture. The very sky seemed to have been brushed in like the sky in an English water-colour, the light to filter down through an atmosphere more dense and more conscious. You cross a ferry, disembark at the foot of the rock on unmistakably foreign soil, and then begin to climb into the city proper – the city *intra muros*. These walls, to the American vision, are of course the sovereign fact of Quebec; you take off your hat to them as you clatter through the gate. They are neither very high nor, after all, very hoary. Our clear American air is hostile to those mellow deposits and incrustations which enrich the venerable surfaces of Europe. Still, they are walls; till but a short time ago they quite encircled the town; they are garnished with little slits for musketry and big embrasures for cannon; they offer here and there to the strolling bourgeoisie a stretch of grassy rampart; and they make the whole place definite and personal.

Before you reach the gates, however, you will have been reminded at a dozen points that you have come abroad. What is the essential difference of tone between street-life in an old civilisation and in a new? It seems something subtler and deeper than mere external accidents – than foreign architecture, than foreign pinks, greens, and yellows plastering the house-fronts, than the names of the saints on the corners, than all the pleasant crookedness, narrowness and duskiness, the quaint economised spaces, the multifarious detail, the brown French faces, the ruddy English ones. It seems to be the general fact of detail itself – the hint in the air of a slow, accidental accretion, in obedience to needs more timidly considered and more sparingly gratified than the pressing necessities of American progress. But apart from the metaphysics of the question, Quebec has a great many pleasant little ripe spots and amenities. You note the small, boxlike houses in rugged stone or in stucco, each painted with uncompromising *naïveté* in some bright hue of the owner's fond choice; you note with joy, with envy, with momentary self-effacement, as a New Yorker, as a Bostonian, the innumerable calashes and cabs which contend for your selection; and you observe when you arrive at the hotel, that this is a blank and gloomy inn, of true provincial aspect, with slender promise of the "American plan". Perhaps, even the clerk at the office will have the courtesy of the ages of leisure. I confess that, in my case, he was terribly modern, so that I was compelled to resort for a lodging to a private house near by, where I enjoy a transitory glimpse of the *vie intime* of Quebec. I fancied, when I came in, that it would be a compensation for worse quarters to possess the little Canadian vignette I enjoy from my windows. Certain shabby Yankee sheds, indeed, encumber the foreground, but they are so near that I can overlook them. Beyond is a piece of garden, attached to nothing less than a convent of the cloistered nuns of St. Ursula. The convent chapel rises inside it, crowned with what seemed to me, in view of the circumstances, a real little *clocher de France*. The "circumstances", I confess, are simply a couple of stout French poplars. I call them French because they are alive and happy; whereas, if they had been American they would have died of a want of appreciation, like their brothers in the "States". I do not say that the little convent-belfry, roofed and coated as it is with quaint scales of tin, would, by itself, produce any very deep illusion; or that the whispering poplars, *per se*, would transport me to the Gallic mother-land; but poplars and belfry together constitute an "effect" – strike a musical note in the scale of association. I look fondly even at the little casements which command this prospect, for they too are an old-world heritage. They open sidewise, in two wings, and are screwed together by that bothersome little iron handle over which we have fumbled so often in European inns.

If the windows tell of French dominion, of course larger matters testify with greater eloquence. In a place so small as Quebec, the bloom of novelty of course rubs off; but when first I walked abroad I fancied myself again in a French seaside town where I once spent a year, in common with a large number of economically disposed English. The French element offers the groundwork, and the English colony wears, for the most part, that half-genteel and migratory air which stamps the exiled and provincial British. They look as if they were still *en voyage* – still in search of low prices – the men in woollen shirts and Scotch bonnets; the ladies with a certain look of being equipped for dangers and difficulties. Your very first steps will be likely to lead you to the market-place, which is a genuine bit of Europeanism. One side of it is occupied by a huge edifice of yellow plaster, with stone facings painted in blue, and a manner of *porte-cochère*, leading into a veritable court – originally, I believe, a college of the early Jesuits, now a place of military stores. On the other stands the French cathedral, with an ample stone façade, a bulky stone tower, and a high-piled, tin-scaled belfry; not architectural, of course, nor imposing, but with a certain gray maturity, and, as regards the belfry, a quite adequate quaintness. Round about are shops and houses, touching which, I think, it is no mere fancy that they might, as they stand, look down into some dull and rather dirty *place* in France. The stalls and booths in the centre – tended by genuine peasants of tradition, brown-faced old Frenchwomen, with hard wrinkles and short petticoats, and white caps beneath their broad-brimmed hats, and more than one price, as I think you'll find – these, and the stationed calèches and cabriolets complete a passably fashionable French picture. It is a proof of how nearly the old market-women resemble their originals across the sea that you rather resentfully miss one or two of the proper features of the type – the sabots for the feet and the donkey for the load. Of course you go into the cathedral, and how forcibly that swing of the door, as you doff your hat in the cooler air, recalls the old tourist strayings and pryings beneath other skies! You find a big garish church, with a cold high light, a promiscuity of stucco and gilding, and a mild odour of the seventeenth century. It is, perhaps, a shade or so more sensibly Catholic than it would be with ourselves; but, in fine, it has pews and a boarded floor, and the few paintings are rather pale in their badness, and you are forced to admit that the old-world tone which sustains itself so comfortably elsewhere falters most where most is asked of it.

Among the other lions of Quebec – notably in the Citadel – you find Protestant England supreme. A robust trooper of her Majesty, with a pair of very tight trousers and a very small cap, takes charge of you at the entrance of the fortifications, and conducts you through all kinds of incomprehensible defences. I cannot speak of the place as an engineer, but only as a tourist, and the tourist is chiefly concerned with the view. This is altogether superb, and if Quebec is not the most picturesque city in America, this is no fault of its incomparable site. Perched on its mountain of rock, washed by a river as free and ample as an ocean-gulf, sweeping from its embattled crest, the villages, the forests, the blue undulations of the imperial province of which it is warden – as it has managed from our scanty annals to squeeze out a past, you pray in the name of all that's majestic that it may have a future. I may add that, to the mind of the reflective visitor, these idle ramparts and silent

courts present other visions than that of the mighty course of
the river and its anchorage for navies. They evoke a shadowy
image of that great English power, the arches of whose empire
were once built strong on foreign soil; and as you stand where
they are highest and look abroad upon a land of alien speech,
you seem to hear the echoed names of other strongholds and
provinces – Gibraltar, Malta, India. Whether these arches are
crumbling now, I do not pretend to say; but the last regular
troops (in number lately much diminished) are just about to be
withdrawn from Quebec, and in the private circles to which I
have been admitted I hear sad forebodings of what society will
lose by the departure of the "military". This single word is elo-
quent; it reveals a social order distinctly affiliated, in spite of
remoteness, to the society reproduced for the pacific
American in novels in which the hero is a captain of the army
or navy, and of which the scene is therefore necessarily laid in
countries provided with these branches of the public service.
Another opportunity for some such reflections, worthy of a
historian or an essayist, as those I have hinted at, is afforded
you on the Plains of Abraham, to which you probably adjourn
directly from the Citadel – another, but I am bound to say, in
my opinion, a less inspiring one. A battlefield remains a battlefield, whatever may be done to it; but the scene of Wolfe's
victory has been profaned by the erection of a vulgar prison,
and this memento of human infirmities does much to efface
the meagre column which, with its neat inscription, "Here
died Wolfe, victorious," stands there as a symbol of exceptional virtue.

II.

To express the historical interest of the place completely, I
should dwell on the light provincial – French provincial –

aspect of some of the little residential streets. Some of the houses have the staleness of complexion which Balzac loved to describe. They are chiefly built of stone or brick, with a stoutness and separateness of structure which stands in some degree in stead of architecture. I know not that, externally, they have any greater charm than that they belong to that category of dwellings which in our own cities were long since pulled down to make room for brown-stone fronts. I know not, indeed, that I can express better the picturesque merit of Quebec than by saying that it has no fronts of this luxurious and horrible substance. The greater number of houses are built of rough-hewn squares of some more vulgar mineral, painted with frank chocolate or buff, and adorned with blinds of a cruder green than we admire. As you pass the low windows of these abodes, you perceive the walls to be of extraordinary thickness; the embrasure is of great depth; Quebec was built for winter. Door-plates are frequent, and you observe that the tenants are of the Gallic persuasion. Here and there, before a door, stands a comely private equipage – a fact agreeably suggestive of a low scale of prices; for evidently in Quebec one need not be a millionaire to keep a carriage, and one may make a figure on moderate means. The great number of private carriages visible in the streets is another item, by the way, among the Europeanisms of the place; and not, as I may say, as regards the simple fact that they exist, but as regards the fact that they are considered needful for women, for young persons, for gentility. What does it do with itself, this gentility, keeping a gig or not, you wonder, as you stroll past its little multicoloured mansions. You strive almost vainly to picture the life of this French society, locked up in its small dead capital, isolated on a heedless continent, and gradually consuming its principal, as one may say – its vital stock of memories, traditions, superstitions. Its evenings must be as dull as the evenings described by Balzac in his *Vie de Province*; but has it the same ways and means of dullness? Does it play lotto and "boston" in the long winter nights, and arrange marriages between its sons and daughters, whose education it has confided to abbés and abbesses? I have met in the streets here little old Frenchmen who look as if they had stepped out of Balzac – bristling with the habits of a class, wrinkled with old-world expressions. Something assures one that Quebec must be a city of gossip; for evidently it is not a city of culture. A glance at the few booksellers' windows gives evidence of this. A few Catholic statuettes and prints, two or three Catholic publications, a festoon or so of rosaries, a volume of Lamartine, a supply of ink and matches, form the principal stock.

In the lower class of the French population there is a much livelier vitality. They are a genuine peasantry; you very soon observe it, as you drive along the pleasant country-roads. Just what it is that makes a peasantry, it is, perhaps, not easy to determine; but whatever it is, these good people have it – in their simple, unsharpened faces, in their narrow patois, in their ignorance and naîveté, and their evident good terms with the tin-spired parish church, standing there as bright and clean with ungrudged paint and varnish as a Nürnberg toy. One of them spoke to me with righteous contempt of the French of France – "They are worth nothing; they are bad Catholics." These are good Catholics, and I doubt whether anywhere Catholicism wears a brighter face and maintains more docility at the cost of less misery. It is, perhaps, not Longfellow's *Evangeline* for chapter and verse, but it is a tolerable prose transcript. There is no visible squalor, there are no rags and no curses, but there is a most agreeable tinge of gentleness, thrift, and piety. I am assured that the country-people are in the last degree mild and peaceable; surely, such neatness and thrift, without the irritability of the French genius – it is true the genius too is absent – is a very pleasant type of character. Without being ready to proclaim, with an enthusiastic friend, that the roadside scenery is more French than France, I may say that, in its way, it is quite as picturesque as anything within the city. There is an air of completeness and maturity in the landscape which suggests an old country. The roads, to begin with, are decidedly better than our own, and the cottages and farmhouses would need only a bit of thatch and a few red tiles here and there to enable them to figure creditably by the way-sides of Normandy or Brittany. The road to Montmorency, on which tourists most congregate, is also, I think, the prettiest. The rows of poplars, the heavy stone cottages, seamed and cracked with time, in many cases, and daubed in coarse, bright hues, the little bourgeois villas, rising middle-aged at the end of short vistas, the sunburnt women in the fields, the old men in woollen stockings and red nightcaps, the long-kirtled curé nodding to doffed hats, the more or less bovine stare which greets you from cottage-doors, are all so many touches of a local colour reflected from over the sea. What especially strikes one, however, is the peculiar tone of the light and the atmospheric effects – the chilly whites and grays, the steely reflections, the melancholy brightness of a frigid zone. Winter here gives a stamp to the year, and seems to leave even through spring and summer a kind of scintillating trail of his presence. To me, I confess it is terrible, and I fancy I see con-stantly in the brilliant sky the hoary genius of the climate brooding grimly over his dominion.

The falls of Montmorency, which you reach by the pleasant avenue I speak of, are great, I believe, among the falls of the earth. They are certainly very fine, even in the attenuated shape to which they are reduced at the present season. I doubt whether you obtain anywhere in simpler and more powerful form the very essence of a cataract – the wild, fierce, suicidal plunge of a living sounding flood. A little platform, lodged in the cliff, enables you to contemplate it with almost shameful convenience; here you may stand at your leisure and spin analogies, more or less striking, on the very edge of the white abyss. The leap of the water begins directly at your feet, and your eye trifles dizzily with the long, perpendicular shaft of foam, and tries, in the eternal crash, to effect some vague notation of its successive states of sound and fury; but the vaporous sheet, for ever dropping, lapses from beneath the eye, and leaves the vision distracted in mid-space; and the vision, in search of a resting-place, sinks in a flurry to the infamous saw-mill which defaces the very base of the torrent. The falls of Montmorency are obviously one of the greatest of the beauties of nature; but I hope it is not beside the mark to say that of all the beauties of nature, "falls" are to me the least satisfying. A mountain, a precipice, a river, a forest, a plain, I can enjoy at my ease; they are natural, normal, self-assured; they make no appeal; they imply no human admiration, no petty human cranings and shrinkings, head-swimmings and similes. A cataract, of course, is essentially violent. You are certain, moreover, to have to approach it through a turnstile, and to enjoy it from some terribly cockneyfied little booth. The spectacle at Montmorency appears to be the private property of a negro innkeeper who "runs" it evidently with great pecuniary profit. A day or two since I went so far as to be glad to leave it behind, and drive some five miles farther along the road, to a village rejoicing in the pretty name of Château-Richer. The village is so pretty that you count on finding there the elderly manor which might have baptized it. But, of course, in such pictorial efforts as this Quebec breaks down; one must not ask too much of it. You enjoy from here, however, a revelation of the noble position of the city. The river, finding room in mid-stream for the long island of Orleans, opens out below you with a peculiar freedom and serenity, and leads the eye far down to where an azure mountain gazes up the channel and responds to the dark headland of Quebec. I noted, here and there, as I went, an extremely sketchable effect. Between the road and the river stand a succession of ancient peasant-dwellings, with their backwindows looking toward the stream. Glancing, as I passed, into the apertures that face the road, I saw, as through a picture-frame, their dark, rich-toned interiors, played into by the late river light and making an admirable series of mellow *tableaux de genre*. The little curtained alcoves, the big household beds, and presses, and dressers, the black-mouthed chimney-pieces, the crucifixes, the old women at their spinning-wheels, the little heads at the supper-table, around the big French loaf, outlined with a rim of light, were all as warmly, as richly composed, as French, as Dutch, as worthy of the brush, as anything in the countries to which artists resort for subjects.

I suppose no patriotic American can look at all these things, however idly, without reflecting on the ultimate possibility of their becoming absorbed into his own huge state. Whenever, sooner or later, the change is wrought, the sentimental tourist will keenly feel that a long stride has been taken, roughshod, from the past to the present. The largest appetite in modern civilisation will have swallowed the largest morsel. What the change may bring of comfort or of grief to the Canadians themselves, will be for them to say; but, in the breast of this sentimental tourist of ours, it will produce little but regret. The foreign elements of eastern Canada, at least, are extremely interesting; and it is of good profit to us Americans to have near us, and of easy access, an ample something which is not our expansive selves. Here we find a hundred mementoes of an older civilisation than our own, of different manners, of social forces once mighty, and still glowing with a sort of autumnal warmth. The old-world needs which created the dark-walled cities of France and Italy seem to reverberate faintly in the steep and narrow and Catholic streets of Quebec. The little houses speak to the fancy by rather inexpensive arts; the ramparts are endued with a sort of silvery innocence; but the historic sense, conscious of a general solidarity in the picturesque, ekes out the romance and deepens the colouring.

XX.

NIAGARA.

1871.

My journey hitherward by a morning's sail from Toronto
across Lake Ontario, seemed to me, as regards a certain dull
vacuity in this episode of travel, a kind of calculated prepara-
tion for the uproar of Niagara – a pause or hush on the
threshold of a great impression; and this, too, in spite of the
reverent attention I was mindful to bestow on the first seen, in
my experience, of the great lakes. It has the merit, from the
shore, of producing a slight ambiguity of vision. It is the sea,
and yet just not the sea. The huge expanse, the landless line of
the horizon, suggest the ocean; while an indefinable shortness
of pulse, a kind of fresh-water gentleness of tone, seem to con-
tradict the idea. What meets the eye is on the scale of the
ocean, but you feel somehow that the lake is a thing of smaller
spirit. Lake-navigation, therefore, seems to me not especially
entertaining. The scene tends to offer, as one may say, a sort
of marine-effect missed. It has the blankness and vacancy of
the sea, without that vast essential swell which, amid the
belting brine, so often saves the situation to the eye. I was
occupied, as we crossed, in wondering whether this dull
reduction of the main contained that which could properly be
termed "scenery". At the mouth of the Niagara River, however, after a sail of three hours, scenery really begins, and very
soon crowds upon you in force. The steamer puts into the

narrow channel of the stream, and heads upward between channel embankments. From this point, I think, you really enter into relations with Niagara. Little by little the elements become a picture, rich with the shadow of coming events. You have a foretaste of the great spectacle of colour which you enjoy at the Falls. The even cliffs of red-brown earth are crusted and spotted with autumnal orange and crimson, and, laden with this gorgeous decay, they plunge sheer into the deep-dyed green of the river. As you proceed, the river begins to tell its tale – at first in broken syllables of foam and flurry, and then, as it were, in rushing, flashing sentences and passionate ejaculations. Onwards from Lewiston, where you are transferred from the boat to the train, you see it from the edge of the American cliff, far beneath you, now superbly unnavigable. You have a lively sense of something happening ahead; the river, as a man near me said, has evidently been in a row. The cliffs here are immense; they form a *vomitorium* worthy of the living floods whose exit they protect. This is the first act of the drama of Niagara; for it is, I believe, one of the commonplaces of description that you instinctively convert it into a series of "situations". At the station pertaining to the railway suspension-bridge, you see in mid-air, beyond in interval of murky confusion produced at once by the farther bridge, the smoke of the trains, and the thickened atmosphere of the peopled bank, a huge far-flashing sheet which glares through the distance as a monstrous absorbent and irradiant of light. And here, in the interest of the picturesque, let me note that this obstructive bridge tends in a way to enhance the first glimpse of the cataract. Its long black span, falling dead along the shining brow of the Falls, seems shivered and smitten by their fierce effulgence, and trembles across the field of vision like some enormous mote in a light too brilliant. A moment later, as the train proceeds, you plunge into the village, and the cataract, save as a vague ground-tone to this trivial interlude, is, like so many other goals of æsthetic pilgrimage, temporarily postponed to the hotel.

With this postponement comes, I think, an immediate decline of expectation; for there is every appearance that the spectacle you have come so far to see is to be choked in the horribly vulgar shops and booths and catchpenny artifices which have pushed and elbowed to within the very spray of the Falls, and ply their importunities in shrill competition with its thunder. You see a multitude of hotels and taverns and stores, glaring with white paint, bedizened with placards and advertisements, and decorated by groups of those gentlemen who flourish most rankly on the soil of New York and in the vicinage of hotels; who carry their hands in their pockets, wear their hats always and every way, and, although of a stationary habit, yet spurn the earth with their heels. A side-glimpse of the Falls, however, calls out your philosophy; you reflect that this may be regarded as one of those sordid foregrounds which Turner liked to use, and which may be effective as a foil; you hurry to where the roar grows louder, and, I was going to say, you escape from the village. In fact, however, you don't escape from it; it is constantly at your elbow, just to the right or the left of the line of contemplation. It would be paying Niagara a poor compliment to say that, practically, she does not hurl away this chaffering by-play from her edge; but as you value the integrity of your impression, you are bound to affirm that it suffers appreciable abatement from such sources. You wonder, as you stroll about, whether it is altogether an unrighteous dream that with the slow progress of taste and the possible or impossible growth of some larger comprehension of beauty and fitness, the public conscience may not tend to confer upon such sovereign phases of nature something of the inviolability and privacy which we are slow to bestow, indeed, upon fame, but which we do not grudge at least to art. We place a great picture, a great statue, in a museum: we erect a great monument in the centre of our largest square, and if we can suppose ourselves nowadays to build a cathedral, we should certainly isolate it as much as possible and expose it to no ignoble contact. We cannot enclose Niagara with walls and a roof, nor girdle it with a palisade; but the sentimental tourist may muse upon the contingency of its being guarded by the negative homage of empty spaces and absent barracks and decent forbearance. The actual abuse of the scene belongs evidently to that immense class of iniquities which are destined to grow very much worse in order to grow a very little better. The good humour engendered by the main spectacle bids you suffer it to run its course.

Though hereabouts so much is great, distances are small, and a ramble of two or three hours enables you to gaze hither and thither from a dozen standpoints. The one you are likely to choose first is that on the Canada cliff, a little way above the suspension-bridge. The great fall faces you, enshrined in its own surging incense. The common feeling just here, I believe, is one of disappointment at its want of height; the whole thing appears to many people somewhat smaller than its fame. My own sense, I confess, was absolutely gratified from the first; and, indeed, I was not struck with anything being tall or short, but with everything being perfect. You are, moreover, at some distance, and you feel that with the lessening interval you will not be cheated of your chance to be dizzied with mere dimensions. Already you see the world-famous green, baffling painters, baffling poets, shining on the lip of the precipice; the more so, of course, for the clouds of silver and snow into which it speedily resolves itself. The whole picture before you is admirably simple. The Horseshoe glares and boils and smokes from the centre to the right,

drumming, itself into powder and thunder; in the centre the
dark pedestal of Goat Island divides the double flood; to the left
booms in vaporous dimness the minor battery of the
American Fall; while on a level with the eye, above the still
crest of either cataract, appear the white faces of the hither-
most rapids. The circle of weltering froth at the base of the
Horseshoe, emerging from the dead white vapours – absolute
white, as moonless midnight is absolute black – which muffle
impenetrably the crash of the river upon the lower bed, melts
slowly into the darker shades of green. It seems in itself a
drama of thrilling interest, this blanched survival and recovery
of the stream. It stretches away like a tired swimmer, strug-
gling from the snowy scum and the silver drift, and passing
slowly from an eddying foam-sheet, touched with green lights,
to a cold, verdantique, streaked and marbled with trails and
wild arabesques of foam. This is the beginning of that air of
recent distress which marks the river as you meet it at the lake.
It shifts along tremendously conscious, relieved, disengaged,
knowing the worst is over, with its dignity injured but its
volume undiminished, the most stately, the least turbid of tor-
rents. Its movement, its sweep and stride, are as admirable as
its colour, but as little is its colour to be made a matter of
words. These things are but part of a spectacle in which
nothing is imperfect. As you draw nearer and nearer, on the
Canada cliff, to the right arm of the Horseshoe, the mass
begins in all conscience to be large enough. You are able at last
to stand on the very verge of the shelf from which the leap is
taken, bathing your boot-toes, if you like, in the side-ooze of
the glassy curve. I may say, in parenthesis, that the importunities one suffers here, amid the central din of the cataract, from
hackmen and photographers and vendors of gimcracks, are
simply hideous and infamous. The road is lined with little
drinking-shops and warehouses, and from these retreats their

occupants dart forth upon the hapless traveller with their competitive attractions. You purchase release at last by the fury of your indifference, and stand there gazing your fill at the most beautiful object in the world.

The perfect taste of it is the great characteristic. It is not in the least monstrous; it is thoroughly artistic and, as the phrase is, thought out. In the matter of line it beats Michelangelo. One may seem at first to say the least, but the careful observer will admit that one says the most, in saying that it *pleases* – pleases even a spectator who was not ashamed to write the other day that he didn't care for cataracts. There are, however, so many more things to say about it – its multitudinous features crowd so upon the vision as one looks – that it seems absurd to begin to analyse. The main feature, perhaps, is the incomparable loveliness of the immense line of the shelf and its lateral abutments. It neither falters, nor breaks nor stiffens, but maintains from wing to wing the lightness of its semicircle. This perfect curve melts into the sheet that seems at once to drop from it and sustain it. The famous green loses nothing, as you may imagine, on a nearer view. A green more vividly cool and pure it is impossible to conceive. It is to the vulgar greens of earth what the blue of a summer sky is to artificial dyes, and is, in fact, as sacred, as remote, as impalpable as that. You can fancy it the parent-green, the head-spring of colour to all the verdant water-caves and all the clear, sub-fluvial haunts and bowers of naiads and mermen in all the streams of the earth. The lower half of the watery wall is shrouded in the steam of the boiling gulf – a veil never rent nor lifted. At its heart this eternal cloud seems fixed and still with excess of motion – still and intensely white; but, as it rolls and climbs against its lucent cliff, it tosses little whiffs and fumes and pants of snowy smoke, which betray the convulsions we never behold. In the middle of the curve, the depth of the recess, the converging walls are ground into a dust of foam, which rises in a tall column, and fills the upper air with its hovering drift. Its summit far overtops the crest of the cataract, and, as you look down along the rapids above, you see it hanging over the averted gulf like some far-flowing signal of danger. Of these things some vulgar verbal hint may be attempted; but what words can render the rarest charm of all – the clear-cut brow of the Fall, the very act and figure of the leap, the rounded passage of the horizontal to the perpendicular? To say it is simple is to make a phrase about it. Nothing was ever more successfully executed. It is carved as sharp as an emerald, as one must say and say again. It arrives, it pauses, it plunges; it comes and goes for ever; it melts and shifts and changes, all with the sound as of millions of bass-voices; and yet its outline never varies, never moves with a different pulse. It is as gentle as the pouring of wine from a flagon – of melody from the lip of a singer. From the little grove beside the American Fall you catch this extraordinary profile better than you are able to do at the Horseshoe. If the line of beauty had vanished from the earth elsewhere, it would survive on the brow of Niagara. It is impossible to insist too strongly on the grace of the thing, as seen from the Canada cliff. The genius who invented it was certainly the first author of the idea that order, proportion and symmetry are the conditions of perfect beauty. He applied his faith among the watching and listening forests, long before the Greeks proclaimed theirs in the measurements of the Parthenon. Even the roll of the white batteries at the base seems fixed and poised and ordered, and in the vague middle zone of difference between the flood as it falls and the mist as it rises you imagine a mystical meaning – the passage of body to soul, of matter to spirit, of human to divine.

Goat Island, of which every one has heard, is the menagerie of lions, and the spot where your single stone – or, in plain prose, your half-dollar – kills most birds. This broad insular strip, which performs the excellent office of withholding the American shore from immediate contact with the flood, has been left very much to itself, and here you may ramble, for the most part, in undiverted contemplation. The island is owned, I believe, by a family of co-heirs, who have the good taste to keep it quiet. More than once, however, as I have been told, they have been offered a "big price" for the privilege of building an hotel upon this sacred soil. They have been wise, but, after all, they are human, and the offer may be made once too often. Before this fatal day dawns, why should not the State buy up the precious acres, as California has done the Yo-Semite? It is the opinion of a sentimental tourist that no price would be too great to pay. Otherwise, the only hope for their integrity is in the possibility of a shrewd prevision on the part of the gentlemen who know how to keep hotels that the music of the dinner-band would be injured by the roar of the cataract. You approach from Goat Island the left abutment of the Horseshoe. The little tower which, with the classic rainbow, figures in all "views" of the scene, is planted at a dozen feet from the shore, directly on the shoulder of the Fall. This little tower, I think, deserves a compliment. One might have said beforehand that it would never do, but, as it stands, it makes rather a good point. It serves as a unit of appreciation of the scale of things, and from its spray-blackened summit it admits you to an almost downward peep into the green gulf. More here, even, than on the Canada shore, you perceive the unlimited *wateriness* of the whole spectacle. Its liquid masses take on at moments the likeness of walls and pillars and columns, and, to present any vivid picture of them, we are compelled to talk freely of emerald and crystal, of silver and marble. But really, all the simplicity of the Falls, and half their grandeur, reside in their unmitigated fluidity, which excludes all rocky staging and earthy commixture. It is water piled on water, pinned on water, hinging and hanging on water, breaking crashing, whitening in shocks altogether watery. And yet for all this no solid was ever so solid as that sculptured shoulder of the Horseshoe. From this little tower, or, better still, from various points farther along the island-shore, even to look is to be immersed. Before you stretches the huge expanse of the upper river, with its belittled cliffs, now mere black lines of forest, dull as with the sadness of gazing at perpetual trouble, eternal danger. Anything more horribly desolate than this boundless livid welter of the rapids it is impossible to conceive, and you very soon begin to pay it the tribute of your own suddenly-assumed suspense, in the impulse to people it with human forms. On this theme you can work out endless analogies. Yes, they are alive, every fear-blanched billow and eddy of them – alive and frenzied with the sense of their doom. They see below them that nameless pause of the arrested current, and the high-tossed drift of sound and spray which rises up lamenting, like the ghosts of their brothers who have been dashed to pieces. They shriek, they sob, they clasp their white hands and toss their long hair; they cling and clutch and wrestle, and, above all, they appear to *bite*. Especially tragical is the air they have of being forced backward, with averted faces, to their fate. Every pulse of the flood is like the grim stride of a giant, wading huge-kneed to his purpose, with the white teeth of a victim fastened in his neck. The outermost of three small islands, interconnected by short bridges, at the extremity of this shore, places one in singularly intimate relation with this portentous flurry. To say that hereabouts the water leaps and plunges and rears and dives, that its uproar makes even one's own ideas about it inaudible, and its current sweeps those ideas to perdition, is to give a very pale account of the universal agitation.

The great spectacle may be called complete only when you have gone down the river some four miles, on the American side, to the so-called rapids of the Whirlpool. Here the unhappy stream tremendously renews its anguish. Two approaches have been contrived on the cliff – one to the rapids proper, the other, farther below, to the scene of the sudden bend. The first consists of a little wooden cage, of the "elevator" pattern, which slides up and down a gigantic perpendicular shaft of horrible flimsiness. But a couple of the usual little brides, staggering beneath the weight of gorgeous cashmeres, entered the conveyance with their respective consorts at the same time with myself; and, as it thus carried Hymen and his fortunes, we survived the adventure. You obtain from below – that is, on the shore of the river – a specimen of the noblest cliff-scenery. The green embankment at the base of the sheer reel wall is by itself a very fair example of what they call in the Rocky Mountains a foot-hill; and from this continuous pedestal erects itself a bristling palisade of earth. As it stands, Gustave Doré might have drawn it. He would have sketched with especial ardour certain parasitical shrubs and boskages – lone and dizzy witnesses of autumn; certain outward-peering wens and warts and other perpendicular excrescences of rock; and, above all, near the summit, the fantastic figures of sundry audacious minor cliffs, grafted upon the greater by a mere lateral attachment and based in the empty air, with great slim trees rooted on their verges, like the tower of the Palazzo Vecchio at Florence. The actual whirlpool is a third of a mile farther down the river, and is best seen from the cliff above. From this point of view, it seems to me by all odds the finest of the secondary episodes of the drama of Niagara, and one on which a scribbling tourist, ineffectively playing at showman, may be content to ring down his curtain. The channel at this point turns away to the right, at a clean right-angle, and the river, arriving from the rapids just above with stupendous velocity, meets the hollow elbow of the Canada shore. The movement with which it betrays its surprise and bewilderment – the sudden issueless maze of waters – is, I think, after the Horseshoe Fall, the very finest thing in its progress. It breaks into no small rage; the offending cliffs receive no drop of spray; for the flood moves in a body and wastes no vulgar side-spurts; but you see it shaken to its innermost bowels and panting hugely, as if smothered in its excessive volume. Pressed back upon its centre, the current creates a sort of pivot, from which it eddies, groping for exit in vast slow circles, delicately and irregularly outlined in foam. The Canada shore, shaggy and gaudy with late September foliage, closes about it like the rising shelves of an amphitheatre, and deepens by contrast the strong blue-green of the stream. This slow-revolving surface – it seems in places perfectly still – resembles nothing so much as some ancient palace-pavement, cracked and scratched by the butts of legionary spears and the gold-stiffened hem of the garments of kings.

THE END.